LIVING IN EARLY VICTORIAN LONDON

LIVING IN EARLY VICTORIAN LONDON

MICHAEL ALPERT

PEN & SWORD
HISTORY

AN IMPRINT OF PEN & SWORD BOOKS LTD.
YORKSHIRE - PHILADELPHIA

First published in Great Britain in 2023 by
PEN AND SWORD HISTORY
An imprint of
Pen & Sword Books Ltd
Yorkshire – Philadelphia

ISBN 978 1 39906 084 4

Typeset in Times New Roman 11/13.5 by
SJmagic DESIGN SERVICES, India.
Printed and bound in the UK by CPI Group (UK) Ltd.

Pen & Sword Books Limited incorporates the imprints of Atlas, Archaeology,
Aviation, Discovery, Family History, Fiction, History, Maritime, Military, Military
Classics, Politics, Select, Transport, True Crime, Air World, Frontline Publishing,
Leo Cooper, Remember When, Seaforth Publishing, The Praetorian Press,
Wharncliffe Local History, Wharncliffe Transport, Wharncliffe True Crime and
White Owl.

For a complete list of Pen & Sword titles please contact
PEN & SWORD BOOKS LIMITED
47 Church Street, Barnsley, South Yorkshire, S70 2AS, England
E-mail: enquiries@pen-and-sword.co.uk
Website: www.pen-and-sword.co.uk

Or
PEN AND SWORD BOOKS
1950 Lawrence Rd, Havertown, PA 19083, USA
E-mail: Uspen-and-sword@casematepublishers.com
Website: www.penandswordbooks.com

Contents

Preface   vi

Acknowledgements   viii

Note on Currency   ix

Chapter 1   The Largest, Richest, Most Populous and
Refined City in the World   1

Chapter 2   A Woman's Place?   12

Chapter 3   What They Ate, Where They Shopped and
What They Wore   24

Chapter 4   In Sickness and In Health   47

Chapter 5   Money, Housing and Class   64

Chapter 6   Learning, Literature and Liturgy   81

Chapter 7   Outsiders   98

Chapter 8   Communications   116

Chapter 9   'A burst of applause which made the building ring'   134

Chapter 10   Crime, Police, Detectives and the Manning Murder   154

Chapter 11   Trial and Execution   170

Chapter 12   Elation and Sorrow   181

Bibliography   189

Notes   193

Index   207

Preface

This book is about living in London between 1837, when Victoria came to the throne, and the early 1850s, when three major and memorable events took place. In 1851 people came from all over to visit the Great Exhibition in Hyde Park. Many Londoners, perhaps for the first time, saw and heard foreigners as well as visitors from remote parts of Britain. In 1852 Londoners in their thousands watched the funeral procession of the Duke of Wellington. Finally, 1853 brought the first quarter of Victoria's sixty-four-year reign to an end. In that year Britain took a step which would involve it in the Crimean War, the first conflict with a European nation since Wellington had vanquished Napoleon at Waterloo in 1815.

Four years earlier, between August and November 1849, Londoners' attention had been gripped by a murder. Maria and Frederick Manning had killed Patrick O'Connor and buried his corpse under flagstones in their kitchen. Maria had fled to Scotland on the railway; Frederick had taken the train and boat to Jersey. Both were traced, with the help of the telegraph, by members of the new Scotland Yard detective service. The couple were brought back to London by train, tried and convicted at the Old Bailey, and hanged in public before a roaring crowd.

Setting aside their murderous character, the Mannings were an ordinary, lower middle-class couple, who lived a humdrum life in a two-storey, rented, terraced house in Bermondsey, a not very smart part of the capital. The record of their trial provides a wealth of description and references to the lives that people like them lived in the London of the early part of Queen Victoria's reign,

My choice of what to describe about the lives of ordinary lower middle-class Londoners is inevitably arbitrary, but I have in mind how people lived, what concerned them, their ambitions and their pleasures. Thus this book uses a multiplicity of sources, contemporary as far as possible, to illustrate where people lived, how they dressed, washed, shopped and cooked. I aim to investigate aspects of the world of middle-class work, what people earned and what things cost, how Londoners moved about their city, how they amused themselves, their illnesses, and the medicines they took.

I am interested in what they read, in their religious and moral principles and their political fears and prejudices.

Londoners in the early Victorian years lived on the cusp of modernity. The penny post, the telegraph, and cheap newspapers and books were relatively new to them. They had had the Metropolitan Police and the horse-drawn omnibus at their disposal since 1829 and the railway since 1837. They could install domestic gas lighting if they could afford it. By the late 1840s, they had the benefit of anaesthesia. As yet, however, they did not have the advantage of the underground railway, which would allow many people to live at a distance from their work. Better public government of London, basic education for all, a mass press, electricity, surgical asepsis, expanded opportunities for women, and the cheap tram were still to come, as was mass slum clearance and the long-awaited clean and reliable supply of water together with a massive sewer system which would put an end to the ever-looming danger of cholera. In some ways, early Victorian Londoners lived as their ancestors had for centuries, but in other ways, they enjoyed the most advanced features of modern cities.

Acknowledgements

A number of friends have been of great help to me, in particular Professor Donald Hawes who helped me with his wide knowledge of nineteenth-century literature, Dr. Gordon Higgott, an architectural historian who enlightened me about the habits of early Victorian builders; Dr. Barry Hoffbrand, who read the pages about medicine and saved me from making inevitable howlers. My friend and ex-colleague Francis McFarland listened to me read the text and pointed out infelicities. I am in debt to my editor whose skills and care contributed to preparing the book for the press.

Note on Currency

The change brought about by the decimalisation of the currency in 1971 was not merely a question of arithmetic, but also of the vocabulary and even the oral expression of how much something cost.

In the early Victorian age, there was a pound coin (also known as a sovereign) and a half-sovereign. The pound was divided into twenty shillings (the 'guinea' was not a coin but the sum of one pound and one shilling). Each shilling was divided into 12 copper, later bronze, pence. There were quarter-pence called 'farthings', sometimes pronounced 'fardens', half-farthings and half-pennies, pronounced 'hayp'nce' ('hayp'ny' in the singular). The sum of a penny and a halfpenny was expressed orally as 'three- hayp'nce'. Two pence was pronounced 'tupp'nce' and three pence (for which there was a silver coin) sounded like 'thrupp'nce'. The stress was on the number, not as now on the word 'pence', so one would have heard for example 'TENpence' and not 'Ten PENCE'. Pence were abbreviated in writing to d., thus a price would be marked as 2d.

Shillings were abbreviated to *s* or /-, so one pound and five shillings was written £.1.5s or 25/-. One usually said 25 shillings. An account might total, say, £1.5.4.1/2d., or one pound, five shillings and fourpence and one half-penny. People would say 'One pound, five and fourp'nce hayp'ny' or 'twenty-five and fourp'nce hayp'ny'.

If shillings or pence were mentioned together the sum would be expressed, for example, as 7/6 or 7s.6d., that is seven shillings and six pence. Colloquially, one said 'seven and six', adding perhaps the word 'pence' and where necessary the words 'hayp'ny' or 'farthing' or 'three farthings'. The shilling was called a 'bob' and the sixpence a 'tanner'.

The silver coinage consisted of the 3d, 6d and shilling pieces, although there was also a 'groat' worth 4d. There was a florin, worth two shillings, and the half-crown, which most people called 'half a crown', worth two shillings and six pence, or one-eighth of a pound.

The following table shows equivalent values for pre-and post-decimalised British currency (approximate for amounts under 6d.)

'Old' money	*Decimalised*
1d	½ p
2 ½d	1 p
6d	2 ½ p
1/-	5 p
2/-	10 p
2/6d	12 ½ p
5/-	25 p
10/-	50 p
15/-	75 p

Inflation has made sums of money mentioned nearly two centuries ago meaningless unless we know people's incomes. Income tax began once one was receiving £150 per year, which was considered the minimum on which one could live a 'lower' middle-class life. A working man who had a regular thirty shillings or £1.10s a week could live with some ease, but many earned far less and suffered occasional or even regular unemployment or short time.

MICHAEL ALPERT: MAY 2022

Chapter 1

The Largest, Richest, Most Populous and Refined City in the World

Today, if you walk from the south to the north bank of the River Thames via London Bridge, the oldest crossing over the river rebuilt in 1831, and then stroll eastwards along the footpath on the north bank towards the Tower of London, you are actually walking along some of the most bustling of the nineteenth-century wharves and quays. Until 1800, the City of London, which jealously guarded its medieval prerogatives, had jurisdiction as far up the river as the tide rose. It allowed ships to unload their cargoes only on that short stretch of the north bank. However, so little space was available that most ships had to moor in the river and discharge their contents onto barges and lighters. Ships and their attendant craft negotiated the river amid a torrent of shouting and cursing, whistles and hooters; stevedores and coal-whippers strained and sweated to unload the colliers which brought vast quantities of coal from north-east England for London's consumption, while others manhandled boxes, crates and casks out of the holds of the tall sailing ships which had brought their cargoes of rum, sugar, wine, tobacco, cocoa, coffee, indigo, India rubber and other raw materials from all over the world to feed the burgeoning British economy and the demands of industry.

A Forest of Masts, Yards and Cables

As the import and export trade of London grew in the boom years after the defeat of Napoleon in 1815, so the Pool of London, as that stretch of the river is called, grew ever-more congested. In the end, over £5 million was spent to build new wharves further downriver. The West, India, East India, Surrey, London and St. Catherine's docks were constructed over the next thirty years. By mid-century, as many as six hundred ships could be moored at the quaysides of the Port of London. Every day over one hundred vessels came into the docks, not counting the steam tugs which pulled the great

1

sailing ships into place, and the passenger steamers which took people up the Thames to Richmond, and down as far as Gravesend and Margate, or overseas.

By mid-century, even after the new docks had been built, from a distance the ranks of masts still crowding the Port of London looked like a forest to travellers as they sailed up the Thames Estuary. In 1852, Baron Dupin, who had represented France at the Great Exhibition of 1851, said in a speech he gave at the Paris *Conservatoire des Arts et Métiers:*

> Imagine the ships of all countries lying in order at anchor from the last of the bridges (*London Bridge; Tower Bridge had not been built*) arrayed ... in transversal ranks, succeeding each other almost without interval for a league in length ...Imagine five groups of floating docks ... a surface of water always available, never subject to the rise and fall of tides ... Imagine around these docks an establishment of warehouses and workshops for the rigging and armament of ships of commerce and of war[1]

And the French historian Hippolyte Taine left this more dramatic, if perhaps excitable, description, after visiting London in the 1860s:

> But that which carries the impression to its height, is the sight of the canals through which the docks communicate with the sea; they form cross streets, and they are streets for ships; one suddenly perceives a line of them which is endless; from Greenwich Park where I ascended last year, the horizon is bounded with masts and ropes. The incalculable indistinct rigging stretches a spiders' - web in a circle at the side of the sky ... an inextricable forest of masts, yards and cable[2]

Ships were anchored in the River Thames two or three abreast in two tiers as far as the eye could see, and steamboats, barges and boats of all sizes skilfully navigated their way through the long lines of vessels just arrived from far-off lands, laden with exotic goods such as palm oil or ivory, or swarmed over by the bawling, perspiring dockers as they lowered cases full of Birmingham metalware or cotton goods from Manchester into the holds. What a sight to stand and stare at as one walked or rode on a horse-drawn omnibus across London Bridge!

Have You Anything to Declare, Sir?

Standing imposingly by London Bridge was the Custom House, where all imports had to be cleared. In 1840, three years after Queen Victoria succeeded to the throne, its famous Long Room collected over £11 million pounds per year, almost half the total amount of dues paid in the country. Today, with over a century of dirt removed, it looks as new as when it was rebuilt in 1825.

Yet smuggling was rife, and it meant severe loss to the national revenue, for in the 1840s Customs and Excise duties were the largest source of Government income. They were worth far more than the £10 million which arose from taxes on income and property. Duty on tobacco was three shillings per pound weight, a high proportion of the retail price that the smoker paid. It was hardly surprising that people smuggled, even though 2,187 tobacco smugglers were convicted between 1843 and 1845 in England alone.[3] Visitors to Britain, complained Flora Tristan, the French socialist and feminist writer, in her memoir of England, suffered cruelly from the over-officious nature of British customs officers' behaviour. They even had the power to sequester a whole ship with its goods if a sailor was caught with contraband items.[4] The American writer and author of *Moby Dick*, Herman Melville, had 'infinite trouble' with the 'cursed customs' at the East India Docks when he went to recover his personal baggage.[5] On 13 November 1843 even the majestic London daily newspaper *The Times* thundered against the draconian powers of customs officers and the courts which supported them.

Yet, at the same time, the Customs themselves had suffered scandalous frauds and was a hotbed of corruption. Patrick O'Connor, murdered in 1849 by Maria Manning and her husband, in a case which became notorious, was himself involved in lucrative smuggling from his position in the Customs and Excise Department, which he had secured through pulling influential strings.

A clever and a lucky man, O'Connor was one of the 26,000 inhabitants of London, about one in a hundred, who enjoyed an official position, and one of the 2,228 attached to the Port of London Customs and Excise Department.[6] Originating from the Irish Catholic middle class, O'Connor had arrived in England in 1832 armed with a letter of introduction from his brother, the principal of Thurles College in Tipperary, addressed to a barrister in London, who in turn gave him a note of recommendation for Commissioner Richard Mayne of the Metropolitan Police. However, the Commissioner had no high-level appointments to distribute. O'Connor would have to start at the bottom and, as police constables' wages were low and the work challenging, he went in for tobacco smuggling and money-lending.

Technically, he was known as a tide-waiter, an official who waited for ships, boarded and inspected them. Soon he became a gauger, one who estimated the contents of casks and other containers. The report of the trial of his murderers revealed that he had become a wealthy man, with investments in railway shares and a healthy bank balance.[7]

On the fatal Thursday of his murder, 9 August 1849, O'Connor was last seen walking over London Bridge walking south in the direction of Bermondsey, where Maria Manning and her husband lived. As the Irishman crossed over the bridge among the hundred thousand pedestrians who were reputed to use it daily, he would have glanced downstream at the serried rows of ships in the Pool, and upstream towards Southwark Bridge, built in 1819. The weather was hot that August day; people were lighting coal fires only for cooking, so perhaps for once, this city, the largest in the world, was not covered by the permanent haze of smoke that characterised it.

The Monster City

Some years later, the investigative journalist Henry Mayhew took a balloon flight over London. Below him, he wrote:

> ... lay the Leviathan Metropolis, with a dense canopy of smoke hanging over it, and reminding one of the fog of vapour that is so often seen steaming out of the fields at early morning. It was impossible to tell where the monster city began or ended, for the buildings stretched, not only to the horizon on either side, but far away into the distance, where, owing to the coming shades of evening and the dense fumes from the million chimneys, the town seemed to blend into the sky, so that there was no distinguishing earth from heaven.[8]

London was a universe. By mid-century, it stretched nine miles from Fulham in the west to Poplar in the east, and seven miles from Highbury in the north to Camberwell in the south, with areas of suburbia such as Paddington and Lambeth. It was twice the size of Paris, four times that of Vienna and six times that of Berlin. No city in the British Isles approached it.

4

Despite its size, parts of London were even more congested than today. And it was ugly, despite some new and attractive buildings such as the Bank of England, completed in 1827, the British Museum and the Gothic mass of the new Houses of Parliament, which rose steadily between 1837 and 1847 beside Westminster Bridge to replace the old Palace of Westminster which had burnt down in 1834.

London had not been redesigned when it was rebuilt after the Great Fire of 1666, so its streets were narrow and winding, particularly in the City, but also behind the great avenues of Regent Street, Oxford Street and the Strand. It had spread northwards past the New Road, today the Marylebone and Euston roads, opened in the late eighteenth century between Paddington and Battle Bridge (today's King's Cross) in order to bypass the most crowded parts and provide a quick route to the City. London was spilling over the New Road into the slum of Agar Town, which would soon become railway yards and where the new British Library would be built a century and a half later. And from the top of Tottenham Court Road London had stretched across the New Road as far as Camden Town and was beginning to move up the hill towards Hampstead. The sheds, stables and warehouses of the London and North Western railway stretched for over a mile up the line from Euston, as far as the engine shed known from its shape as the Round House, and the opening of the Primrose Hill tunnel on the line to Birmingham.

London was a huge concentrated market for goods. It pulled merchandise into its huge maw by sea, canal and increasingly even before the beginning of Victoria's reign, by rail. Although London had no staple industrial base like the northern cities, it employed 15 per cent of the labour force engaged in manufacturing in England and Wales. There were hundreds of little factories and workshops, mostly in the City and the inner suburbs, making clothing in Stepney and Bethnal Green, furniture in the Tottenham Court Road, and scientific instruments and clocks in Clerkenwell. Along the river flourished industries such as sugar-refining, soap-making, rubber, chemicals, paint and tobacco-blending. Southwark, and specifically Bermondsey, was a centre of tanning, brewing and flour-milling. Downriver there were shipbuilding yards in Limehouse, Millwall and Rotherhithe. Like other big cities in later epochs, London's building industries were a magnet for both skilled and unskilled men, and the capital drew people into employment in government, medicine, the law, education, shipping, banking, insurance and clerking in general, as well as a massive host of all sorts and classes of domestic servants.

In the years after the Duke of Wellington's defeat of Napoleon in 1815 and up to the late 1830s, an economic boom had stimulated London's population surge. The city had been growing at the rate of a quarter of a million each decade, but with the arrival of railways in the 1830s, the population had multiplied even faster. The census of 1851 counted 2,363,141 people, which was between one-fifth and one-sixth of the total figure for England and Wales.

The inns, churches, ancient houses and Old Curiosity Shoppes of Charles Dickens's early novels were now being swept away or overshadowed by railway tracks, stations, sidings and viaducts, and by the terraces and villas of suburbia. Trafalgar Square had been laid out in 1844 with the new National Gallery on its north side. The almost 17-foot high statue of Admiral Lord Nelson was displayed in Charing Cross in 1842, where thousands admired it briefly, after which the column itself was reared to its height of nearly 170 feet in Trafalgar Square to commemorate Nelson's great victory off the Spanish coast over the French and Spanish fleets on 21 October 1805. Later the relief depicting the death of Nelson at Trafalgar would be inserted on the south face of the column.

Hungerford Market, where Charing Cross railway station is now, had been rebuilt in 1845, together with a footbridge across the river. By 1847 New Oxford Street had been driven through the foetid, deprived and criminal slums of St. Giles – one of the so-called 'rookeries', because the inhabitants seemed to disappear into holes in the walls and the ground, just like rooks. But as yet Shaftesbury Avenue and Charing Cross Road had not been driven through their own warrens of filthy slums. There were no purpose-built blocks of flats, no Victoria Embankment, no Tower Bridge and no new Royal Courts of Justice in the Strand.

In the early Victorian era, thousands of Londoners were thrown out of their homes to make space for the railway lines as the building work neared the planned terminuses in the capital, and to build major thoroughfares, but no arrangements were made for rehousing them. As a result, the existing slums became even more crowded. Men had to live close to where they worked if they wanted to be at the head of the queue for whatever jobs were on offer at six in the morning when work began in the docks and on building sites. The fast and cheap Metropolitan Railway would not come until the 1860s. Omnibuses had rattled over cobblestoned streets since 1829, but they were too expensive for working men. They were also very slow, stopping whenever hailed and struggling to make their way through narrow streets congested with carts and multitudes of moving humanity. Consequently, most people walked or, if they could afford it, took a cab.

London was chaotically administered. Except for the Metropolitan Police, established in 1829, no single authority covered all of London and none would do so until the Metropolitan Board of Works began to rebuild

London's inadequate sewers in 1855. The original City of London itself was governed by a small, self-perpetuating, tightly-knit and wealthy Court of Aldermen and the Court of Common Council, as well as by its influential and ancient trade guilds. This created an obstinate unwillingness to accept any proposal which might involve expense outside the City's boundaries. The suburbs were governed by parish vestries, to which the right of election was very limited. The vestries themselves did not have full responsibility for matters such as relieving the poor, drainage, lighting, cleaning the streets and paving, for which there were some two hundred other bodies, created *ad hoc* by a chaotic web of individual Acts of Parliament over many years. The parish of St. Pancras, for instance, had eighteen separate paving trusts in its four square miles.[9] And, most importantly for London's public health, the eight metropolitan commissioners of sewers did not see that it was their responsibility to ensure the removal of anything but surface water.[10] The vast mass of London's people had only eighteen members of Parliament to represent their interests, one for every 131,285 inhabitants, though only 6,870 had the right to vote even after the Reform Bill of 1832 had extended the suffrage. Secrecy and corruption reigned. All attempts at intervention clashed with local interest. London's administration was totally inadequate for its huge size and its immense population.

Central London's noise and gloom struck most observers. The American novelist Herman Melville looked over the city from Primrose Hill in the north. 'Cityward it was like a view of Hell', he wrote of the heavy pall of smoke that covered London. The sky was dull; the rattle of wooden and iron wheels across cobbled streets was ceaseless and was now, in some areas, punctuated by the puffing, whistling and rattling of the railway, which only added to the smoke. Thomas Carlyle, the Scottish historian, wrote to his sister Jean that, even in semi-rural riverside Chelsea, where they took a house in 1834, he and his wife Jane were close to the 'noisiest Babylon that ever raged and fumed (with coal smoke) on the face of this planet'.[11] For the admittedly hyper-sensitive Carlyle the noise was constant: 'men, women, children, omnibuses, carriages ... steeple bells, door bells, gentleman raps, twopennny post raps, footmen showers-of-raps'.[12] Flora Tristan wrote admiringly about the 'magic brightness' of the gas lighting of London's main streets, which had begun when Pall Mall was lit by gas in 1807. Nevertheless, in the autumn and winter a dense and permanent canopy of gloom hung over the city, and every now and then there came a 'London Particular', a fog brought about by low cloud, still air and the rising mass of sulphurous smoke pouring out of the multi-chimneyed roofs that still today rise, though unused, from the skylines of London's Victorian districts. Even the flaring gaslights about which Mme. Tristan enthused did not succeed in preventing the gloom created by the three and one half million tons of coal burnt every year. Indeed, she also complained about the British capital's smoke, soot, thick fog and what would later be known as *smog*.[13]

Mud, Gloom and Starvation

According to the season, the carts, cabs and omnibuses sent up fountains of dirty water, mud and horse dung, or whirlwinds of dust, straw and dry dung. London was foul and mephitic. Its narrow streets squelched with mud and dung ('the mud lay thick upon the stones,' wrote Dickens in *Oliver Twist*). Those streets which were not cobblestoned or macadamised with small pieces of broken granite pressed together by a roller were poorly paved and easily broken up by traffic. Ladies lifted their skirts delicately to cross the road and gave a coin to the ragged boys employed as crossing-sweepers, who brushed away some of the dung, mud or dust. Near the meat market and the slaughterhouses of Smithfield, they whisked away the blood and the flies and, in many parts of London, human excrement. And, like Jo in Dickens's *Bleak House*, who had no parents and no friends, who had never been to school and lived in the rookery which the novelist called 'Tom All-Alone's', the poor and the destitute, the sick, the starving and the freezing were everywhere.[14]

Henry Colman, an American visitor, wrote to his Bostonian friends in 1849:

> In the midst of the most extraordinary abundance, here and there men, women and children are dying of starvation, and running alongside of the splendid chariot, with its gilded equipages, its silken linings and its liveried footmen, are poor, forlorn, friendless, almost naked wretches[15]

Colman had a parlour and a bedroom in a London Hotel for 30 shillings a week, including breakfast and tea. He paid extra for coal and candles, items which a hotel guest would use as much or as little as he chose. He paid a shilling – which makes one wonder whether he was overcharged – to have his boots cleaned, and he tipped the chambermaid. Colman's compatriot Herman Melville rented a room at 25, Craven Street, just off the Strand in central London, for only 1/6d more. He paid a guinea and a half or £1.11.6d. per week and considered the rate cheap. On the unfashionable south side of the river, he could have had as good a place for only a pound. Such prices were far beyond the pockets of the poor, who earned and spent in pennies and rarely saw silver coinage, leave alone gold sovereigns.

Colman thought that Londoners were very civil, but this was perhaps because he had been given introductions to polite society. He also thought London was very clean, contrary to most other visitors' impression. He wrote that he had scarcely seen a smoker. He probably had not seen anyone chewing tobacco and spitting out the juice, as the journalist and famous novelist Charles Dickens saw with disgust when visiting the United States. Colman also said that he had not heard a profane word or a risqué story, even though he recounts a visit to the slums. However, his experience was hardly surprising because he was a Unitarian minister and presumably dressed the part. Yet, despite his praise for the general public order of the British capital, he contrasts the French fishing port of Boulogne, where people were neatly dressed and well-fed, with the hunger, squalor and drunkenness of the British capital.[16]

Rookeries

A visitor could hardly fail to notice the street urchins, the barefoot and ragged crossing sweepers, the men who ran for miles behind a cab in order to earn a few pennies for unloading luggage, the children turning cartwheels in the mud for coins, sleeping in the streets, eating when and where they could, the mudlarks of the river, ragged, filthy, starved and prematurely active sexually, illiterate and in some cases probably bound for gaol. They were among the 150,000 who lived in London's rookeries where the houses were high and narrow and the largest possible number of dwellers were crowded together. Some areas became rookeries as soon as they were built, such as Agar Town just north of the New Road, a district which eventually disappeared under railway sidings and coal yards. A speculative builder might design his houses for middle-class tenants, and find that for some reason he could not attract them. To maintain his cash flow, he would have to let the houses cheaply in flats which were soon subdivided into rooms into which landlords might admit more than one family, each occupying a corner. The district would become poorer and rowdier, and would stay like that until the slum was finally demolished, often not until a century later. Other rookeries were the abandoned houses of prosperous folk who had moved away. In the early Victorian age, one of the most notorious rookeries was St. Giles, where New Oxford Street meets Shaftesbury Avenue today. Occupied by totally indigent Irish immigrants, and by labourers, vagrants and a criminal class, St.Giles housed up to eight men and women living and sleeping literally cheek by jowl in the same room, often on the floor or on some straw, most likely alive with bugs.

Here is the appalling and hair-raising description of a rookery written by the journalist George Augustus Sala in 1859:

From a hundred foul lanes and alleys have debouched on to the spick and span new promenade unheard-of human horrors. Gibbering forms of men and women in filthy rags, with fiery heads of shock hair, the roots beginning an inch from their eyebrows, with eyes themselves bleared and gummy, with gashes filled with yellow fangs for teeth, with rough holes punched in the nasal cartilage for nostrils, with sprawling hands and splay feet, tessellated with dirt – awful deformities, with horrifying malformations of the limbs and running sores ostentatiously displayed ... They hang around your feet like reptiles, or crawl round you like loathsome vermin, and in a demonic whine beg charity from you. One can bear the men, ferocious and repulsive as they are; a penny and a threat will send them cowering and cursing to their noisome dens again. One cannot bear the women without a shudder and a feeling of infinite sorrow and humiliation. They are so horrible to look upon, so thoroughly unsexed, shameless. Heaven-abandoned and forlorn, with their bare liver-coloured feet beating the devil's tattoo on the pavement, their lean shoulders shrugged up to their sallow cheeks, over which falls their hair either wildly dishevelled or filthily matted, and their gaunt hands clutching at the tattered remnant of a shawl, which but sorrily veils the lamentable fact that they have no gown – that a ragged petticoat and undergarment are all they have to cover themselves ... Look at the lanes themselves, with the filthy rags flaunting from poles in the windows in bitter mockery of being hung out to dry after washing: the threshold littered with wallowing infants, and revealing beyond a Dantean perspective of infected back yard and cloacal staircase. Peer as well as you may through the dirt-obscured window-panes, and see the dens of wretchedness where people dwell – the sick and infirm, often the dying, sometimes the dead, lying on the bare floor, or at best covered with some tattered scraps of blanketing or matting: the shivering aged crouching over fireless grates, and drunken husbands bursting through the rotten doors to seize their gaunt wives by the hair, and bruise their already swollen faces, because they have pawned what few rags that remain to purchase gin[17]

The novelist Mrs. Gaskell's more objective and less-emotional description in her *Mary Barton* (1848) of a Manchester slum could easily apply to London:

> [The street] was unpaved and down the middle a gutter forced its way, every now and then forming pools in the holes with which the street abounded. Never was the old Edinburgh cry of 'Gardez l'Eau!' more necessary than in this street. As they passed, women from their doors tossed household slops of every description into the gutter; they ran into the next pool, which overflowed and stagnated. Heaps of ashes were the stepping-stones on which the passer-by who cared in the least for cleanliness took care not to place his foot[18]

The 'slops of *every* (italicised in the original) description' was a euphemism for human excrement.

Quite a lot of money could be made from letting rooms in these slums, even for just a few pence per week. There was one – Calmel Buildings off Portman Square, close to some of the most elegant properties in the capital – which consisted of a courtyard 22 feet wide surrounded by 26 three-roomed houses. A malodorous open sewer ran down the middle. In the houses lived 426 men and 518 women, an average of 36 per house. Each house brought its owner £20 to £30 per year.[19]

Even though the Metropolitan Association for Improving the Dwellings of the Industrious Classes, founded in 1845, erected the Albert Dwellings in the east London district of Stepney in 1849, with flats containing a kitchen, scullery, two bedrooms, a piped water supply and a water-closet, at rents of 3/6d and 4/6d per week, which were required to make them financially feasible, they were beyond slum-dwellers' ability to pay. Victorian manuals of household economy reckoned 10 per cent of income should go to paying rent. But only a skilled man earning an unlikely £2 per week could pay 10 per cent of this, which was four shillings. Few working men earned such wages, and very many suffered regular unemployment. A labourer earning fifteen shillings per week might be paying 2/6d per week rent, one-sixth of his meagre income, for a room for himself and his wife and family. It did not take much, illness, an accident at work, unemployment, an extra mouth to feed, to bring a person down to the lowest level in early Victorian London.

Chapter 2

A Woman's Place?

Long Live Her Majesty!

The wretched, mud-spattered and often starving side of her capital was hidden from Queen Victoria when she was driven to her coronation in Westminster Abbey on 28 June 1838. She was a young woman, carefully, even restrictively brought up by her mother, and she would look forward to marriage and a family. It was unlikely that she had heard or seen anything of the distress of the extreme poor of London. Moreover, her first Prime Minister, Lord Melbourne, believed that social reform legislation was rarely effective.[1]

The coronation was intended by the Prime Minister to revive the reputation of the British royal family. It was the first coronation since the great Reform Bill of 1832 and Melbourne intended to make it a major public event by starting the procession to the Abbey from Buckingham Palace, newly modernised and from then onwards the official residence of the British sovereign. The drive would take a full hour. Some main roads in London were now more smoothly paved so that a coach ride was less uncomfortable than it had been over cobblestones.

The cavalcade of military and civil dignitaries and foreign ambassadors in their carriages was followed by royal dukes and other members of Victoria's family. The new Queen rode in the Gold State Coach, with an escort of Life Guards and Yeoman of the Guard, and was accompanied by mounted bands of the Household Brigade.

Artillery salutes began at four in the summer dawn. By eight o'clock that morning the stands which had been ordered by the Government to facilitate the view for the spectators around St. George's Hospital at Hyde Park Corner were already full of well-dressed ladies and gentlemen, who were charged 2/6d for a place. The United States' embassy, in particular, had been overwhelmed by requests for tickets. Early cloud had dispersed when, starting at ten that morning Victoria drove through the cheering crowds up Constitution Hill to Hyde Park Corner, where her coach turned right, passing Apsley House, home of the Duke of Wellington, known as 'No.1, London', and continued along Piccadilly, turning right at St. James's Street. The long procession went down to Pall Mall and then turned towards Charing Cross and along Whitehall to Westminster and the Abbey. The journey took the expected hour. The royal coach returned along the same route, starting at a quarter past four that afternoon, thus giving many thousands the chance to see and cheer their young new queen. That day, Alexis Soyer, the famous chef of the Reform Club, founded two years earlier in Pall Mall, prepared a breakfast for two thousand guests.

Many of the 400,000 spectators who were estimated to have lined the streets to wave as they saw Victoria pass had arrived in London in special excursion trains at the recently-built main line stations of Euston Square and London Bridge, or had left the trains at the temporary 'termini' of Nine Elms or Bishops Bridge Road (Victoria and Paddington Stations not having yet opened). Many of them encamped in the royal parks, where entertainment and catering were provided. There was a huge fair in Hyde Park, which went on for two days by popular demand, as well as bands and a balloon ascent. A firework display in Green Park enlivened that joyful summer night.

'It seems to me a March of the Dead'

Observers of that June day of national rejoicing remarked on the elegance of the ladies who occupied the reserved places along the route of the coronation procession.[2] However, London was the home of many other young women, of the same age as Victoria, brought up perhaps in conditions of filth, drunkenness, immodesty and foul language. They, or single working girls, particularly in the abysmally low-paid dressmaking trade, domestic servants, or orphans, might become the girlfriends of young, wealthy bachelors who amused themselves with women of a lower social class before they themselves were ready to marry into society.

The girl would enjoy the high life for a time, until the man married and dumped her, or if she gave birth to one of the 42,000 illegitimate children (nearly 7 per cent of all births) registered as born in 1851, or others whom they farmed out or even did away with.[3] She would have lost her reputation and perhaps, even if she had parents, have been thrown out of her family home. She might have had to go on the streets in the higher class of trade in St James's, or prowl the theatre bars at Drury Lane or Covent Garden.[4] The Haymarket and Lower Regent Street, favourite places to solicit custom, were not yet separated by Piccadilly Circus from the similar Lisle, Wardour and Windmill Streets.

Instead of driving down Regent Street in a glossy carriage, stopping to finger expensive materials displayed seductively behind the brightly-lit plate glass, from early evening onwards, she would walk the Haymarket and the pavement of the Colonnade where Regent Street curved into Coventry Street and today into Piccadilly Circus. When the Colonnade was demolished in the 1840s the prostitutes had to move to Burlington Arcade, which was frequented by men about town. City clerks would go there to cut a dash, to fantasise as they ogled the expensive tarts as they strolled around, typically between three and five o'clock in the afternoon, awaiting a signal from similarly strolling gentlemen, after which prostitute and client would meet upstairs.[5] Rooms above milliners' and trinket shops were known to be devoted to the trade in flesh. Because dressmakers were paid so poorly to sew garments that they could only yearn to wear themselves, they were exposed to irresistible temptation by the promise of fine clothes, and attracted to 'gay' living (the term implied not homosexuality as now but sexual looseness in general) in the big city. When Ralph Nickleby in Chapter 10 of Dickens's novel *Nicholas Nickleby* finds his niece Kate a job at Madame Mantalini's dressmaking workshop, readers would have understood that Ralph was a scoundrel, who knew the dangers to which he was exposing Kate Nickleby.[6]

The police rarely intervened. In 1841 only 9,409 prostitutes, mostly of the poorest class, were arrested, and this was probably for associated crimes of theft or public disorder.[7]

As powder and paint became less effective in concealing the effect of the passing years, the London prostitute's earnings might drop from the £20 or £30 that these high spenders were reputed to be able to demand at the height of their attractiveness. She might move to Portland Place at the top of Regent Street and join the detachment of females who offered their services there, or to the narrow streets at the top end of the Haymarket. Later she would look for trade in the Vauxhall and Cremorne Pleasure Gardens, well-known haunts of erotic activity, then along the ill-lit Edgware Road which led due north from Hyde Park, but finally and perhaps inevitably she would tumble to the rough end of the vice trade. The very worst part of London for prostitution was dockland, where pox-marked and foul-mouthed drabs paraded half-dressed in second-hand finery from pub to pub as they fought other women who tried to muscle in on their trade among the seamen who were spending their accumulated wages. The men who used her would decline in behaviour and fastidiousness until she reached the bottom, when she could be had up against the wall for the price of a glass of gin or a bed for the night. For the wretched, drink-sodden slattern, her ill-clad body at the mercy of wind and rain, her careworn, bitter face bedaubed with rouge, it was a toss-up whether she died of a beating-up, alcoholism or syphilis.

Foreign observers were taken aback by the extent and the brazenness of London prostitution. Hippolyte Taine reported that you could not walk one hundred yards down the Haymarket or the Strand without being accosted for money for gin or to pay the rent. 'It seemed as if I was watching a march-past of dead women,' he wrote. 'Here is a festering sore, the real sore on the body of English society.'[8]

One of the streets in a newish district that Flora Tristan visited, off the Waterloo Road, south of the bridge of that name, contained, according to the 1841 census, 24 houses inhabited by 57 young women, whose age and the absence of men suggests that they were all prostitutes.[9] Flora Tristan reported that, on the summer night when she visited the area, the women were naked to the waist, at the windows and the doors. She thought that their situation was the inevitable result of the injustice of women's lives, and she was very aware of the protectors, pimps or 'bullies' who were with the women at the windows. She also described in detail the so-called 'finishes' where well-off men would go to end an evening of debauchery. She refers to them as 'splendid taverns', where very expensive women – Flora claimed, perhaps with some exaggeration, that some could demand fifty or even one hundred pounds – were displayed on the stage for men to select and entertain at tables.[10]

Flora Tristan quoted a contemporary investigation of London prostitution to state that eighty to one hundred thousand women were selling their bodies nightly in the capital. Numbers, nevertheless, were inevitably little more than guesswork or extrapolations of statistics of arrests or admissions to lock hospitals for venereal disease where a prostitute would be treated with mercury, the only remedy available. There was no clear law defining a prostitute. A police magistrate declared vaguely:

> About this town, within our present district of Westminster, or halfway down the Strand towards Temple Bar (where the City of London begins), there would every night be found about five hundred or one thousand of that description of wretches; how they can gain any profit from their prostitution one can hardly conceive[11]

Unlike some Continental cities, it was not possible to establish statistics because London prostitutes were not required to register with the Police, to have regular medical examinations or to conduct their trade in special licensed brothels.

The absence of control made the situation even worse. Until 1875 twelve was the legal age for consent to sexual intercourse. Mothers sold their twelve-year-old daughters, or girls whom they claimed to be such. The customer would be assured that he was the girl's first man, an important point because it was commonly believed that intercourse with a virgin could cure a sexually-transmitted disease. In any case, however, adolescent girls were often outside parental control; promiscuity was frequent among the delinquent or semi-criminal class of young people who lived in cheap lodging houses or in London's rookeries. The London Society for the Prevention of Juvenile Prostitution had been founded in 1835 and reported that young boys were also bought and sold in London.

There was no lack of organisations set up to try to reform prostitutes. In 1847 Charles Dickens was instrumental in cooperating with the philanthropist Angela Burdett-Coutts to find a suitable house, which he called by the homely name of Urania Cottage, in Shepherd's Bush, in the western suburbs of London. The women were carefully selected, disciplined firmly though not harshly, and encouraged to learn appropriate domestic skills. Many ended by emigrating to America and Australia.[12]

The lowest figures for London prostitutes were the Metropolitan Police statistics of around ten thousand. The press blew these likely under-estimated figures up to a probably exaggerated one hundred thousand. In 1848 the shopkeepers of Regent Street went as far as getting the Georgian and Regency architect John Nash's famous arcade in the Regent Street Quadrant demolished because prostitutes sheltered under it from inclement weather. One correspondent to *The Times* protested strongly, appealing to Londoners to say if they had ever been annoyed by the 'helpless creatures' who now had nowhere to take refuge.[13] A decade later, on 8 January 1858, *The Times* proclaimed that in no other European capital city was there 'daily and nightly such a shameless display of prostitution as in London'.[14] Ladies on shopping expeditions in Regent Street and Piccadilly might well find themselves challenged by prostitutes who assumed that they were competitors. Even worse, women were being solicited by the equivalent of modern 'kerb crawlers', which also suggests that prostitutes were not necessarily identifiable at first glance. In some ways, prefiguring the modern polemic about whether women should be advised to dress modestly, ladies were warned to wear poke-bonnets, thus hiding their faces except from the direct onlooker, and to avoid wearing red, which as Lola Montes, the leading figure in a contemporary legal case, discovered to her cost, was understood to be the uniform of ladies of the night.

Dark and Exotic: Lola Montes

Lola Montes or Montez was one of the great adventuresses of the time, who filled many columns of the London press in 1849.[15] She was born Eliza Gilbert in Ireland in 1820, the daughter of an army officer. Her father was posted to India where he died of cholera and she eloped at the age of sixteen with Lieutenant Thomas James. Her marriage broke up and soon she was back in England, living it up on money given to her by her generous stepfather and driving matched ponies and a glittering phaeton in Hyde Park in the company of several male friends including Lieutenant George Lennox. In time, the money ran out. Eliza was disgraced when Lennox admitted what was discreetly called *crim.con*, short for 'criminal conversation' (meaning adultery) and paid Lieutenant James a token £100 to settle his action. The beautiful and talented Eliza went off to Andalusia to study Spanish dancing, adopting the name of Maria Dolores, or Lola for short. Meanwhile, on 15 December 1842, James obtained a separation from Eliza in the Ecclesiastical Court. It was not a divorce, so any subsequent marriage was illegal.

Under her stage name of Lola Montes, Eliza became the toast of Paris, where she was 'protected' by wealthy men and combined her undoubted talents as a dancer with daringly erotic movements and the minimum of clothing, especially in her famous Spider Dance in which she pretended to search in her clothes and intimate parts of her body for a spider which had crawled in there.

On a visit to London, she tried to attract press attention by going to the Princess Theatre in Oxford Street wearing a revealing crimson dress, a colour which was taken as identifying the woman who wore it as a prostitute. Her gamble for notoriety failed. People looked away, Lola, a known adulteress, was ostracised, but this would be no more than a temporary hiccup in her career.

Performing in Munich in 1846 she was noticed by Ludwig I of Bavaria, a minor sovereign in his sixties, a mediocre poet and builder of neo-classical edifices. Ludwig was irresistibly smitten by the dark and exotic Lola, whom he made Gräfin or Countess of Landsfeld. Here, on her estates, and in the Bavarian capital, Lola behaved like a modern spoiled pop idol, beating her servants, breaking windows in a bad temper, refusing to pay the large bills she incurred, and finally prevailing on Ludwig to close the local university in order to suppress the protests of the students against Ludwig's extravagance and his excessive spending on his mistress. Moreover, she became so inextricably involved in political intrigue that the cabinet resigned and in 1848 Ludwig was eventually forced to abdicate.

Carrying a fortune in jewels that the doting king had given her, Lola returned to London and, still irrepressible, took a costly ten-roomed apartment at 27, Half-Moon Street, off Piccadilly. A stage production about her Bavarian adventure was so scandalous that the Lord Chamberlain, who was in charge of censuring plays, banned it. Snubbed by high society, Lola nevertheless caused a general sensation. Everybody talked about her, women copied her hair and her clothes, while tradesmen put her picture on fans for women to envy, and on snuffboxes for men to pass around to their leering friends.

Lola married George Stafford Heald, an eligible bachelor, at the fashionable St. George's, Hanover Square, on 19 July 1849. It was an error, for soon afterwards, as they returned from their honeymoon, Lola was arrested and charged with bigamy.

On 6 August, amid feverish public interest, Lola and George Heald appeared at the magistrate's court at Great Marlborough Street, in London's West End. The reporter for *The Times* wrote, somewhat ungallantly, that Lola claimed to be 24 years old, though she was 28, but looked 30 and was 'quite unembarrassed' by her predicament. Readers were informed in great detail about her appearance and her clothes. She claimed that she had been granted a legal dissolution of her early runaway marriage to Thomas James. She was sure, she insisted, that she was allowed to contract another marriage. Lola wore black silk, a close-fitting black velvet jacket and a white straw bonnet trimmed with blue. She was plump, with prominent cheekbones and large blue eyes framed with long black lashes. Her bigamous husband had a turned-up nose, which gave him a look of 'great simplicity'. He was only 21. The charge of bigamy had been laid by his unmarried aunt, concerned that Lola the adventuress had her hooks into his income of six or seven thousand pounds a year.

Lola was granted bail in the huge sum of £2,000, but preferred not to appear in court. She and Heald jumped bail, and slipped over the Channel. Their marriage soon failed. Lola continued her dancing career on the Continent, in the United States and in Australia where she was contracted to entertain the gold miners of Ballarat. Finally, she decided on a new life in the United States, where she married twice more. The rest of her life was a decline into nostalgia for her glamorous past. In the end, she took to religion and expressed regret for her earlier conduct. Always a heavy smoker, a habit she had picked up while studying dance in Spain, she suffered a series of strokes and died on 17 January 1861. She was just under forty years old. Hers was a short life, but happier than that of many other women. In her earlier years, Lola Montes would probably not have agreed with the sententious proclamation which appeared in a publishing phenomenon of the time:

Martin F. Tupper's banal moralisation in his *Proverbial Philosophy*. 'Yea, there is no cosmetic like unto a holy conscience.' Millions did agree with it however, for by 1849, it had reached its ninth edition. It sold half a million copies in Britain and a million in the United States.[16]

Beauty For Ever

Women anxious about the effect of years, or whose faces were their fortune, would patronise Madame Rachel's establishment in New Bond Street, the heart of fashionable London, where, just after mid-century, they could have their hair dyed and their wrinkles concealed by a method called 'enamelling' together with many other treatments, none costing less than one guinea. Other beauty applications included the use of toothpaste, shampoo and eye-shadow, expensively supplied by Madame Rachel, while others contained no more than water and common druggist's items, among them the two guinea a bottle Magnetic Rock Dew Water of Sahara, which was later discovered to be a mixture of lead, starch, hydrochloric acid and distilled water. Madame Rachel had, however, obtained a possibly genuine recipe for luxuriant hair from a doctor at a hospital where illness had caused her own locks to fall out. All these were described in Madame Rachel's promotional brochure entitled *Beauty For Ever*. This slogan was echoed, somewhat grotesquely, by Coventry Patmore's poem 'Faithful for ever', later incorporated into his poem 'The Angel in the House', which was an idealisation of the Victorian wife.[17] Madame Rachel's advertising was carried on placards by two women parading behind each other in the street. First came the beauty and then another, whose faked ugliness was meant to indicate how the beauteous one had looked before putting herself in Madame Rachel's hands. In the end, Madame Rachel, who had earlier sold fried fish in Clare Market and functioned as a procuress in the back corridors of Drury Lane Theatre, found herself in the dock at the Old Bailey and was gaoled for obtaining money under false pretences. The charge was not, however, that she deceived the credulous women who flocked to her establishment. Her crime was to have extracted £7,000 from a wealthy widow by forging amorous letters to her from a lusty young nobleman, which had encouraged the ageing lady to buy Madame Rachel's full range of costly rejuvenating treatments. Madame Rachel was sentenced to a term of imprisonment at hard labour.[18]

Madame Rachel's salon at 47a New Bond Street was also known as a place where married women could meet their lovers, for, despite the advance of piety and respectability, London had a bubbling world of upper-class sexual vice, reflected in the flourishing market in pornography centred in Holywell Street, off the Strand, where in 1865 William Dugdale's shop was raided by the police, who removed 822 books, 3,870 prints and a large amount of other material.[19]

It was not, however, necessary to consult pornography to obtain information about what people got up to, because the newspapers offered salacious accounts of actions for *crim.con*, even before the Divorce Act of 1857 gave them many more opportunities to report fashionable adultery, 'in the public interest'.

By mid-century, rectitude, chastity and seriousness (a Victorian vogue word) were replacing the easier-going sexual attitudes of the Regency Age, As Victoria's reign advanced, high-class sexual impropriety ceased to be a light-hearted matter. Lord Palmerston, the Home Secretary, found this to his cost in 1840 when he was discovered in the bedroom of one of Victorias's ladies-in-waiting. The Queen's long-lasting hostility to 'Pam' stemmed from this escapade.[20]

Marriage, Divorce and a Woman's Place

Opportunities to earn a living wage were so hard to find that for a poor woman there was often no alternative to selling her body. 'Most women', wrote the novelist Charlotte Brontë in her novel *Shirley*,

> had no earthly employment but household work and sewing:
> no earthly pleasure but an unprofitable visiting, and no hope,
> in all their life to come, of anything better[21]

Charlotte Brontë published these words in 1849 under the male pseudonym of Currer Bell, because she did not want to be judged as a woman author who might be thought to be exaggerating. Her words indicate that the situation was not only seen from the angle of the enormously altered economic, social and legal position of women today, but as she and some other women of her time saw their own lives.

Women's legal status was entirely dependent on that of their husbands. A wife could not be an agent, trustee or executor without her husband's consent. She could not sue or be a party to a contract or make a will without her husband's permission. He could even confine her against her will, as Mr Rochester does in Charlotte Brontë's *Jane Eyre*. In sum, she had no independent legal existence. Her property was his unless it had been settled on her by trust. Her earnings, if any, legally belonged to him.

She was, however, protected against divorce by him. If a husband wanted to divorce his wife for infidelity, he would have to bring an action against her lover for *crim.con*, that is adultery. He would ask for damages and then institute a case in a Church court for a divorce *a mensa et thoro* – 'from table and bed' – which was probably the legal separation that had been granted to Lola Montes. Otherwise, a divorce *a vinculo*, that is from the 'bond' of marriage, was only possible if the marriage itself could be declared illegal, either because one party was already married, or because the blood relation was too close or perhaps because there had been some error in the original ceremony.[22] Divorce, in any case, would make a wife into a marked woman, especially if her husband could prove her adulterous behaviour. She, of course, could counter that he had consented, but this would leave them exposed to an accusation of collusion, which itself would make divorce impossible. For all practical purposes, the immense majority of unhappy couples were married, as the marriage service said, till death did them part.

In the mid-nineteenth century view, social order relied on sexual stability. So the predominant atmosphere of piety, evangelism and social discipline took an ascetic view of sex. A 'serious' person was not only faithful to his or her spouse, but also self-controlled or Malthusian, that is aware of the demographic consequences of over-enthusiastic copulation. The serious middle class, whose view had spread to the upper classes and was imposed on those below, required society to be protected against the rampant sexuality of the mob. This would be done by requiring the aristocracy to show a good example, and then by relieving the ignorance and squalor in which the lower classes lived. The earnest or evangelical stance was not hostile to love or marriage. The angelic wife was projected as a form of domestic saviour, which was all the more reason for the horror felt for hard-as-nails murderess Maria Manning in the notorious case of 1849. She did not reflect the Victorian concept of the wife as the angel of the hearth dedicated to preserving the home as a refuge from the abrasive outside world. Maria's adultery and of course her French accent (she came from French-speaking Switzerland), associated her with over-the-Channel immorality and barred her from fitting the ideal of the Victorian wife, who was thought to lack sexual passion – not the case, as later became known, of Victoria herself,– and to be so frightened of it that she preferred never to be naked in front of her husband.[23] Dr William Acton's much-reprinted *Functions and Disorders of the Reproductive Organs* of 1857 laid down that: 'As a general rule, a modest woman seldom desires any sexual gratification for herself'.[24]

What Acton really seemed to be saying was that women who liked sex were immodest. A liberal attitude towards sex was impossible for most Victorians because it was associated with atheism and revolutionary extremism in an England which, in the general view, had had the good fortune to escape the excesses of the French Revolution and of the social and political uprisings which had spread over much of Continental Europe in 1848.

Women in Trousers!

Fear of defeminisation was widespread. In 1851 there was a violent reaction to a campaign to relieve women of their cumbersome clothing. The garments devised by Mrs Amelia Bloomer, the highly-respectable editor of an American temperance journal, were based on Turkish trousers gathered at the ankle and worn beneath a calf-length skirt. There was nothing immodest about them except that the trousers suggested the presence of legs under the skirt. Mrs Bloomer, who was in London to visit the Great Exhibition in Hyde Park, walked along Piccadilly on 11 September 1851 distributing handbills and dressed in her 'rational' outfit, When she reached St. James's Park, threats to duck her in the pond made her take to her heels, a flight incidentally facilitated by her clothes.[25] It would be forty years before her 'bloomers' were adopted by women who took up cycling. In 1851 they provoked masses of articles and cartoons revealing profound anxiety about the advance of campaigns for women's rights. Saintly femininity was seen as the protection against the depravity of the squalid lives of the male mob, Sexual decency and self-restraint were the guardians of respectable society. Charles Dickens, hardly a reactionary, asked:

> should we love our Julia better if she were a Member of Parliament, a Parochial Guardian, a High Sheriff, a Grand Juror, or a woman distinguished for her able conduct in the Chair? Do we not, on the contrary, rather seek in the society of our Julia, a haven of refuge from Members of Parliament, Parochial Guardians, High Sheriffs, Grand Jurors and able Chairmen?[26]

'Falling' Pregnant

The two and one-quarter year marriage of the murderers Maria and Frederick Manning was childless. So, were Maria or her two partners, Patrick O'

Connor and Frederick Manning, infertile, or was she determined and able enough to avoid 'falling' pregnant?

Since women might give birth, as Charles Dickens's wife did, to as many as ten children in thirteen years, breastfeeding acted as a natural inhibitor of conception. In the intervals, contraception consisted usually of withdrawal by the man before he climaxed, known as *coitus interruptus*. Abortion was common and products which could bring about abortion were widely, though euphemistically, advertised as 'restoring female regularity'. Indeed until 1837 abortion had not even been criminal when carried out by the woman herself, at least not until the foetus began to quicken, or stir in the womb. Women used all sorts of dangerous preparations, usually with the aim of producing violent spasms with the aid of an explosive mixture of gin and gunpowder, or with emetics, cantharides ('Spanish Fly'), or purgatives such as aloes, juniper or ergot. Sophisticated contraceptive methods such as a sponge soaked in a spermicide or the condom were recommended in pamphlets such as Richard Carlile's *Every Woman's Book* or *What is Love*, published in 1826. But these items were quite difficult to get hold of even if a woman had ever heard of them. Rubber condoms were not considered appropriate for married people, difficult to find and in any case, cumbersome. The American Dr Charles Knowlton's *Fruits of Philosophy* of 1834 recommended douching, which was probably the most frequently used contraceptive method after withdrawal. Knowlton's forty-page book, however, sold poorly for forty years. Sales took off only after the 1877 prosecution of the freethinkers Charles Bradlaugh and Annie Besant for republishing it.[27]

The London public was morbidly excited and primed for the two scandalous cases of 1849: Lola Montes' bigamy and Frederick and Maria Manning's murder of Maria's lover, for neither woman fitted the cult of purity and moral inspiration personified in Coventry Patmore's expression of domestic bliss in his poem 'The Angel in the House', which would sell a quarter of a million copies.[28]

> Her disposition is devout,
> Her countenance angelical.
> The best things that the best believe,
> Are in her face so kindly writ,
> The faithless, seeing her, conceive
> Not only Heaven, but hope of it.

Chapter 3

What They Ate, Where They Shopped and What They Wore

Would you like to join us for dinner...?

Maria and Frederick Manning planned to murder Patrick O'Connor. They invited him to dine at their house in Bermondsey at 5.30pm. on Thursday, 9 August 1849. The time when people ate their evening meal was a marker of their social class. 5.30 had been the usual upper-class time in the eighteenth century, but a couple of generations later dinner for high society had been put off until 7.30.[1] For the 'middle' middle class, dinner was served at 6pm. The Mannings were at the foot of the middle class, so they dined a half-hour earlier than this.

It was smart, however, to dine even later. The thousands of readers of George Reynolds's very successful serial *The Mysteries of London*, of 1846, read that:

> The banquet was served up at seven precisely. Mr. Greenwood
> had gradually made his dinner an hour later as he had risen
> in the world; and he was determined that if ever he became
> a baronet he would never have that repast put on the table till
> half past eight o'clock[2]

For ordinary working folk, the word 'dinner' did not mean the evening meal but their main meal, which they ate at midday or 1pm. At night, men did not finish work until eight or even later. They took time off for their 'tea' at about four in the afternoon and had a meal called 'supper' much later. Well after dark the children of the poor would be sent out for an ounce of ham and a few pieces of cheese for dad's supper. They could be observed selecting the most savoury pieces of plaice or flounder in the fried fish shop. Fried potatoes or chips, however, as Flora Tristan complained, were as yet not a familiar accompaniment to fried fish and could not be found in London.[3]

The working man's supper time could be as late as 11pm, wrote the journalist George Augustus Sala. He added, perhaps with tongue in cheek:

when, by the steady and industrious mechanic, the final calumet is smoked, the borrowed newspaper read, the topics of the day, the prospects of the coming week discussed with the cheery and hardworking helpmeet who sits by the side of her horny-handed lord, fills his pipe, pours out his beer and darns the little children's hose[4]

What did they eat? What did it cost?

There were lots of takeaways, as they would be called today, to be had from a shop or a stall: puddings, pies, halfpenny potatoes baked with butter and salt, hot eels and pea soup. The poor, who ate whenever they had money, and who possessed few cooking facilities, such as pots and pans or even plates, had no well-provided table to look forward to at home, so they bought food where and when they could, and ate what they fancied. One trader in the poor East End district of Whitechapel told the investigative journalist Henry Mayhew that he could sell three hundred penny pies a day, mostly to boys. 'Is it just up?' they would ask, 'I likes it 'ot.'[5]

The fictional David Copperfield's account of his early life reflects Charles Dickens's memories of the time when, as a ten-year-old boy, he worked putting paper labels on bottles at Warren's boot-polish factory near Hungerford Bridge. In the novel, David's lodgings at the Micawbers are paid for by his stepfather, the cruel and appropriately named Mr Murdstone, but every penny of the six to seven shillings he earns every week goes on his food. He breakfasts on a penny 'loaf' or more likely a roll, and a pennyworth of milk (probably warm as it was newly milked in the street or a neighbouring cowshed). He sups on another penny loaf and a piece of cheese. If the cheese costs a penny he would spend two shillings and fourpence a week, leaving him perhaps four shillings a week for his main meal. Sometimes he is so hungry that he cannot wait for midday dinner and buys some of the stale pastry put outside the bakeries at half-price, or:

> a stout, pale pudding, heavy and flabby, and with great, flat raisins in it, stuck in whole at wide distances apart. It came up hot at about my time every day, and many a day did I dine off it

When he saves his money until the evening, David has a saveloy sausage and a penny loaf, or a fourpenny plate of beef, or bread and cheese and a glass of beer. 'Tea' is a pint of coffee and a slice of bread and butter. The older David, looking back at his childhood, recalls that, not surprisingly for a ten-year-old boy who worked from morning till night and walked from Camden Town down to the Thames and back again, he was hungry all the time and spent any extra money he could obtain on food. His breakfast and supper were nutritionally poor as well as monotonous. This would not have mattered so much if he had eaten a properly balanced meal during the day. Yet how many working London children did not even have David's six or seven shillings to spend on their week's nourishment?

For all but the wealthiest, food was the largest item in family budgets, and bread the largest item in the family food bill. The stodgy, soggy, greyish-coloured quartern loaf, called by that name because it was often cut into quarters for sale, and which, by the London Bread Act of 1822, was required to weigh four pounds and fifteen ounces, that is just under five pounds or 2.2 kilograms, cost eightpence halfpenny in 1846.[6] When the Corn Laws were repealed in that year to allow cheap corn to be imported, the price of the loaf fell slightly, though not till the development of railways in the USA and Russia, and the cheapening of sea freight by the widespread use of steam power for ships, did the poor of London benefit from the vast production of the wheat fields of those still distant lands.[7]

A 'Nice Cuppa'

Prior to 1833, the East India Company had enjoyed a monopoly in importing the tea leaf, which kept the price high. Tea was also heavily taxed. With the duty, tea in the early years of Victoria's reign cost a substantial three shillings per pound. This led people to brew their tea weak and watery, so consumption was quite low.[8] However, as in so many aspects of life, change was coming. In 1853, the duty on tea was reduced, while new sources in India and Ceylon were steadily being developed. Consequently, tea consumption began to rise.

Milk on its own was not drunk very much. In any case, most people had no way of keeping it fresh, especially in the summer, so Londoners would buy a jugful every day from a milkmaid who milked a backyard cow and carried two heavy tubs of the fluid around the local streets suspended from a yoke over her shoulders. Weak tea with little or no milk was made palatable by sugar, which had fallen in price to fivepence a pound. The huge amount of thirty-six pounds per head of sugar was consumed in England and Wales, with all that the addiction would mean for the extent of dental decay among people who were unfamiliar with the use of a toothbrush.[9]

The sort of food that one ate, as well as the quantity, depended on one's income. Bacon was considered cheap at eightpence per pound. It was easy to cook over an open fire, but economy-minded housewives who had some

26

skill in cooking, and the time for it, could also buy coarse cuts of butcher's offal for fourpence a pound or less. Best butcher's meat was expensive and could not be so carefully eked out, nor so easily cooked as bacon.

Another consideration, for poorer people at least, was the facilities they had for preparing food. Many did not have a hearth or fireplace of their own, or possess more than a frying pan. And if women worked as hard as men during the day, perhaps sewing for a pittance, or doing the laundry for a better-off family, the time it took to prepare food was ill-affordable. The manicured vegetables and fruit sold in supermarkets in the latter part of the twentieth century, together with the ready-made meals and the meat tailored to the need for quick-cooking on today's reliable gas or electric cookers, contrast with life even in the first half of the twentieth century when, not so differently from a century earlier, the greengrocer offered the London housewife, particularly in the winter, a poor choice of no more than a few earth-covered and battered potatoes, some tired looking cabbages, twisted carrots and wormy apples, while a chicken, which she had to draw and pluck herself, was a luxury.

Family Food Budgets

The desperate poor lived almost entirely on potatoes. At a slightly higher level, hunger could be assuaged only by bread, potatoes and gruel, this last a staple in prisons and workhouses, like the one in which Dickens's Oliver Twist is so hungry that he asks famously for more. The London labourer, or even Bob Cratchit, Ebenezer Scrooge's underpaid clerk in Dickens's *A Christmas Carol*, earning fifteen shillings a week, with a family to keep, had little choice of food. If his wife was really economical, and a skilled manager and housewife, she could buy for herself, her husband and their children, the following basket of food.

	s.	d
5 quartern loaves at 8½d	3	6½
5 pounds of meat at 5d	2	1
7 pints of porter (beer) at 2d	1	2
Half hundredweight (56 pounds) of coal		9½
40 pounds of potatoes	1	4
3 ounces of tea; 1 pound of sugar	1	6
1 pound of butter		9
Total	11	2

Three-quarters of that family's income went on food and coal. The remainder of the fifteen shillings was spent on rent for their one room, and on candles and odd purchases. Nothing remained for clothes, shoes, medicine or for any emergency or pleasure at all.

That diet was not, in any case, ideal. The amount of protein obtained from the meat was not inconsiderable, but there were hardly any fats save the pound of butter to be shared among five people. They drank no milk. Bread and potatoes provided the required bulk. Father had to have his daily pint of beer, which provided the calories he needed for his heavy labour. The children's sweet tooth seems to have been well-provided for by the pound of sugar consumed every week. But no fruit or green vegetables came home in this family's shopping basket.

A better-paid workman, earning perhaps £1.5/- a week, and especially if he was in regular employment, could eat meat daily, and add bacon and cheese to his diet, but when times were hard, during the winter, for example, in the building trade, meat might disappear from the table, to be replaced by the appetite-satisfying bread and potatoes, with or without butter or the dripping which butchers sold separately.

A much better-off middle-class man with an income of £250 per year, with two or three children and a live-in servant, had a weekly diet, according to Mrs Rundell's *New System of Domestic Economy*, of 1825, of 3½ pounds of butter, that is over half a pound per person, a quarter of a pound each of cheese and a staggering 4½ pounds of sugar, that is approaching a pound per head. They ate eighteen pounds of meat, but only sixpence-worth of vegetables and fruit.[10]

Families enjoying a still high income ate even more meat and butter. Thomas Carlyle, author of the famous history of the French Revolution, his wife Jane and their servant, with income from land as well as from his writing, ate 10 pounds of potatoes and 2½ pounds of butter between them every week, but consumed little or no fresh fruit or green vegetables. Christmas dinner was soup, stewed mutton and bread pudding, followed by mince pies. Vegetables are not mentioned. Yet Carlyle lived to the age of 86. His diet does not seem to have done him much harm.[11]

How They Cooked

If a housewife bought a duck, goose or chicken, the butcher might draw and pluck it, but if she bought it from a drover who had chivvied a few head of poultry to market, she would probably have to carry out such difficult, unpleasant and time-consuming tasks herself, with demanding children hanging around her skirts.

English cooking was plain, according to the popular recipe books of the early Victorian age. Garlic and sauces were foreign and therefore to be avoided. Interestingly, in contrast to the popularity for British palates that Indian and Chinese food would acquire later, a high-selling recipe book of the 1840s, Eliza Acton's *Modern Cookery for Private Families*, published in 1845, devoted only fifteen of its 250 pages to foreign dishes.

Middle-class families would advertise for 'a good, plain cook'. She would be expected to provide straightforward English food, exemplified by this weekly menu:

SUNDAY: Roast beef, Yorkshire, potatoes and greens.
MONDAY: Hashed beef and potatoes.
TUESDAY: Broiled [grilled] beef and vegetables.
WEDNESDAY: Fish, chops and vegetables.
THURSDAY: Boiled pork, pease pudding, greens.
FRIDAY: Pea soup, pork.
SATURDAY: Stewed steak and suet dumplings[12]

Meat was eaten every day. The Wednesday fish is not specified, but was to be eaten with a chop. It is striking that vegetables, besides potatoes, greens and peas, are mentioned often in this weekly menu. Salads are, however, not often listed because raw food was thought too hard to digest. The presence of vegetables is explained possibly by the fact that the author of the book in which this menu appeared was Alexis Soyer, the famous French chef of the Reform Club between 1837 and 1850. Soyer had fled the 1830 revolution in France, and had repaid English hospitality by setting up soup kitchens in Leicester Square in central London during a period of high unemployment and distress, as well as in Ireland to bring some relief to people who were starving during the potato blight of 1847. Later, in 1853, he would go out to the Crimea to help nurse Florence Nightingale set up field kitchens to improve the diet of soldiers lying sick and wounded in the military hospital at Scutari.

Soyer's menu appeared in his *The Modern Housewife or Ménagère*, published in 1849. The book sold so well that it was reprinted after the first fortnight, and by 1851 it had sold 21,000 copies.[13] So well known was Soyer's book that the humorous weekly *Punch* published a piece on 15 September 1849 in which two married women, 'Mary A.' and 'Eliza B.', complained about how much more demanding their husbands had been since the work appeared. Perhaps the hostess at the house where the

Reverend Dan Greatorex dined out in 1856 had studied Eliza Acton's and Soyer's works closely. Greatorex noted in his diary that he had eaten roast lamb, boiled chicken, apple tarts and cherry pudding.[14]

How the Food arrived: Shopping in London

In the early Victorian period, the railways were not yet bringing into the city the vast amounts of food that London required for its teeming two million inhabitants. Every day, in the light of the early summer dawn or still in winter darkness, hundreds of horses plodded in from the fields of the neighbouring or 'home' counties of Essex, Middlesex and Surrey, while women walked long distances carrying produce from the market gardens of Hammersmith, Fulham or Deptford, to supply Covent Garden and London's other large markets. The wholesalers bought produce from the market gardeners between five and seven in the morning. One of the specialities of poor Irish immigrant women was to buy small quantities of vegetables and carry them in baskets to all parts of London. As for meat, the main roads into the capital were thronged with people driving ducks and geese, while 152,804 head of cattle and 1,582,530 sheep were sold at Smithfield meat market in 1828.[15]

All this would change with the coming of the railway. It was already beginning to make a difference. By 1853, seven railway companies were bringing over one million head of live cattle per year to the capital. A striking example of how the railways could bring down costs came from St Thomas's Hospital. For years St Thomas's had bought milk for its patients from local dairies at a cost of a shilling a gallon. From 1854 onwards, however, the hospital began to buy milk 25 per cent more cheaply from an Essex dairy farmer and have it brought by the Eastern Counties railway. Eastern Counties carried 750,000 gallons of milk that year, much of which went to London.[16] Fruit, not yet a major component of diet, also fell in price once it could be brought from cheaper producers abroad, discharged at Southampton or Liverpool and brought to London by the railway. It does not seem, however, to have been popular. Jane Carlyle, indeed, thought it was of no use at all and merely gave one the colic. Yet even the exotic West Indian pineapples were beginning to appear. Charles Dickens reported having seen them in the main market at Covent Garden as early as the late 1830s.[17] They were, however, very dear. Thomas and Jane Carlyle's maidservant was rumoured to have a wealthy great-uncle who thought nothing of paying £2.10s for a pineapple.

However, it would be the invention of refrigeration, and its use on cargo ships, that would finally cut the cost of imported foodstuffs so greatly that later in the Victorian century the economy of much of English agriculture collapsed. Meat would then be brought frozen into Britain when previously it had to be imported on the hoof from Argentina much more expensively.

The housewife could shop on Saturday nights, once she had been supplied with money by her husband, who had just received his weeks' wages. As an aspiring middle-class lady, the murderess Maria Manning could walk to Borough Market from her home in Bermondsey, or to the New Cut off the Waterloo Road, and, stepping daintily so as to avoid splashing mud on her white cotton stockings, her merino wool dress and her dark blue or black shawl (all of which would later be listed on the police inventory of her possessions), ignoring the vulgar repartee of the stall-holders, might point disdainfully with a gloved forefinger at the heaps of earth-covered potatoes or carrots and other vegetables. Perhaps she would buy a shilling's worth of mackerel, a plateful of sprats or a quart of mussels. Oysters, today an expensive delicacy, were cheap and a favourite dish.

One may doubt whether middle-class people, or those who aspired to be considered such, would have deigned to buy a baked potato from the 'baked tater' man, leave alone a penny mutton pie or a penny's worth – a 'penn'orth' in London speech – of the cockney favourite, stewed eels, sold in little metal dishes. Not only was eating in the street vulgar, but who knew whether such delights were really what they claimed to be?

> PUBLICAN: 'Looks like rain.'
> DRINKER: 'Yes, I thought it wasn't beer.'

Whether there was much, if any, real mutton in the pie sold by the 'flying pieman', as one famous purveyor of that particular delicacy styled himself, might be doubted. There was virtually no control over the genuineness of what was being offered, and food was widely adulterated. This is known, curiously enough, because about this time books were published which, in due course, led to something being done about the scandal. In 1848, for example, John Mitchell published his *Treatise on the Falsifications of Food and the Chemical Means used to detect them.* Greed and great competition to reduce costs led to widespread adulteration of food. This was particularly so in the case of bread and beer, as well as of heavily-taxed products such as tea. Bakers ground up potatoes and beans into their flour, or mixed alum, chalk, ashes and powdered bones into their product, already falsified by the stone dust that the millers had added to the flour. Brewers and publicans were among the worst culprits. The former used not only the toxic *cocculus indicus* but also *nux vomica*, another poisonous berry from the East Indies, together with the pungent *capsicum* and coriander, as substitutes for malt and hops by which the diluted beer was given flavour and strength. New beer could be rapidly matured with sulphuric acid; old and sour beer could be restored with oyster shells, while iron sulphite allowed diluted beer to froth. Sulphuric acid and white arsenic were added to gin.

As for grocers, they sold loose 'tea' well mixed with ash, sloe or elder leaves. In the 1840s there were eight 'factories' in London specialising in recycling tea leaves.[18] The used leaves were dried, coloured with chemicals and mixed with the genuine article. Elsewhere, copper was added to give colour to pickles, and red lead and pepper dust were added to the rind of cheese. Zinc, iron and even arsenic were used for similar purposes.[19] The purpose was as deceitful, if more dangerous, as today's habit of placing tired meat under bright lights to suggest falsely exaggerated freshness. On 25 August 1849, *Punch* quipped that the anti-diarrhoeic chalk mixture prescribed during the current cholera epidemic could easily be replaced by the adulterated milk that people were being sold. Let the milkman advertise 'Genuine Chalk Mixture' and he would make his fortune.

Attitudes towards official interference, even for the benefit of the public in controlling the adulteration of food and drink, as well as the purity of the water supply, were seen as intolerable Continental-style snooping on the individual free British citizen. It is hard to understand why the uniformed French inspectors who checked the weight of Parisian bakers' loaves were held up as examples of the police state that might come about in Britain if people were not vigilant, until one takes into account how unpopular even the idea of a patrolling police force was before people grew accustomed to seeing the constables. Nevertheless, opinion, echoed as so often by Charles Dickens, was coming round to the view that the traditional London authorities were far from competent to administer a modern, heavily-populated and pulsating city. If, for example, cab drivers in Paris were better regulated than their foul-mouthed, cheating London opposite numbers because they were centrally controlled, then let us have 'centralisation', even though this was the current bogey word, wrote Dickens.[20] Probably his plea would have been echoed by the twenty guests who had been taken ill at a public banquet in Nottingham in the 1850s. They had been served blancmange for their dessert, whose green colour had been intensified by the addition of arsenite of copper. Fortunately for the survivors, only one died.[21]

Let's Eat Out

As for eating out, there were only a few hotel dining-rooms open to the public in London. The best restaurants, according *to Murray's Handbook to London* of 1851, were Verrey's in Regent Street, Bertolini's and Giraud's off Leicester Square, and Mouflet's in Knightsbridge.

'Restaurants' had been opened in London during the French Revolution by the unemployed chefs of guillotined aristocrats. The word 'restaurant' still had French connotations and was probably pronounced as in French. All these restaurants served 'French' dinners, advised *Murray's Handbook*. Ladies are said not to have eaten unaccompanied in such places. Yet, when Jane Carlyle was being driven to distraction by the builders, who seemed never to be going to finish the repairs and alterations to her Chelsea house, she went for her 'dinner', which she preferred to have at about 2pm, at Verrey's. Here Jane ordered a chop and a glass of bitter ale. It cost only 1/5d. On another day she ate in a restaurant in the Strand. Her dish there was half a roast chicken, a large slice of ham and three new potatoes, all for a mere shilling. She must have been a little doubtful about the propriety of eating on her own, for she noted that she was reassured to see other ladies, as respectable-looking as herself, dining alone.[22] Times were evidently changing.

What you ate was firmly marked by your social class, or perhaps it was the other way round. There were grimy eating places, like the 'greasy-spoons', patronised by working men in overalls, where house painters in white paper hats and paint-stained corduroy trousers sat with carpenters and plumbers. These were skilled men a cut above mere labourers and navvies who brought their food wrapped in a pocket handkerchief. Men in suits sat in 'dining-rooms' at partitioned-off tables. Today still, in rows of shops in gloomy Victorian inner London suburbs awaiting the demolition men, the fascia board of a long-closed shop bearing the words 'Dining-Room' is sometimes revealed beneath more modern shop signs. Here, diners in their black coats sat in enclosed wooden booths, hanging their hats on the corner of the partitions and eating their chop and potatoes as they read the newspaper propped up against the cruets. In the City, there were 'chop-houses', where the man of affairs could enjoy his steaming mutton-chop or his plate of boiled beef, accompanied perhaps by a potato or two. At a higher level still, unmarried men and retired military officers, such as the novelist Thackeray's Major Pendennis, ate at their private clubs. You could have a well-served dinner at the Athenaeum for 2/10d, which was a lot more than Jane Carlyle paid for her meals out, but good value if compared with what three Dickensian law students consumed when they had a rambunctious meal out.

Phiz's illustration in Chapter XX of *Bleak House* shows Mr Jobling, Mr Guppy and the young Bart Smallweed sharing a booth in the type of eating house known, Dickens tells his readers, as a 'slap-bang', perhaps because of the unceremonious way the meal was served. The clerks push the boat out and spend recklessly. Smallweed reckons up what they have eaten, adding the cost of each item to the total as he goes along:

> Four veals and hams is three [shillings], and four potatoes is three and four, and one summer cabbage is three and six, and three marrows is four and six, and six breads is five, and three Cheshires [cheese] is five and three, and four half pints of half and half is six and three, and four small rums is eight and three, and three Pollies [tip for the waitress] is eight and six

The meal costs each clerk a sizeable two shillings and ten pence, although without the rum each bill would have been sixpence less. It is still extravagant for men earning a little over a pound a week, though Guppy gets £1.15s. Henry Colman, the Bostonian visitor to early Victorian London, reckoned that he could dine for between 1/6d and 2/- without wine. A plate of meat was eightpence, potatoes a penny, celery twopence, greens twopence, bread a penny; apple pie was 4d, a pint of ale a penny. With a penny for the waiter, the total cost was 1/8d, close to Jane Carlyle's bill at Verrey's.[23]

Eat it and Like it

The quality of the product in shops, the cooking in restaurants, and the service was another matter. It was not done to make a fuss about any of them. You ate what you were given and liked it. In any case, people who depended on credit in their local shop could not afford to complain. It would be a long time before multiple grocers such as Lipton's and the famous Home and Colonial opened shops in London's high streets, and competed with the smaller shops in price and quality. One critic of about 1850 dared to complain, but only anonymously, about being served in a London eating-place with:

> parboiled ox-flesh with sodden dumplings floating in a saline, greasy mixture, surrounded by carrots looking red with disgust and turnips pale with dismay[24]

The American Herman Melville went out for his breakfast on 18 November 1849 to a chop house near the Temple, close to the Strand where he was staying. He noted that he was served 'a villainous cup of coffee, a large dirty roll and a strip of bacon', though he paid no more than 4d, so perhaps his expectations were too high.[25] In contrast, the Austrian dramatist Franz Grillparzer dined at the London Coffee House, on:

> Salmon, too grand for an emperor, roast beef surpassing every conception, currant tart for Great Britain's palate, peas boiled in water, salads to eat raw, which we did not, Stilton cheese to which there is nothing equal[26]

Few of these eating-houses, dining-rooms or chop houses were patronised by women, who did not usually eat out alone – perhaps Jane Carlyle's experience was exceptional – until much later in the century when the new department stores began to open refreshment rooms, and even later when J. Lyons & Co and the Aerated Bread Company or ABC opened teashops where the female office workers who handled the new typewriting machines and telephones could have something to eat in their dinner hour, away from the overwhelming masculine atmosphere of the chop houses and 'slap-bangs' with their avuncular or gloomy waiters, their sawdust and spittoons, stained table cloths and heavy, coarse crockery and cutlery.

'Tis my Delight on a Friday Night'

Better-off people could round off an evening at a West End theatre with supper, perhaps at the Café de l'Europe in the Haymarket, ordering a partridge, fillet steak or truffles, or plain English chops, steak and kidney, sausages or Welsh rarebit, washed down with a glass of stout. The gentleman could finish off his meal with a cigar and a glass of brandy and water. If their funds did not run to such luxuries, they could buy a tired ham sandwich or some poor quality pig's trotters from an old woman wearily carrying her tray in the street. At the least, they could finish off the evening in the Royal Albert at the junction of the Haymarket and Coventry Street with a halfpenny baked potato.[27]

Fish probably offered the best value for eating out. Shellfish were relatively cheap in London, and oysters, in particular, were known as food for the poor. At the famous Greenwich fair stallholders sold pennyworths of pickled salmon with fennel, oysters and whelks, the latter unfamiliar to Charles Dickens who wrote that he thought they were called *wilks*.[28] There was a shop in the Haymarket where oysters, lobsters, crabs, pickled salmon and sprats were to be enjoyed. One ate them standing up at the wooden counter, with crusty bread and butter and a pint of stout. However, there were no napkins, even of the paper variety, and one wiped one's hands on a common roller towel.

Sprats were a favourite treat for supper. The tune of 'The Lincolnshire Poacher' was given the words:

> Oh! 'Tis my delight on a Friday night,
> When sprats they isn't dear,
> To fry a couple of score or so,
> Upon a fire clear.

Another treat on a bright summer day was to take an excursion on a steamer down the river to Lovegrove's East India Tavern at Blackwall, where you could have the speciality of the house: whitebait with a squeeze of lemon and cayenne pepper, or salmon, eels or stewed carp, accompanied by brown bread and butter and washed down with iced punch, followed by a fruit tart with custard.

Posh Eating

This was quite different. The upper class dined starting with soup, then fish followed by the entrée and the roast. After that came the savoury and a dessert. Dinner might be served *à la française*, where there were two courses, each with a wide choice of dishes, or *à la russe*, where each dish was presented in turn. Really wealthy folk employed French chefs (Alexis Soyer served at several noble houses in turn), following the example of the Prince Regent, who had paid one thousand pounds a year to his chef, somewhat contradictorily named Carême, which means 'Lent'.

Society festivities were catered for by Robert Gunter of Mayfair's elegant Berkeley Square, a renowned pastry cook. Gunter supplied lavish parties with trifles, ice cream, lobster salads, turkey in jelly, ham in broth and the like, and you always went to Gunter's for your daughter's wedding cake. Gunter's also supplied the china and the glass, as well as the requisite number of black-clad men with grave faces and butler-like mien. If not Gunter's, the wealthy patronised Fortnum and Mason of Piccadilly, which dated back to 1707 and is still attracting well-heeled tourists and country cousins.[29] Fortnum's speciality was hampers for picnics.

Shopping in Town

Usefully, considering its unreliable weather, London provided covered shopping in arcades and bazaars. The Adelaide Gallery in the Lowther Arcade near Trafalgar Square was eighty yards long and had shops which were lit by skylights and sold jewellery, millinery, cutlery, perfumes and fancy goods. Marks and Spencer in Oxford Street stands today on the site of what was called the Pantheon, a bazaar for accessories and fancy goods, toys, wax flowers and crochet work, The Pantheon employed beadles with gold-laced hatbands at the Oxford Street and Great Marlborough Street ends to prevent undesirables wandering in and annoying the customers. The beadles welcomed female customers with a bow. Inside there were stalls with fancy items, toys and papier-mâché ornaments for the table, dolls and children's dresses, wax flowers and crochet-work, and wares of all sorts to attract women. The Pantheon employed female assistants. A contemporary journalist wrote about them:

> The gentlemen, I am pleased, though mortified, to say, they
> treat with condescension mingled with a reserved dignity
> which awes the boldest spirit[30]

At a corner of Soho Square stood the Soho Bazaar, where women rented the stalls for between two and three shillings a day. All the merchandise: millinery, lace, gloves, jewellery and the like was for high-spending women, whose private carriages were to be seen lined up outside.

The young women serving at the stalls were, of course, very 'respectable'. They were supervised by a matron and required to wear plain, dark dresses.[31] Along Oxford Street the later famous department stores, now mostly gone, of Peter Robinson, Dickens and Jones and Marshall and Snellgrove were flourishing as linen drapers. In West London's wealthy suburbs, Henry Harrod, the tea merchant, had taken over a grocery shop in the Brompton Road, but Whiteley's in Westbourne Grove would not open until 1863.

Regent Street was the prime shopping centre for fancy and unnecessary luxuries. It had been completed in 1820. In 1837, the year Victoria came to the throne, it was described thus:

> The buildings of this noble street chiefly consist of palace-like
> shops, in whose broad showy windows are displayed articles
> of the most splendid description, such as the neighbouring
> world of wealth and fashion are daily in want of. The upper

parts of these elegant structures are mostly let as apartments to temporary visitors of the metropolis.

The Circus [*Regent, now Oxford Circus*] unites Regent-Street with Oxford-Street. It is a continuous style of architecture with the houses above it. Its form is one of the best which could be devised for the purpose; it gives an air of grandeur and space to the streets, and a free circulation of air to the houses. It affords facilities to carriages and horsemen in turning from one street to the other, and is as elegant in form as useful in application[32]

Oxford Street, running west to east through the centre of the West End, did not entirely share the high social status of Regent Street, which crossed it at Regent Circus, but it was the centre of women's fashion, and already in 1817 had premises for thirty-three linen drapers, twenty-four boot and shoe manufacturers, seventeen hosiers and glovers, as well as a variety of other shops catering for women.[33]

Henry Colman, the Bostonian Unitarian minister, admired the elegance of the shop windows of Regent Street, with their plate glass, gaslight and gilding, stuccoed frontages, gold lettering, carpets and massive pillars:

> Indeed, I think one of the most beautiful sights I have seen in London has been on a ride down Regent Street, on the box-seat of an omnibus, in the evening, when the streets are crowded with people elegantly dressed and the shops ... with their illuminated windows of immense length ... the whole of this magnificent street seems converted into the hall of an oriental palace[34]

Regent Street was 'a great trunk road to vanity fair' wrote the journalist George Augustus Sala in 1859. Between two and four in the afternoon was the fashionable time for shopping. In Regent Street, the assistants in the expensive and modish shops gave themselves airs as they showed silk stockings at four shillings a pair, lace cuffs at three shillings and shawls at two guineas, all with a languid air of indifference.

Indeed, the strange behaviour of London shop assistants and even proprietors until almost the present day was remarked on by a Parisian visitor in 1856:

> The detached attitude of shopkeepers in London is amazing ...
> they seem quite indifferent as to whether you make or do

not make a purchase … the cashier took my money with the attitude of a man receiving a subscription for some charitable purpose[35]

In smart shops to bargain would have seemed the height of foreign-style vulgarity, yet the price of an article was not always indicated and had to be asked about. Nor were the customers invited to inspect the goods at their leisure. Not until the drapers' shops became department stores with fixed and clearly-indicated prices, selling for cash and not credit (cash was seen by many as vulgar), did things change.

Clothes make the Woman

The wealthy had their clothes made personally for them by a tailor or a dressmaker. When they no longer wanted them they gave them away to their servants, who passed them on to the poor in the streets or sold them to the abundant market in second-hand garments. Hippolyte Taine, the French historian and critic, observing English behaviour, thought that the wearing of second-hand finery by the London poor was grotesque and debasing. The French workman and peasant wore their own clothes. 'In England,' he wrote, 'the poor resign themselves to being other people's doormats.'[36]

The record of the trial of Maria and Frederick Manning reveals much about female clothing. Maria wore items given to her by her employers, Lady Palk and Lady Blantyre, who would probably wear certain dresses, shoes and kid gloves only once or twice. Maria, however, had the skill to alter the dresses and to establish her image of respectable and stylish neatness. And she had a vast quantity of clothes. When she fled to Edinburgh after murdering Patrick O'Connor, she took so many trunks and boxes with her that the police later found a receipt for excess baggage in her purse. She had already left so many clothes in the boxes that she had deposited at London Bridge Station that their inventory occupied four foolscap sheets of the police clerk's copperplate penmanship. Among them were eleven petticoats, nine gowns, twenty-eight pairs of stockings, seven pairs of drawers, nineteen pairs of kid gloves, as well as sheets, tablecloths, napkins and the astonishing number of twenty-seven pillow cases.[37] This, nevertheless, was minor in comparison with the property she took with her to Edinburgh: morning wrappers, petticoats, nightgowns, handkerchiefs, shifts and chemises, stays, a mantilla, silk and cotton stockings, silk handkerchiefs, veils, aprons, gowns of sarsnet (a fine soft silken material), of merino wool and satin, a worsted shawl, lace flounces, lace veils, tippets, collars and gloves, thirty pieces of silk and satin, other dress-lengths, skirts and bodices, and much more.

Maria sewed by hand. Sewing machines came into widespread use later, although ten patents for them were filed in 1849.[38] She had a wide choice of fashion magazines at her disposal, including *Le Petit Courrier des Dames* and *The Lady's Gazette of Fashion*. Later on, the fashion magazines would compete for readers by including free paper dress patterns in each issue.

The press described in detail the dresses and accessories that Maria wore at her trial. She dressed neatly, in good-quality clothes, and with sober and elegant taste. She wore the wider skirts which came into fashion after the simple lines of the Regency period began to go out of style just as Victoria ascended the throne, but she went to her death before the introduction of the exaggeratedly hooped skirt which was called the crinoline because it was stiffened by an underskirt made of horsehair (*crin*, in French). Nevertheless, the wider skirts of the 1840s required an ever-growing number of petticoats to support them and bulk them out. Maria wore as many as seven flannel or starched calico petticoats in order to produce the dome-like appearance of a skirt which was several feet in circumference. To create the essential small waist and generously pushed-up bosom of the times, she wore high-laced stays. These were essential, and to leave them off for comfort was considered indecent and produced an unfamiliar outline of the female form. In very young and slim women, however, such as Marian Halcombe, whom the novelist and friend of Dickens Wilkie Collins introduces in Chapter 5 of *The Woman in White*, published in 1860, the waist was 'visibly and delightfully undeformed by stays'.

Stays could be made to measure but also bought ready-made. They laced up behind, though there was a version called 'the new corset', which did up more conveniently at the front. Maria Manning wore white cotton stockings. These were kept up with garters, which could be bought at Harvey Nichols's for 4/11½ d a pair, though a serviceable version could be found in poorer districts like Bermondsey, where Maria lived, for no more than 4½ d.

The police inventory of Maria's clothes also lists several pairs of drawers, a garment which came in before the crinoline, although it is often said that drawers were invented to avoid serious lapses in modesty when the wind got under the enormous 'cage' hoops of the 1850s, blowing women over and their skirts in the air. Wearing drawers was a mark of Maria's social class aspiration, for working women adopted the garment much later.[39]

Maria's clothes were described in great detail in the reports of her and her husband's trial. On her head, she wore black or white lace or muslin caps. No respectable women went out without a bonnet, and on all formal occasions, Maria wore a coal-scuttle shaped hat, which she had bought perhaps in Swan and Edgar on the corner of Regent Street and Piccadilly, trimmed with ribbons and with lace or muslin framing her face, which could be seen only straight on, for women did not want to appear to be trying to invite attention.

The pictures of Maria, drawn in court by artists for the press, make it difficult to see how she wore her hair. In one, she seems to have dressed it in ringlets or curls cascading over her forehead and down the side of her face.[40] In the photographs of Madame Tussaud's wax model, however, Maria wears her hair with a parting in the middle and drawn firmly down on each side of her head. She wears a lace cap, tied under her chin, so that the back of her head is not visible, but she probably had her hair tied firmly back over her ears and drawn together with a ribbon at the back.[41] Perhaps this was how she was required to wear her hair in prison.

In court, she wore elegant shawls in suitably matching colours. Certainly, had Hippolyte Taine, the critical French observer, seen her, he would not have written, as he did about Englishwomen – Maria was Swiss – that her clothes were

> Badly-matched, striped, fussed, overdone, loud, with excessively numerous colours swearing at each other[42]

The American Henry Colman thought that upper-class Englishwomen were very neat, compared with the 'dirty pantalets bobbing about the ankles of our women'.[43] English women, he wrote, did not wear false curls or dye their hair as, he implied, American women did. By the end of 1843, however, his letters show that he was less sure about the good taste of women in England, for he writes that 'the dress and appearance of the middle classes, with many exceptions, are much inferior to ours'.[44] Colman, however, was prone to frequent changes of opinion.

Show me how you dress and...

As for men, a combination of evangelical seriousness and the dirty atmosphere of the city streets contributed to their clothes growing ever more sombre.[45] Gone were the padded shoulders and the flamboyant waistcoats of the Regency. The new professions of policemen, station-masters and men of some authority wore top hats, as did some coachmen and even grocers, but not all were made of silk. You could even get them in papier-mâché.[46] The humorous journalist and dramatist Douglas Jerrold's fictional Mr Caudle once treated himself to a beaver hat which his wife said was worth 23/-, but after a night out with his friends, he picked up somebody else's headgear for which, as his wife sneered next morning, no second-hand dealer would give him fivepence.[47] Mrs Caudle was probably exaggerating because in the 1830s Thomas Carlyle wore a beaver hat which cost only 6/6d., which was dear enough.

When Dickens wrote *Nicholas Nickleby* in the late 1830s, in Chapter 2 he dressed the eponymous hero's uncle Ralph Nickleby in a decidedly old-fashioned mode, with a bottle-green coat called a spencer over a blue jacket, a white waistcoat, grey mixture pantaloons and a frilled shirt. In 1834, Thomas Carlyle acquired a 'rifle-green' (perhaps the colour of the uniform of Rifle regiments of the British Army) frock coat. By the late 1840s, however, men were wearing frock coats in brown, grey, dark blue or black, or black cutaway coats. Later, Jane Carlyle bought her husband a striking sky-blue coat with yellow buttons, but this may have been her rather than his taste. In London, the American Herman Melville's green coat 'plays the very devil with my respectability here' he wrote on 13 December 1849, and he had to buy what he called a darker 'paletot', which was a general word for an overcoat.[48]

Carlyle wore a satin stock and a starched collar. Underneath he wore flannel, muslin or cambric shirts, according to the weather, which Jane sewed for him. In the winter, he wore carpet slippers made of 'shag' a heavy worsted cloth, which buttoned up. They cost 5/6 a pair and were usually worn by women, but he ordered them bespoke at a costly nine shillings a pair.[49]

Men's waistcoats could be white and their gloves lavender. Trousers might have checks or be made of 'pepper and salt' material, but usually, the entire suit would be in the same drab colour. A black neckcloth usually hid the upper part of the white shirt, which by the end of a week in London's smoke and fog was getting somewhat grimy. If tied tightly enough, the neckcloth held the shirt collar high up against the ears. Except among the dandified swells and their vulgar imitators, the 'natty gents' with their flashy jewellery, greasy hair and false-fronted shirts, men's clothes, if they were to be 'decent' and 'respectable' – both terms suggested aspirations to something higher than one's class implied – had to be monotonous and inconspicuous.

A wedding was the only appropriate time for wearing brighter colours. In 1831, for his wedding, Mr Caudle wore a blue coat with bright buttons and a white, watered-satin waistcoat.[50] In the 1840s, Dickens's Mr Dombey was similarly colourfully wed in a blue coat, fawn-coloured pantaloons and a lilac waistcoat.[51]

Where did Frederick Manning obtain his clothes? One cannot imagine Maria consenting to him poking about in the second-hand shops of Middlesex Street, near Aldgate, still known today as 'Petticoat Lane', or in the slums of Whitechapel and St Giles. Nor would he have worn the simple work clothes known as 'slop'. On the other hand, people like the Mannings with little more than £100 a year, although they considered themselves as belonging to the middle class, could not afford clothes made to order. A great many of them patronised the most widely-advertised men's outfitter in London, Elias Moses and Son, a firm with its headquarters on the corner of Aldgate and the Minories, and with branches on the corner of Tottenham Court Road and the New Road, as well as in New Oxford Street. Beginning as a maker of 'slop', E. Moses sold jackets, trousers, waistcoats and ladies' riding-habits. He offered bespoke men's suits, and others whose fit was assured by 'self-measuring', which probably meant that he could supply a range of sizes from his stock. In any case, alterations were cheap enough. Unlike other shops, Elias Moses and Son neither embarrassed people by not labelling their goods with prices, nor expected them to bargain. Moses displayed his fixed prices on tickets, which was considered highly vulgar by those who had their clothes made for them by George Stulz of Bond Street, the tailor of fashionable male London.

E. Moses and Son did not miss a trick in self-promotion. Their name was emblazoned on the sides of omnibuses and on hoardings along the approaches to London's railway main railway stations, where boys thrust handbills into the hands of travellers as they stepped down from the carriages. E. Moses took advertising space in the newspapers and was on the front page of the august *The Times*, which at that time contained not news but only advertisements and notices. The firm arranged for little publicity booklets to be inserted into the first four numbers of Dickens's serial novel *Martin Chuzzlewit* in 1843-1844, and regularly bought space on the inside of the wrapper of succeeding parts of Dickens's novels. Some of E. Moses's advertising copy was flowery prose and some was no more than doggerel verse, related to the season of the year or even to episodes in the particular part of the novel being serialised.[52] One particular rhyme ran thus:

> Attend to my ditty, attend, ev'ryone!
> For I owe my existence to MOSES and SON.
> I am viewed as the very perfection of dress,
> And wherever I go I am met with success.

> My fashion and elegance none will dispute,
> But all have pronounced me 'a beautiful suit'

These and the sixteen lines that followed were high poetry in comparison with the doggerel of:

> Our waistcoats shall rival all others by far,
> And our trowsers shall prove that our House is the star.[53]

E. Moses and Son understood that if they were going to sell, as they claimed, 'ready-made suits that Beau Brummel would have been proud to wear, at prices that a mechanic could afford to pay' – which was an exaggeration at both ends of the phrase – their shops would have to be different from the hushed pomposity of the traditional gentleman's tailor, as well as from the rough and ready crudeness of the second-hand clothes shop or market stall. The assistants at E. Moses's large emporia were polite. They were trained to be neither smarmy nor snooty but to sell by putting people at their ease. The premises were brilliantly lit with candelabra with a reputed seven hundred gas burners. The German tourist, Max Schlesinger, wrote about E. Moses's

> many thousands of gas flames, forming branches, foliage and arabesques, and sending forth so dazzling a blaze that this fiery column of Moses is visible at the distance of half a mile, lighting up the haze which not even the clearest evening can wholly banish from the London sky[54]

There were Corinthian columns, sculptured panels and soft carpets. Moses sold everything, as a contemporary journalist wrote, 'from a tin shaving pot to a Cashmere shawl',[55] as well as hosiery, hats, boots and shoes to everyone 'from prince to peasant'. By 1860, he was claiming that 80 per cent of the population were buying ready-made clothes. This was not surprising, if there was any truth in Thackeray's poem published in *Punch* on 25 March 1848, which proclaimed that 'the poor are not done and the rich are not fleeced by E. Moses and Son'. No longer did ordinary people need to look, as in the French observer Taine's comment, like ludicrous caricatures of high life because they wore aristocratic dress which had been handed down to them by their employers.

That most of these advertising puffs came from E. Moses and Son's own publications does not necessarily mean they were not to a considerable extent true, as they would be decades later of Moses's own cultural successors,

Montague Burton and the Fifty Shilling Tailor. These were outfitters who could make a man look respectably middle class in a new suit that fitted him, even if to the trained eye it was not adapted to all the peculiarities of his body and was made in a standard style rather than to the customer's personal taste.

Jane Carlyle made some of her husband Thomas's shirts herself, but the garments could be bought very cheaply indeed, for as little as 4½ d. each, but only because thousands of women were 'sweated', that is grossly overworked and underpaid by shops in harsh competition with each other. 'Sweating' was at the root of much destitution, disease and prostitution among the 197,000 sewing outworkers in London, one-quarter of those in England and Wales in 1861.[56] In 1843, *Punch* printed an anonymous poem called 'The Song of the Shirt'.

> With fingers weary and worn
> With eyelids heavy and red
> A woman sat, in unwomanly rags,
> Plying her needle and thread –
> Stitch! Stitch! Stitch!
> Danger and dirt.

When Elias Moses was accused of 'sweating', that is paying the lowest wages to the people who made his clothes, he defended himself fiercely, insisting that he paid more than other employers, particularly more than the widely-advertised H.J. Nicoll of Regent Street, who engineered the dismissal of the investigative journalist Henry Mayhew from the *Morning Chronicle* by threatening to remove his advertising after Mayhew had accused Nicoll of sweating.[57]

Beaver!

Illustrations of the age show many men with clean-shaven faces, although military men affected moustaches. Facial hair was in fact considered a sign of mental imbalance, eccentricity, immorality, or being a revolutionary and very likely foreign into the bargain. Henry Mayhew's comic novel about Mr and Mrs Sandboys and their trip to London to see the Great Exhibition contains obsessive references to 'mustachioes', and bearded Frenchmen. Beards became so unfashionable that an enthusiast for them, W. H. Henshaw, felt impelled to publish a pamphlet in 1847 entitled *Beard Shaving, and the Common Use of the Razor, an Unnatural, Irrational, Unmanly, Ungodly and Fatal Fashion among Christians.*[58] The clean-shaven fashion changed, however, when conditions during the Crimean War of 1854-1856 obliged British troops to grow full facial hair, at which point hirsuteness became fashionable among civilians and would remain so until it became once more associated with anarchist assassins and bomb-throwers towards the end of the century.

One of the most widely advertised hair products for men was Rowland's Macassar Oil. While chemical analysis in 1850 discovered that its major ingredient was olive oil, it gave its name to the piece of white cloth which was laid over the backs of armchairs until almost contemporary times, known as an antimacassar.[59]

At the other end of the body, for their shoes or more commonly boots, men used Warren's boot blacking, made in the factory close to Hungerford Bridge, where the young Dickens worked and which he portrayed in *David Copperfield* as Murdstone and Grinby's. The paste, costing a sizeable sixpence or one shilling per pot or bottle, was advertised with a picture of a cat taken aback at its own reflection in a shiny boot.

An important discovery was made in 1849 which in time would make a great difference to people's smartness. A Parisian tailor spilt turpentine over the tablecloth and noticed that it had removed some stains. This was the origin of *nettoyage à sec* or dry cleaning, a technique brought to England by Achille Serre in 1870. Stains would be removable from lighter coloured cloths, making it less necessary for men to wear very dark clothes.

The principles of style changed slowly. Despite the brighter fabrics that chemical dyes would in due course permit, the dark suit and the black dress would always stay in fashion. But it would be the grand-daughters of early Victorian women who, entering the mass labour market in the 1914-1918 war, shortened their skirts and relaxed their stays, while men continued to wear detached wing collars, long-sleeved vests and long-legged underpants, heavy boots and wide-waisted trousers until American styles came in well after 1945 and the Second World War. The wing collar, not to speak of the corset, survived into the age of terylene.

Chapter 4

In Sickness and In Health

Physicians and Surgeons

Although the general medical practitioner was becoming a common figure, wealthy people consulted physicians. These were high-status gentlemen with the title of 'Doctor' and Oxford or Cambridge degrees. They had page-boys, who wore patent leather pot-shaped hats and who brought written prescriptions round to the wealthy who could afford to pay the bills which these lords of the medical world issued once a year, unless the fee (expressed in guineas, much superior to the vulgar pound) was discreetly handed to them enclosed in a piece of paper when they left their patient's house. The physician recommended drugs, or 'physic'. He did not bandage injuries or perform surgical operations, but merely took the sick person's pulse and glanced at his or her urine. He would then prescribe the requisite medicine or pills, which would be supplied by the apothecary, who gave medical advice but, not being qualified, was not permitted to charge for it. He made his living from selling his drugs. He was thus 'in trade' and of a lower social status than the physician.

Most people when sick would have recourse to traditional remedies. They might rub their chests with goose fat if suffering from a chill, and apply a hot poultice for boils. To counter sleeplessness, and to relieve pain and fever, people would buy morphia, opium and even arsenic and mercury over the counter. Constipation could be tackled efficiently if somewhat violently with a dose of castor oil or liquorice powder. Laudanum, a tincture of opium in alcohol, was the common painkiller, pacifier of babies and general tranquilliser. It could be taken as a cough suppressant or for binding the loose bowels which were so common in the unhygienic conditions of a London summer.

In Chapter 8 of Dickens's novel *Nicholas Nickleby*, which he published in serialised form in 1838-1839, he describes how, at Wackford Squeers's 'school' or rather place for boarding out unwanted boys, Mrs Squeers forces each child to swallow a large wooden spoonful of the well-known cure-all brimstone (another word for sulphur) and molasses or treacle. Mrs Squeers claims that she gives it to the boys because without they would always be ill with something or other.

Physicians sensibly recommended diet, exercise, rest, baths and massage, together with a battery of treatments of less efficiency, including purges and enemas, bleeding and sweating, which were intended to rid the body of whatever was causing its malaise. Physicians also prescribed arsenic-based remedies for a number of illnesses, including fevers, epilepsy and even the deficiency disease of rickets. Thomas Carlyle, the historian, self-medicated his rather vague ailments with castor oil and the 'blue pill', which consisted of five grains of mercury. Mercury was dangerous, but Carlyle, who lived a long life, may have taken it in liquid form, which was swiftly eliminated from the organism. His wife Jane's lack of appetite and poor digestion was treated by the doctor with quinine, as well as with a substance called pepsin, scraped from bears' stomachs, boiled, distilled, bottled and taken in drops. She also used morphia. Both Carlyles, who seem to have suffered from constipation, used senna pods.[1]

Medicines were still very much the stock-in-trade of patent medicine manufacturers. Most were either palliatives of pain or simple laxatives. Enormous quantities were sold. Forty thousand bottles of Atkinson's 'Infant Preservative', which was mostly laudanum, were sold annually in the 1840s, while 'Godfrey's Cordial' and 'Daffy's Elixir' served generations of mothers to silence their infants, perhaps permanently, while they went out to work or got on with the thankless tasks of the household.[2]

'Holloway's Pills', invented by Thomas Holloway, were recommended for every illness from ague and asthma, through constipation, dropsy and gout, to jaundice, lumbago and piles, ending the alphabet with ulcers and venereal disease. In case the advertising copywriter suspected that those ailments he had omitted to mention would have been thought incurable by Holloway's Pills, he added, 'and weakness from whatever cause'. When analysed, Holloway's Pills were found to contain aloes, rhubarb, saffron and Glauber's Salt (sodium sulphate). As a cure for constipation, which must have been endemic among people who consumed so few vegetables and fruit, the best one could say was that Holloway's Pills would not have done much harm. In addition, the newspapers carried advertising for 'Parr's Life Pills', which were reputed to have allowed the possible inventor, Thomas Parr, to have reached the age of 152 when he died in 1635.[3]

'Morison's Vegetable Universal Pills' were announced as recommended by the 'British College of Health'. This bogus institution happened to occupy the same address as the manufacturers of the pills, who were Morison and Moat in the New Road near King's Cross. The pills had a purgative effect and no more, which did not prevent them selling one million boxes in 1834.[4] Another patent medicine was 'Barry's Revalenta Arabica', whose exotic name suggested mysterious cures from the Orient but turned out to be mostly powdered lentils.[5]

In fact, few diseases were curable or even identifiable. Heart disease related to heavy smoking would not be recognised for another century. A doctor might have prescribed foxglove, known pharmaceutically as digitalis, a diuretic, to stimulate the heart if it was affected by rheumatic disease, but there was no known medical treatment available for cancer, save extirpating a visible tumour, and none for arthritis, diabetes or asthma. Nor were there any techniques available to analyse or even to identify blood. William Odling, the twenty-year-old son of the police surgeon at the Manning trial, who had studied chemistry, could not state positively under oath that the stains on Maria Manning's dress were those of blood. Even if his tests could have ruled out iron oxide or rust, he could not have proved whose blood it was, whether that of the victim or, as defence counsel delicately suggested, Maria's own.

If he used a stethoscope, a doctor might have recognised symptoms of advanced tuberculosis, though his main diagnostic tool would have been the patient's own medical history. Stool analysis and bacteriology were unknown. Liver and kidney disease, unless there was jaundice or a stone present, were often not recognised. Doctors had little knowledge of resuscitation techniques, and there was no blood transfusion or intravenous fluid technique. For a patient who had suffered a multiple limb fracture with skin break or artery obstruction, and there was a risk of gangrene, amputation by a surgeon was the only solution.

Surgeons were considered to belong to a profession which was somewhat inferior to that of physician. They were known as 'Mr' but prized for their practical skills. They usually learned 'on the job' and some were highly able. They had a limited range of techniques. They could set bones and lance boils, deal with some external conditions and operate swiftly in places which they could reach with instruments. The leading practitioners amputated limbs very skilfully and rapidly for compound fractures, cut for stone in the bladder, removed some cancerous tumours, repaired strangulated hernias, incised abscesses and carbuncles and couched the eyes to remove cataracts. All these procedures brought great apprehension to the patient, immeasurable pain, often brought thankfully to an end by unconsciousness, and frequently great loss of blood. The lack of asepsis in operating theatres, added to infection in the recovery ward, meant that surgery was very chancy even if the patient did not die from shock. Thus people would not submit themselves to the scalpel if they could possibly avoid it. Not till 1865 did Joseph Lister discover the antiseptic qualities of carbolic acid spray when used in surgical operations.

In pain shalt thou bring forth children

Sufferers from toothache usually had the decayed tooth pulled out with a carpenter's pliers. However, the early Victorian age saw the introduction of anaesthesia. The power of nitrous oxide and sulphuric ether to render a person unconscious had been known about earlier, but the first surgical operations under anaesthesia began to be undertaken in the United States in the 1840s. In London, in November 1846, ether was demonstrated at the Medical-Chirurgical Society on a Dr Duncan, whose arm was pricked with pins as he lay unconscious. Francis Booth administered ether before extracting a tooth on 19 December 1846, and two days later ether was again used at University College Hospital before the famous surgeon Robert Liston amputated a Belgravia butler's leg. Very soon the use of ether, shortly to be replaced by the safer chloroform, became common in the United States and Britain, as well as in many Continental European countries.

Despite some religious objections based on the Scriptural statement that Eve's sin required women to give birth in pain, other authorities quoted the earlier verse 'And the Lord caused a deep sleep to fall on Adam', before extracting his rib, in order to demonstrate divine approval of anaesthesia. In 1849 Charles Dickens's wife was soothed with chloroform at home by a Bart's Hospital doctor who claimed to have administered it four or five thousand times already. She said she had felt no pain and she was quite well the following day. Providing the anaesthetist was careful and watched his patient carefully, Dickens thought that chloroform ' is as safe in its administration as it is miraculous and merciful in its effects.'[6]The argument became academic, or rather theological, when the daughter of the Archbishop of Canterbury was anaesthetised while giving birth, and when in April 1853 Queen Victoria availed herself of chloroform – she referred to her experience as 'soothing, quieting and delightful beyond measure' – to ease the birth of Prince Leopold. For Victoria's next child, Prince Albert himself administered the chloroform through a handkerchief, until his ministrations were taken over by more qualified hands.[7] The argument against chloroform for women giving birth was quietly dropped. Anaesthesia was now quite respectable.[8]

Medicine, however, was on the brink of great advances. Between 1801 and 1850 8,000 university-educated men entered the medical profession in

Great Britain. The number of practitioners was keeping pace with the increase in population. The hospitals of London, Bart's, Guy's, the London, the Westminster, St Georges and the Middlesex, relied on voluntary contributions. These hospitals took in emergency cases, and, if recommended by a governor, non-urgent ones who could not afford to pay a physician to visit them at home and to employ a nurse. Connections were, of course, useful.

Some hospitals, among them the older Bart's and St Thomas's, were wealthy. Hippolyte Taine was impressed by the order and cleanliness of the wards at Bart's and the quality of the food.

Among more modern hospitals was St Mary's in Praed Street, Paddington. This was a general hospital founded in 1851. Specialised medicine was being practised in the many new hospitals founded in the first half of the century, including the London Fever Hospital, the Kensington Children's Hospital and the Free Cancer Hospital in Fulham. There were also a few hospitals for chest diseases, the famous Great Ormond Street for children, and the general hospitals and medical schools associated with the recently-founded University College and King's College, rivals of Oxford and Cambridge.[9] By 1850 there was hospital accommodation for more than twice as many patients as in 1801.

By mid-century many more drugs were available than in 1800, among them quinine, atropine, and codeine. Many diseases, among them emphysema, bronchitis and pneumonia, had been described and differentiated from others. In 1850 Richard Bright observed that protein in the urine was associated with a enlarged heart and shrunken kidneys. Bright, Addison, Hodgkin and Parkinson gave their names to the diseases that they identified. Furthermore, knowledge was increasing about the chances of reaching old age.

Short and Nasty Lives

Smallpox caused disfigurement, blindness and death. Conscientious objectors to vaccination helped to keep the disease alive, despite the Act of 1853 which made vaccination compulsory for babies before they were twelve weeks old. And gonorrhoea and syphilis, only partially treatable with mercury, were widespread, infecting wives and being passed on to children.

The annual death rate in England and Wales was about 22 per thousand. By the late 1840s the figure had fallen since the beginning of the century, particularly because of the increase in the number of people vaccinated against smallpox, but it remained obstinately where it was until much later in the century when, with substantial improvements in public health, it began to decline, reaching 14.7 in 1906-1910.[10] Nevertheless, the annual rate of infant mortality was still 156 per 1000 live births as late as 1871-1875, that is ignoring stillborn babies.[11] This figure concealed a wide variation, from a 10 per cent figure of infant deaths among prosperous families to an appalling 30 per cent among the poor. Thus, infant death was a common and accepted feature of Victorian family life. The absence of reliable contraception and the need to engender many children in order that a small number should survive to term and resist the diseases of childhood, such as scarlet fever, diphtheria, measles, whooping cough and many others, meant that the national birth rate in the 1840s was as high as 32.5 per thousand, three times higher than todays.

Death rates, however, were notoriously higher in London than in the rest of the country. The statistics provided by the *Annual Register* for 1849 indicate a death rate of close on 33 per thousand, magnified by high figures for children under fifteen. In 1841, the expectation of life for an adult in England and Wales was 41 years, but in London only 37.[12] Including infantile deaths, however, the average age of death in the capital was 27, among the working class it was 22, and half the burials in London in 1839 were of children under ten years of age. Epidemics, added to the normal high incidence of death, only increased people's familiarity with the Grim Reaper. The black-plumed horse and the hearse were frequent sights in London's streets, and the passer-by would often hear the unmistakable tapping of the undertaker's hammer hitting the brass-headed nails which fixed the black cloth to the coffin.

Dyspepsia and bad teeth, rheumatism, deficiency diseases such as rickets, infections such as ringworm, coughs and colds and 'the flux' (the common expression for diarrhoea), added to badly-treated injuries, boils and sepsis, were part of most people's lives. If one survived childhood the main causes of death were infectious diseases. A quarter of London's population suffered typhoid fever in November and December 1847.[13] The death rate was also kept high by tuberculosis, known as consumption, or by non-choleraic or English summer diarrhoea, which caused 3,899 deaths in 1849, together with the dreaded Asiatic cholera which swept through London in the summer of that year.

'The filthiest place that can be imagined'

Unaired rooms, persistent damp, people living hugger-mugger and the lack of washing and drainage facilities encouraged unsanitary habits and made respiratory illness, bronchitis and intestinal infections prevalent. Diarrhoea, frequently stated as the cause of infant death, came from poor food hygiene and the spread of infection from unwashed hands. There were no facilities for handwashing after using the privy, and it is doubtful if people knew that they should do so before touching other people's food, or putting their fingers into their own mouths. At the same time, the lack of adequate roughage in the diet and the sheer unpleasantness of visiting the privy in the cold and rain led to constipation.

The London sewers were totally inadequate. Edwin Chadwick, Secretary to the Poor Law Commission, produced a report in 1842 entitled *An Enquiry into the Sanitary Condition of the Labouring Populations of Great Britain*, which provided a mass of detail about conditions in the poorer parts of London, now in a very grave state because of the very rapid rise and concentration of the capital's population and the greatly increased number of connections of new water closets to the sewers rather than to cesspools, both of which were becoming growingly choked with faecal material.

Cesspools were brick chambers measuring about 4 feet by six. They were porous and allowed urine to drain into the surrounding ground. As they filled with faeces from an earth closet, such as the one the Carlyles had in their garden, 'night soil men' came periodically to clean them out.[14] The increased volume of water from the water closet, however, tended to make the cesspool overflow. Plumbers directed the flow so that it discharged into the sewer which, not having been designed for human waste but merely surface water, in turn led into the River Thames, from which London's drinking water was drawn.[15] 'Slops', a euphemism for faeces, were often emptied in the street and found their way down the drains – if there were any – to the Thames.

Asiatic cholera, which had killed several thousand in 1832, was again approaching Continental Europe in 1848. What was to be done? The commonest theory was that cholera was caused by the 'miasma' or the prevalent foul odours and emanations in the streets, by the stink from piles of rotten organic material and from human beings who lived and slept in close proximity in ill-ventilated rooms. Certainly, London was foul, not only, as everyone could see, because of the soot in the air, but also because it stood on a subsoil of decay. Broken or insufficient sewers were blocked; they leaked into the wells and water supplies, or backed up into houses even in expensive parts of the West End. The rookeries, where one foul privy might serve the need of dozens of families, were regularly flooded by their own overflowing sewage, while Westminster Abbey itself lay over cesspools crammed with centuries of filth. In certain streets in Whitechapel, no sewers at all had been connected, admitted the local surveyor to Chadwick's enquiries. In the surveyor's own words, the district was 'the filthiest place that can be imagined'.[16]

In 1847 an inspector reported that 'the filth (the propriety of the times meant that he could not bring himself to write 'excrement') was lying scattered about ... so thick and so deep that it was hardly possible to move for it.'[17] Excrement and urine ran down the gutter in the middle of the street until it was stopped up in a court or an alley. Faeces oozed up through the shallow foundations of houses. The soil of London was sodden with filth. In early Victorian London and for several decades later most of the poor simply threw their excrement into the streets where, hopefully, the rain would carry it into the main sewer and then to the river. The same happened to all kinds of dirty water in the absence of sinks and house drainage. In low-lying Bermondsey, a report stated that the whole borough was crossed and crisscrossed with filthy, stinking ditches which, receiving the contents of privies and the overflow from cesspools, sometimes also constituted the water supply for drinking and washing purposes.[18]

The entire area south of the river was ill-drained, especially in the marshy parts close to the Thames, which was not as yet embanked. Privies hung over ditches and sewers, backing up into houses, bringing foul smells. Excrement and other decaying matter were rarely cleared away. Bermondsey included the notorious Jacob's Island, marked today by Jacob's Street, an infamous rookery and the scene of Bill Sike's death in *Oliver Twist*. This is how Henry Mayhew described Jacob's Island in one of his perambulations around the slums:

> we were assured that this was the only water which the wretched inhabitants had to drink, As we gazed in horror at it, we saw drains and sewers emptying their filthy contents into it; we saw a whole tier of doorless privies in the open road, open to men and women, built over it; we heard bucket after bucket of filth splash into it[19]

Dr Simon's Report

The highly concentrated population and trades of the City of London, however, created very special problems for public health. The City Sewers Act of 1848 made a start on improvement by requiring all new houses and all old ones of a certain size to be connected to sewers and to have facilities for water storage in the form of cisterns. In October 1848 the City appointed Dr John Simon as Medical Officer of Health. Highly energetic, Dr Simon sent out Inspectors of Nuisances to compel the cleansing of privies and the removal of waste. He forced the New River Company to supply water twice a day to standpipes (pipes with taps standing upright in the street). In November 1849, with strong support from the influential *The Times*, Dr Simon published his first annual report. It was, according to one historian, 'a classic document in the history of nineteenth-century sanitary improvement'.[20] If the death rate in the City, where large numbers of the poorest still lived, was high at between 30 and 40 per thousand, the causes, according to Dr Simon, were defective drains, an inadequate supply of water, the unhygienic personal habits of the people, and lastly, to offensive trades and shallow burials. Both animal slaughtering and burying corpses in overcrowded graveyards were causes of repellent odours and sights.

'That shameful place'

The huge numbers of cattle, sheep and pigs driven into London daily had to be slaughtered somewhere. There were no regulations about where an abattoir could be opened, and some were to be found in the backyards or cellars of butchers' shops only yards from major and elegant streets. In Newport Market, for instance, the smell, flies and terrified bellowing of the doomed cattle could be perceived by visitors to one of the major tourist sights of the capital, James Wyld's Great Globe, in the middle of the neighbouring Leicester Square.

Hundreds of thousands of animals were driven to slaughterhouses through the packed streets of the City, and their tons of dung were added to that of the horse traffic, the mud and the general filth. Around the great meat market of Smithfield, in particular, the streets were running with blood, gobbets of animal flesh, slimy entrails, hooves and hides, all buzzing with flies. The scenes around Smithfield were Dantesque. Charles Dickens describes them in Chapter 16 of his *Bleak House*:

> The blinded oxen, over-goaded, over-driven, never guided, run
> into the wrong places and are beaten out: and plunge, red-eyed
> and foaming, at stone walls: and often sorely hurt the innocent
> and often sorely hurt themselves

And again, in Chapter 20 of *Great Expectations*, when Pip takes a stroll to get out of the oppressive atmosphere of Mr Jaggers's office:

> So, I came into Smithfield; and the shameful place, being asmear with filth and fat and blood, seemed to stick to me

Dr Simon found Smithfield:

> full of knackers' yards, tripe-dressers, cats' meat boilers, catgut spinners, paunch cookers, bladder blowers and all the stench and brutality of backyard butchery

On the hot Friday evening of 7 September 1849, a bullock which was being driven to slaughter at Smithfield escaped, ran into the machine-room of a newspaper and found itself wedged between two gleaming new state-of-the-art steam presses.[21] The technical brilliance of the age of steam and machinery had met the mediaeval backwardness of the slaughterhouses of London. The situation could not be allowed to continue unreformed.

As so often, reform was obstructed by the interests of people who lived far enough away from the trouble not to be bothered. The City Court of Common Council, a law unto itself, drew close to £10,000 a year from its various taxes on Smithfield and the other City markets, and of course, resisted all attempts at reform.[22] In 1849, however, a Royal Commission recommended that the great meat market be closed. Despite the objections of the Court of Common Council, this 'reeking central abomination' as *The Times* called it, had to go.[23] On 9 January 1859, the new Copenhagen market was opened in Islington, still partly in the country north of the City. It could accommodate 8,000 cattle and 50,000 sheep, as well as large numbers of pigs and horses.

A Nauseating Stench

Throughout the centuries thousands of corpses had been buried in London's churchyards and a few other historic burial grounds. Each layer of bodies took about seven years to decompose, but new burials exceeded the rate of decay. Room was scarce, so graves were re-opened to put in new coffins. Gravediggers beat and scattered the putrefying remains of the dead, raising a nauseating stench. The earth in many graveyards was a heaving mass of rotting corpses at different stages of putrefaction. In George Reynolds's

The Mysteries of London, Tidkins, the 'Resurrection Man' or supplier of recently dead cadavers to anatomists for dissection, observes as a matter of course that even in cold weather the clay does not freeze because the entire graveyard is greasy with human remains.[24] 'Horrible disclosures' were revealed by the rain, announced the *Illustrated London News* on 15 September 1862, appalled by sights which were 'nauseous, disgusting and putrid'. In the words of another writer:

> Adjoining Whitechapel Church ... the ground is so densely crowded as to present one entire mass of human bones and putrefaction ... They are exhumed by shovelfuls and disgustingly exposed ... It appears almost impossible to dig a grave in this ground without coming into contact with some recent interment, and the gravedigger's pick is sometimes forced through the lid of a coffin when least expected, from which so dreadful an effluvium is emitted[25]

Graves were often not filled in until the piled-up coffins reached within a foot or so from the surface. Thus the most recent dead were interred only eighteen inches or so below ground. Half-decomposed corpses, bones and bits of splintered coffins robbed of their brass fittings, lay exposed and were scattered all over the cemeteries.

'King' Cholera

It was in these conditions of public squalor that cholera was anticipated to strike London in early 1849. On 22 September 1848, a case of cholera was diagnosed in Southwark, in the Borough, just south of London Bridge. This was followed by sporadic outbreaks all over the low-lying areas south of the Thames.

Cholera struck suddenly. Within hours it could kill half of those affected, sometimes within a day of the onset of the violent diarrhoea and vomiting which were its main and completely dehydrating symptoms. It struck with a high degree of randomness, sometimes missing entire towns, districts, streets and even sides of streets. By now it was accepted that cholera was not a contagious disease. You did not 'catch' it from other people in the way you caught a cold. Cholera struck even the convict hulk *Justitia*, full of convicts awaiting the departure of the fleet which would transport them to Australia, a practice which would not end until 1857. The *Justitia* was moored in the river with no shore contact at all, so it seemed that cholera was inherent to the place where it broke out. But how could this be so when Millbank Prison, situated on the north bank of the Thames where the Tate Britain art gallery is today, suffered while other prisons such as Pentonville and 'Bedlam' the Bethlehem lunatic asylum, escaped. What was common to some but not others?

There were theories that explained that cholera was caused by unhygienic living conditions, but in what particular way did such conditions cause the disease? The most popular opinion, however, which claimed that the solution was a major campaign against the unsanitary public health conditions of London, was one which believed in miasmatic or atmospheric influences, that there was a poison in the air caused by the lack of hygiene which permitted the emanations of animal and vegetable substances, largely human excrement and human and animal respiration. Ventilation was insufficient, and human waste was not efficiently enough removed from areas where people lived. In other words, excessive crowding together, human and animal effluvia, lack of clean air and dirty habits were the causes of cholera.

As for treatment, Holloway's Pills were touted as a remedy. According to the puff on the pill-boxes, if you took five or six each night and the same quantity the next morning for six weeks, you would be cured. Nitrous oxide or 'laughing gas', was recommended as a quack remedy for the dread disease which killed over fourteen thousand Londoners in 1849. The most popular remedy was opium, though this might be effective only in the earliest stages of the disease. Other treatments used in London hospitals included electricity, brandy, turpentine, cayenne pepper and the internal use of common salts enemas or the injection into the veins of saline solution, which suggests that there was some intimation that cholera had to be treated by the urgent replacement of fluids.

'The paradise at Tooting'

The worst single outbreak of cholera, and the one which changed the issue from a medical one to a question of far-reaching social policy, occurred in Tooting, now a built-up area of South London but then a village in open fields. Here, Bartholomew Drouet ran a home for orphan pauper children until they were old enough to be released into the world. The infants were farmed out by some of the London workhouses, harsh institutions which the poor were obliged to enter for food and shelter. In the first week of January 1849, there were 112 cases of cholera among the 1,300 children boarded out in Drouet's Establishment for the Infant Poor. The Surrey Coroner, under whose jurisdiction the home came, did not think inquests were necessary. It was only because other children suffering from cholera were removed from Drouet's establishment and died in areas subject to other coroners' authority that the scandal of the refuge came to public notice. On 19 January an inquest was held by a coroner, Dr Wakley, founder of the famous journal *The Lancet* and an active medical and social reformer in contrast to many other coroners who did not have medical qualifications. He found that the children in Drouet's care were badly fed, clothed and housed, The Poor Law Guardians of the London district of Holborn, who boarded out the children from their workhouse at Drouet's, obtained a manslaughter verdict against him. Drouet was tried in the criminal court on 13 April 1849 but acquitted because it could not be proved that his negligence had caused the death from cholera of the particular child whose death was being investigated.

Drouet did run his establishment inefficiently and cruelly. He underfed and ill-treated the children. The final death toll from cholera in Drouet's 'home' was 180. The death of so many defenceless children sparked the public conscience in a way that the solid columns of prose in the medical journals and parliamentary reports on public health could not. Probably the most powerful broadside came from the powerful pen of Charles Dickens, who wrote an article with the title 'The Paradise at Tooting' in *The Examiner* of 20 January 1849.

Dr Grainger, a Board of Health inspector, had given evidence that the lack of ventilation, arising from Drouet's habit of nailing up doors and windows 'exceeds in offensiveness anything yet witnessed ... in hospitals or elsewhere occupied by the sick'.[26] Despite warnings, Drouet had overcrowded his accommodation and had put four cholera patients into one bed. They, of course, were covered with each other's diarrhoea, which the inspector described as 'every offensive, indecent and barbarous circumstance that can aggravate the horrors of their condition'. The insufficient food and clothing, together with the cold, damp, dirty and rotten rooms, made it only the more likely that infectious disease would break out.

Nevertheless, these conditions, foul and intolerable as they were, were only the predisposing cause of the cholera rather than its true origin. Was the disease caused by some unidentified agent? The truth was that, contrary to what Dickens wrote and most medical opinion believed, cholera did not spread because Drouet's institution was, in the novelist's words, 'brutally conducted, vilely kept, preposterously inspected, dishonestly defended, a disgrace to a Christian community, and a stain upon a civilised land'.

All these attacks were justified, but the conditions themselves were not the cause of cholera.

The epidemic raged throughout the summer, particularly in the south London districts of Lambeth, Southwark and Rotherhithe. 250 died in June, 2,000 in July, and more than 4,000 in August. By early September 10,142 had perished, two of them stockbrokers who were due to give evidence at the proceedings in the Manning murder case. Bermondsey, where Mr and Mrs Manning lived, stood high in the number of deaths; it had lost 591 of its inhabitants. The death knell tolled from morning till night, and mourners might return from the graveyard to find that yet another sick person in the house had succumbed.

The True Cause – Contaminated Water

If you were lucky, your water supply might not have been contaminated by a broken sewer or leaking cesspit. Perhaps you boiled your water for tea, or drank only beer. Evidence was mounting that the source of cholera was contaminated water. The huge volume of new construction in the early years of Victoria's reign cracked the walls of cesspools and broke sewers, while the introduction of water closets sent faecal material straight into the sewers and from there it emerged finally into the River Thames from where the water companies drew their supplies, pumping them into London's standpipes and cisterns for people to drink. Sewers, privies and open ditches were known to leak into the water pipes and wells. Arthur Hassall's *Microscopic Examination of the Water supplied to the Inhabitants of London* of 1850 revealed that 'some of the inhabitants of the metropolis are made to consume, in some form or another, a portion of their own excrement'.[27]

Nevertheless, the cholera bacillus (*vibrio cholerae*) had not yet been isolated.

A Vast Open Cloaca

The supply of water to London was a common scandal. On 29 September 1849, the *Illustrated London News* thundered:

> The supply of water ought no more to be meted out to us as
> a matter of profits to individuals than the atmosphere and the
> sunshine

London's water was supplied by eight companies, drawing their supplies from the Thames, from deep wells or from the River Lea. The Thames and the Lea were noisome with horse dung, dead and rotting fish and, worst of all, with the discharge from the sewers. In the same year, 1849, as cholera scourged London, the novelist Charles Kingsley wrote:

> I was yesterday ... over the cholera districts of Bermondsey and, oh God, what I saw! People having no water to drink – hundreds of them – but the water of the common sewer ... full of ... dead fish, cats and dogs[28]

In Southwark, adjacent to Bermondsey, of 18,000 houses, only 4,000 had their own supply of water. The inhabitants of the rest drew their water from standpipes in the street, which were turned on quite briefly and not always every day. Cisterns were not always to be found in houses, with the result that all sorts of insufficient and unhygienic containers were used to store water. This slow and irregular supply of water was the occasion for quarrels among the dozens of mostly women waiting to fill their barrels and jars, which in addition could not be properly washed. The water was saved for as long as possible, and was used and reused, and not drunk until it was stagnant and of no further use for any other purpose.

Houses which enjoyed a piped supply to their basement kitchen or to a cistern in the open 'area' just outside were fortunate. It cost a landlord £4 to install a water supply plus about six shillings a year rent to supply one floor and about twice that amount for a four-roomed house. Progress in supplying piped water was very slow because landlords feared that the tenants would steal and sell the lead fittings. Water companies worried that the water, which was not metered, would be wasted. Nor could landlords be sure of sufficient and regular rent to make up for the charge for installing a water supply. Furthermore, London plumbers who provided the internal arrangements of piping and taps were notoriously inefficient, while the cisterns were allowed to become foul. In any case, the water was piped for only two hours each day, or on alternate days, and never on Sundays.

The way to prevent cholera was to keep the drinking water supply away from the sewers. The cure for a person attacked by the violent stomach pains, vomiting and watery discharges of cholera was to replace the lost fluid. The acute dehydration suffered caused total collapse and a rapid drop in body temperature, ending with a disappearing pulse and a wizened and blue corpse. Yet neither the true cause nor the appropriate public or private remedies were generally agreed.

Dr Snow and the Broad Street pump

It was Dr John Snow, the same who administered an anaesthetic to Queen Victoria during her labour, who implicated water as the carrier of cholera. Snow's first publication on the subject, *On the Mode of Communication of Cholera*, came out in 1849, but attracted little attention given the predominance of the miasma theory. Dr Snow continued to study the subject and in 1855 published a book with the same title as his 1849 essay. He demonstrated that the poor, who had little opportunity for washing, came into contact with the cholera bacillus and transferred it to their mouths. Doctors did not catch it because they washed their hands before they ate and in any case avoided consuming food in their patients' houses. Cholera also spread to better-off sections of the community because the bacillus got into the general water supply. Snow carefully crosschecked where people obtained their water with the incidence of cholera. The pump in Broad Street, now Broadwick Street, in Soho in the centre of London's West End, provided water which was contaminated from a nearby cesspool whose brick revetment was cracked, thus allowing the cholera bacillus to enter the water supply. Looking at the water under a microscope, Snow noticed the typical floccules or flakes sloughed from the intestines of cholera sufferers. People who drew water from this pump fell sick with cholera while others who lived close by but took their water from unpolluted wells did not. Final proof of this came when a widow, who had moved from Broad Street to Hampstead but continued to have the particularly sweet-tasting water of the Broad Street pump sent up to her, was the only person in Hampstead, which had its own wells, to contract and die from cholera. Snow persuaded the authorities to remove the handle from the pump and the cholera infections in Broad Street came to an end.

This, however, was a local outbreak. It was the discharge of sewers into the Thames above the part of the stream where some of the water suppliers, especially the Southwark and Vauxhall Water Company, drew their water, which caused the extent of the cholera outbreak of 1849.

On 16 November 1849, the entire nation was summoned to thank the Almighty for the end of the cholera outbreak. Although it was a weekday, shops closed and the railways ran only a Sunday service. Church bells pealed, but *The Times* made the very valid point that:

> It is not the part of a Christian or any rational man to implore
> the Almighty to remove evils nine-tenths of which we can
> remove ourselves[29]

Over fourteen thousand people had died of cholera in London. Not until the end of the first part of the Victorian age did the Act of 1852 give water companies until 1855 to cease taking their supplies from below Teddington, which is 11.7 miles or 18.8 kilometres upstream from central London. The companies were given until 1857 to cover their reservoirs, filter their water and provide a constant supply. When the Lambeth Waterworks Company moved its intake above the tideway in 1853, as required by the Act, the death rate fell dramatically in the area which it served, compared with the area supplied by the Southwark and Vauxhall companies which caused suffered 130 deaths from cholera per 10,000 inhabitants until they also moved their activities to above Teddington.

In 1855, a proper London-wide sewer authority at last came into being when the Metropolitan Board of Works was set up. However, it was not until Members of Parliament were themselves repelled by the stench from the Thames in the summers of 1857 and 1858, and Queen Victoria and Prince Albert were forced to abandon a trip on the river by the nauseating stink stirred up by the paddles of the steamboat in which they were travelling, that the Government gave the Metropolitan Board of Works the power to construct the sewer system it wanted. Its Chief Engineer, Joseph Bazalgette, built eighty-two miles of sewers. By 1865 these were working and collecting 420 million gallons of water and sewage daily and conducting them to outfalls far outside the area of the river from which drinking water was taken. Cholera was finally halted. The problem of a clean, regular and affordable water supply was not, however, entirely solved until the Metropolitan Water Board bought out the water companies in 1902.

Chapter 5

Money, Housing and Class

Filthy Lucre

To maintain a recognisably middle-class household, even if it was modest, required an income of about £300 per year. This assumed that the wife would lead a life of leisure, save perhaps for some easy sewing. A couple of servants were needed, as well as a house suitable for entertaining guests, sufficiently large to accommodate a growing family, and located in an acceptably middle-class part of London.

Nevertheless, many people in middle-class occupations, such as the growing army of clerical workers, earned far less than £300 a year. Charles Dickens's Bob Cratchit receives only 15 shillings a week or £39 a year and seems to be just able to keep his head above water, although his employer, Ebenezer Scrooge in *A Christmas Carol*, admits that he pays Cratchit very little, so perhaps Dickens was intentionally understating Cratchit's pay. £150 a year would be enough to rent a house without needing to take in a lodger and to employ a live-in servant and another to come in daily. This is close to the £120 per year plus a house that the Cheeryble brothers pay Dickens's Nicholas Nickleby. In Wilkie Collins's *The Woman in White*, serialised in 1860, the drawing master Walter Hartwright is offered four guineas per week 'on the footing of a gentleman', to teach drawing and to mount a collection of pictures. Well might he call such terms 'surprisingly liberal'.

Leaving fiction for reality, Frederick Manning, according to his trial record, was employed as a representative for a stationery firm in Holborn, for which he was paid two pounds a week or £104 per year, plus 5 per cent commission. This does not seem to have brought him up to the magic £150 per annum, for the trial also reveals that he and Maria needed to let a room to a lodger in order to pay the rent. Nor could they afford a live-in servant. Frederick Manning's problem was that he was an alcoholic and had never made a go of anything since he had lost his job as a guard on the railway. Maria was a strong and determined woman, but her husband clearly was a hindrance.

The Mannings' victim, the customs officer Patrick O'Connor, demonstrated that money could certainly be made in London. It was helpful to have good connections and to know how to use them, and to discover a niche in offering people what they wanted, which in O'Connor's case were loans. According to the medical student who lodged with the Mannings, Maria had said that O'Connor had amassed a fortune of about £20,000 and had made a will in her favour. Though this sounds optimistic on her part, O'Connor certainly had savings and considerable investments in railway shares.

'There's gold in them thar hills'

Even larger fortunes could be made, however. By 1849, London had been thrown into excited tumult by the news of a gold strike in distant California where, it was said, the precious metal could be picked up from the ground. Enterprising steamship lines began to put on voyages direct from London to the West Coast of America via Cape Horn.[1] The Californian gold rush became one of the topics of the day. Tickets sold out for the farce at the Adelphi Theatre in the Strand called 'Cockneys in California'. At Vauxhall and Cremorne Pleasure Gardens couples danced the 'California Polka' and the 'Golden Polka'. In London's famous supper and drinking rooms, the Cyder Cellars in Covent Garden and the Coal Hole in the Strand, cigar-smoking gentlemen sang 'The Race to California' and the still unforgotten:

> In a cabin, in a canyon.
> Excavating for a mine,
> Lived a miner, forty-niner,
> And his daughter Caroline.

During 1849 *Punch* joked continually about the gold rush. On 13 January the magazine published a cartoon showing a dustman with his three tiny children, his spade and his broom, announcing: 'Oh! I ain't a-going to stop 'ere, looking for teaspoons in cinders. I'm off to Kallifornia, vere there's ''eaps of gold dust to be 'ad for the sweeping.' Appropriately, the ship in which the dustman is going to sail is called the *Moonshine*. Another cartoon of the same date, called 'A few days at the diggings' illustrates the 'Californian prices' that journalists would call the sums that would be demanded later that year for vantage views to watch the Mannings being executed. *Punch*'s caricatured Yankee, Hiram K. Doughboy, was asking the huge amount of thirty dollars (over £6) per day for board and lodging in the goldfields.

In more serious mood, however, *Punch* hoped that the abundance of gold would lead to lower interest rates. On 22 September that same year, the *Illustrated London News* reported the arrival at the Bank of England, under massive police escort, of cartloads of Californian gold and Mexican gold pesos worth more than half a million pounds. The backing of the increased gold reserve allowed greater circulation of paper currency and, as *Punch* had forecast, an expansion of credit from 1850 onwards. Bank rate fell to 2 per cent in April 1851 and a further boom would be created by increased demand during the Crimean War of 1854-1856.

The national funds were called 'Consols', the colloquial name for the Consolidated Bank Annuities. 'Consols' had paid 5.3 per cent interest since 1801, raising the National Debt from £228 million in 1793 to £709 million in 1816, after the end of Britain's colossal struggle against Napoleon. That high rate of interest had been justified during the inflationary period of the Napoleonic Wars. Taking 1794-1795 as 100, by 1818 prices had doubled, but they had subsequently fallen back to pre-war levels.[2] Consequently, in 1841 interest had been slashed to 3.25 per cent. It was a sizeable fall for people for whom the interest on their investments was their entire income. The tumbling interest rate on Consols was responsible for sending a flood of money into speculative shares and foreign bonds. After the 1847 collapse in British railway shares, there was a renewed flow of investment in railways all over Europe, in public utilities and mines, all channelled through the City of London and often on the basis of loans floated by the big merchant banks. Maria Manning's investments, for example, were in French railway shares.

Patrick O' Connor, the Mannings' victim, was a prudent investor, but investment was common by the 1840s even among ordinary folk, including, as a House of Commons report informed Parliament, country parsons, half-pay officers, servants, mail coach and railway guards, butchers, cooks, coachmen and cotton spinners.[3] Many such people would be ruined by the collapse of the schemes in which they invested their life savings or even by dishonest manipulations of the Stock Exchange.

Swindles

Charles Dickens's 'United Metropolitan Improved Hot Muffin and Crumpet Baking and Punctual Delivery Company' in *Nicholas Nickleby* is capitalised at the impertinently audacious and grotesquely exaggerated sum of £5 million in half a million ten pound shares. This, along with the 'Anglo-Bengalee Disinterested Loan and Life Insurance Company' in

Dickens's *Martin Chuzzlewit*, are fictional examples of one of the notorious phenomena of the age: the share swindle. Until the Limited Liability Act of 1856, shareholders of a failed company would lose not just the value of their shares, but also their property which would be forfeited to the creditors. Innocent Nicholas Nickleby, father of the eponymous hero of Dickens's novel, speculates in shares. In Chapter 1:

> a mania prevailed, a bubble burst, four stockbrokers took villa
> residences in Florence, four hundred nobodies were ruined

In Chapter 35 of *David Copperfield*, David's aunt Betsey Trotwood invests in a fanciful scheme for fishing up treasure, which Dickens may have based on a project which was suggested for recovering the riches that the Israelites, even though they were slaves, had supposedly jettisoned in the Red Sea during their biblical escape from Egypt.[4]

Another personage whose frequent appearance in early Victorian fiction reflects his importance in real life was the usurer. Before the age of bank credit, a person in desperate need of capital had recourse to a moneylender. While in traditional fiction the wastrel son of a wealthy family goes for money to a Jewish moneylender because usury was forbidden to Christians, the reality was often otherwise. This was brought out by Charles Reade in his novel *It's Never Too Late to Mend* of 1856, which portrays the Jewish Isaac Levi as mysterious, oriental and noble. John Meadows, the Gentile usurer who charges 20 per cent interest, considers Levi a rival because his rates are lower. Even a rate of 20 per cent, however, was little enough compared with what the fictional Ralph Nickleby charged. In his schooldays, Nicholas's uncle lent at the rate of 'two pence for every halfpenny', that is 400 per cent.

Bankruptcy

If one could not pay one's debts, bankruptcy or insolvency was the consequence. In Chapter 21 of *Nicholas Nickleby*, Mrs Mantalini has the humiliating experience of bailiffs, named 'Scaley' and 'Tix', and smelling of 'stale tobacco and fresh onions', pushing their way uncouthly into her dressmaking workshop in order to try to recover debts of 'fifteen hundred and twenty-seven pound, four and ninepence ha'penny', incurred by Mr Mantalini by 'gaming, wasting, idling and betting on horse races'.

Selling up the property of the insolvent was in the news in 1849, when Count d'Orsay, lover and stepson-in-law of the Countess of Blessington, had to flee to the Continent to escape his creditors. He must have had a great many, to judge from Jane Carlyle's description of his carriage, 'resplendent with sky-blue and silver', from which the Count, known in London society as 'the Prince of Dandies', had just descended. 'Such a beautiful man', as the Carlyle's servant exclaimed, though Jane herself thought that d'Orsay's beauty was 'of that rather disgusting sort'.[5] She meant that he looked effeminate. Howell and James, silk mercers of Regent Street, tried to recover sums incurred for the expensive furnishings of Gore House, Lady Blessington's residence, which stood on the site of the later Royal Albert Hall in South Kensington. In May 1849 the house was sold at auction. Lady Blessington, a novelist, had conducted a fashionable literary salon that the better-known author Thackeray had attended. He was highly offended by the coarse handling of the items up for sale and the vulgarity of the bidders.[6]

Bankruptcy seems to have been a common fate, at least to judge from the list of failures in *The Times* for the first quarter of 1849. While this may well reflect the sequel to the bursting of the railway share bubble in 1847, bankruptcy seems to have been frequent in the rough and tumble of early and mid-nineteenth-century business, and is often depicted in Victorian novels. In a world of investment and share swindles, together with an enterprise culture in which a certain proportion of those involved was bound to fail, bankruptcies were part of the life of a pulsating city such as London. Wages and salaries were low, so a well-invested legacy might make all the difference between a comfortable life and one endured in straightened circumstances.

A person who could not pay his debts and had no property to be seized by the bailiffs would face the debtors' prison, as the twelve-year-old Charles Dickens knew from visiting his father John in the Marshalsea in Southwark. Squalid and dangerous, the Marshalsea was a place of corruption and extortion, as Dickens describes in *Little Dorrit*.

Housing

There were a few large scale builders in London, such as Thomas Cubitt, who built the Calthorp Estate on Gray's Inn Road, and high-quality and expensive estates such Highbury Park, Woburn Place, Gordon Square, a great deal of Belgravia, and most of Pimlico. The brother of the diarist the Reverend Dan Greatorex bought a house at 5, Westbourne Terrace, a very upmarket district, for £800.[7] But short terraces in unfashionable areas such as Miniver (or Minver) Place, Bermondsey, where the Mannings lived and where they murdered Patrick O'Connor, were put up as speculations by small builders.

Over 43,000 new houses were built in London between 1841 and 1851. A small builder would lay the foundations and raise the walls, then finish the house by paying a subcontractor with the aid of a loan of a couple of hundred pounds obtained by mortgaging the house to one of the new 'building societies' which expanded rapidly in the early Victorian period. When the house was complete, the builder would redeem the mortgage by selling the property at a small profit to a landlord who wanted to put a few hundred pounds into an investment which was reputed to reflect safety, giving rise to the expression 'safe as houses'. That was true enough, for the house was always there, but it was profitable only if one could find reliable tenants at a remunerative rent.

The Manning house in Bermondsey was typical of property rented by the lower middle class. In contrast, the house which Thomas and Jane Carlyle rented in semi-rural Chelsea was less typical of London. Unlike the middle-class shopkeeper or clerk, or the skilled and regularly employed working man, Thomas Carlyle, as an intellectual who lived by his pen but had an income from land, worked at home and had no need to be in easy reach of the centre of London.

The usual method of renting a house was through an agent who displayed a baize-covered board in his window on which slips of paper were pinned giving details of properties to let. No.3, Miniver Place was let to the Mannings by the builder himself, James Coleman. As sketched for the weekly penny parts of Robert Huish's sensational *The Progress of Crime; or Authentic Memoirs of Maria Manning*, it was a white-painted terrace house built of brick and rendered with stucco. The front door, with its decorated lintel and keystone, opened onto a corridor and then a staircase leading to the two rooms on the upper floor. On the ground floor were the front and back parlours and there were a front and a back kitchen in the basement. Given that the average number of persons per house in England and Wales in 1851 was 5.5, the Mannings were spaciously housed, even if they had to take a lodger into one of their six rooms.[8] The house would be demolished in the 1960s, presumably because it could not be improved to minimum standards.

Throughout the 1840s, the battles for public health were fought on the general issues of sanitation, overcrowding, alcoholism and social problems rather than on the housing question in particular. Several proposed building reforms were postponed because of builders' objections. In 1844, the

Metropolitan Building Act had legislated on minimum sizes for houses, on street widths and habitable cellars, but the law did not deal with drainage and sanitation until 1855. London was particularly behindhand in matters such as damp-proof courses and ventilation. In any case, the act of 1844 applied only to the Cities of London and Westminster and some adjacent parishes. There were only thirty-three district surveyors employed in London at the time.[9]

The Mannings had a small garden, not well-cared-for, according to the next-door neighbour, though Maria tried to grow a few straggling runner-beans. The only refinement of the house was the railings which implied middle-class self-containment.

A similar property to the Manning house stood in Bayham Street in Camden Town in North London and was rented by Charles Dickens's father at £22 per year plus the various rates and taxes, sums which the tenant was obliged to pay if the rent was more than £20.[10] One would need an income of about £250 a year to rent it, given that 8 per cent of one's income was considered appropriate to allow the rest of a middle-class income to be spent on a suitable standard of living.[11] Subletting was thus normal. William Massey, the medical student who took a room in the Mannings' house, probably paid about four shillings a week, including coal and candles.

Whatever its condition a century later, Miniver Place, later Weston Street, was better than this contemporary description of a Bermondsey slum dwelling.

> The house was one up, one down, with a small scullery and no backyard except a shut-in paved area three feet deep. Drying and washing was done in the front court, where at the other end there was a standpipe for twenty-five houses with the water on for two hours daily, though never on Sundays. There was no place to wash in, no other water to wash in ... there was one w.c. for the twenty-five homes and a cesspit. Queues lined up outside that w.c., men, women and children[12]

At a middle to upper class level, Karl Marx paid £36 per year for an eight-roomed house in North London during the months when he was visiting the Reading Room of the British Museum daily.

These were houses which were within reach of central London by foot. However, Thomas and Jane Carlyle's house in Chelsea, which was considered a high-status semi-rural suburb, separated from Kensington by fields, alongside a cleaner part of the Thames, was larger and altogether better in quality. It had a sizeable rectangular garden with high brick walls, and eight rooms, with a closet, large enough to be used as a dressing room, on each floor, and was well fitted with cupboard space. There was a kitchen range which supplied up to two gallons of hot water as well as a large copper. This was a deep metal cauldron with a lid, with brick around it and built over a fire. It provided hot water for laundry, in particular. There was, nevertheless, no bathroom. The front kitchen faced the street and, because it was below street level, was usually in semi-darkness The back kitchen had a larder and coal store.

The Carlyles rented their house in 1834 for £35 per year. In 1843 they tried in vain to persuade the head leaseholder to part with what was probably an extremely long lease of the house, which had been built in 1704. However, in consideration of the improvements that the Carlyles continued to make at their own expense, including laying on piped water and two cisterns, with a tap over the kitchen sink, the landlord extended the lease, at the same rent, for thirty-one years.[13] Evidently, nobody expected inflation. The Carlyles also had a gas lamp fitted over the front door and in the kitchen where it was practical because oil lamps or candles were fire hazards.

In addition to the rent, there was a water rate of £1.6s per year, and the Church rate of £2.5s, as well as a Lighting, Pavement and Improvement rate, and a Poor Rate. Insurance against fire was also to be paid. These charges pushed the fixed costs up to at least £40 annually.

It was not easy to run a house in early Victorian times without at least one servant. Kitchens were in the basement, which was dark and dank unless they had an 'area' in front, for this would give some light to the front kitchen. The area was known as the 'airy', a word which rhymed with a common Irish surname to create the song heard when children used to play in London streets:

> One, two, three, O'Leary,
> My ball's in the airy

Only better houses had a kitchen range which could heat water. Otherwise, residents had to heat small quantities of water over the open fire in the grate, or in the 'copper'. If water was piped into the house, it was almost certainly to the ground floor only, called 'low service', and only to the sink in the basement kitchen where Maria invited the hapless O'Connor to have a refreshing wash that hot early August evening before she shot him in the back of the head.

'A dandified folly'

Bathrooms were very rare, even in expensive upper-class houses. Sybarites could install cold shower-baths, as Thomas Carlyle did in the kitchen, where he had piped water and a tap. He hauled up buckets of cold water with an apparatus of ropes and a pulley, and, with a device which upended the pail, poured the water over himself. He persuaded his rather sickly wife Jane to do the same. 'The shock is indescribable!' wrote Jane, 'and whether it strengthens or shatters me I have not yet made up my mind.'[14] In Chapter 29 of Thackeray's *Pendennis*, which appeared in monthly parts in 1849, the younger barristers in the Temple have installed showers, but their elderly colleague Mr Grump declares that the practice is 'an absurd, newfangled, dandified folly'.

One of the improvements made by the pressure for sanitary reform in the 1840s was the Public Baths and Wash houses Act of 1846. This came a long time after the tax on soap had been reduced in 1833, to be removed altogether in 1853. The consumption of this necessary aid to hygiene doubled between 1841 and 1851.[15] A large public bathing institution was opened in Goulston Street, Whitechapel, in May 1849, with 94 individual warm and cold baths, as well as steam and sulphur installations.[16] A cold bath cost one penny and a warm shower twopence. The sulphur baths were probably prescribed for the skin disease of scabies.

As for human waste, the usual provision was a privy or 'necessary' at the end of the back garden – if there was one. The excreta fell into a box and were covered with a shovelful of earth. 'Night-soil' men, who often worked as chimney sweeps during the day, came at night and emptied the box, selling the material as fertiliser. This was a safe way of emptying the area of offensive material. In the Manning garden, however, there was a closet connected to a cesspit. It was thought that the couple had thrown the murder weapon into it as well as the crowbar with which Frederick had finished off their victim. The police report spoke of a 'water closet' but did not mean a lavatory with its own cistern.[17] Even though the house was new, it was cheaply built and its inhabitants were not to enjoy this very modern way of relieving themselves. At best, they would have tipped a bucket of water down the privy.

Water, however, was scarce. There was piped water in the kitchen, but the supply was irregular. Yet there was probably no cistern or way of storing any substantial quantity of water in the house. At the Manning trial, evidence was given that Maria had tried to clean the basket that held the quicklime which the Mannings had used to destroy O'Connor's corpse, 'until she had exhausted all the water on the premises'. This suggests that, as was common, she kept water in containers.

Home Cooking

Maria Manning's kitchen had an open fire with enough space over it to hang a roasting spit, but no 'range' or 'kitchener'. This was a coal-burning stove with ovens and hotplates on top for cooking pans. It was just coming into use and was economical of coal and provided hot water also.

Expenditure on coal at the time was a major item. The Carlyles burnt twelve tons a year at 21/ per ton, about the same cost as a servant. However, landlords would not install an expensive range – the average price was £7.5s. plus the cost of fitting – unless they could charge more rent, so ranges were rare in the poorer parts of London.[18] The range in the Carlyles' Chelsea house did not work well. In 1852, Thomas Carlyle agreed to pay for a new one and the landlord promised to refund the cost when the Carlyles moved.[19]

The fire would burn in the grate of the Mannings' basement kitchen all through the year. As well as the spit there was a trivet over the open fire which could support one or more pots at a time, but the food probably tasted of coal smoke. In the winter, what with London grime and fog, the cooking would have made the kitchen greasy and dirty. There was probably a lot of condensation and the floor would have been damp. Washing up was an unpleasant business. The butler sink was unglazed and there was probably only a rough wooden draining board. Nevertheless, the Mannings' new house had a larder in which to store food, and, living as they did in a great city, they could buy food in any quantities they needed when they wanted it.

Home Comforts

Mr Bainbridge, the furniture dealer, prepared an inventory of all the Mannings' furniture, which Frederick had sold to him. Although the details are not mentioned, Bainbridge stated that the secondhand value of the tables and chairs was £13.10s., though Frederick had asked for £16. It had cost £30, much dearer than the price at which one would be able to furnish a house at the end of the century when mass production had brought the cost down to £12.12s. or just under ten weeks' wages for a man on 25 shillings a week.[20]

The fuel for heating and cooking came to London loaded on the seven hundred colliers which carried coal from Tyneside. In the docks, the coal was broken up and bagged by the coal-whippers, brought to the riverside in barges and sold by the ton by merchants who brought it to the houses on carts drawn by powerful shire horses. At Miniver Place the coal cupboard was off the back kitchen. The black coal dust would have filled the Manning house when the coalman tramped down the area steps, plodded through the kitchen, and emptied the bags into the coal store, creating as he did so clouds of coal dust which coated the laundry, the net curtains and the white-scrubbed doorstep.

Rooms were smoky in the winter because the downdraughts blew coal dust down the chimney. The chimneys were none too efficient and carried much of the incompletely combusted fuel out into the air in the form of soot, which created the black pall of smoke that struck all foreign visitors.[21] And, sometimes, during high winds, chimney pots, which the builders had not fixed properly to the chimney stacks, would come crashing down with an explosion of shattered earthenware.

As for lighting, gas was rare even in middle-class homes until the 1850s, when its installation in the new House of Commons reassured many who suspected its safety, even though by the time of Victoria's accession there were already more than two hundred miles of gas mains laid below the streets of London, largely devoted to the lighting of the streets and the most impressive shops. Gas was not very pure and was smelly and stuffy. It left black marks on ceilings. Furthermore, gas light was yellow until incandescent mantles were introduced in the 1880s. It was also quite expensive. Thomas Carlyle had gas put in, but he considered it a great extravagance.

Gas for private houses, as opposed to public buildings, was seen as typical of nouveau-riche show-offs, who made their residences look like brilliantly lit gin palaces. It made the atmosphere even hotter and stuffier than it was already, and the impurities created an unpleasant smell. Gas was also cruel to women's complexions, showing up every blemish.[22] Cooks were reluctant to accept gas, though the famous chef Alexis Soyer used it at the Reform Club, where he produced legendary banquets from 1841 onwards.[23]

The price of gas fell as its use became more widespread, but less well-off people used whale oil or colza, made from oil-seed rape, in their lamps, and in the bedroom smelly tallow or rendered animal fat candles. For the really poor, lighting was expensive, so they used rushes dipped in hot bacon fat, called 'farthing dips'.[24] Candles cost tenpence a pound and were out of the question. Extravagantly, the middle-class Carlyles burned three pounds of candles in ten days, but this was because Thomas liked to stay up late reading.

As for laundry, Maria Manning might have done the washing herself, sent it out or employed a washerwoman to come in once a week. Washing Maria's voluminous petticoats, Fred's underwear, shirts and neckcloths, and the nightdresses, sheets and pillowcases of the household required soaking in a tub, vigorous rubbing, boiling in the copper, rinsing, blueing and starching.

A steady £3 a week was considered to be the minimum income at which one could afford to keep a live-in servant of the least-skilled sort, a 'maid of all work' or 'skivvy', who might earn between £6 and £12 a year with her keep. The Mannings' income did not run to a servant but Maria engaged a charwoman when she needed one, as she did when she brought in twelve-year-old Hannah Firman to clean up after she and Frederick had buried O'Connor's corpse. Hannah usually sold matches, bootlaces and laces for women's stays from a tray in the street. It took her a whole day to clean up the mess of lime and earth produced by the disposal of the victim's body. Maria gave Hannah sixpence. The girl made up for the meanness of her reward by stealing stockings, a petticoat and an egg, as she unwillingly confessed when she gave evidence in court.

Class

Maria Manning had been a lady's maid to a noblewoman. She had never had to soil her hands. Now she was obliged to shop, cook, and clean with little help from an alcoholic and unreliable husband. A few months in Bermondsey with the stink from its tanneries and the general grime of London would have driven her to despair. Though a married woman and no longer a servant, she would have felt that she had dropped in social class. But what was her class?

> Oh! Let us love our occupations,
> Bless the squire and his relations,
> Live upon our daily rations,
> And always know our proper stations.

In Dickens's short novel, *The Chimes*, of 1844, this rhyme, which the author quotes sarcastically but which may well have been taught with all seriousness to children, is set to music by the 'new system' of tonic-sol-fa for Lady Bowley, wife of Sir Joseph Bowley, MP, who wants the men and boys of the village to sing it in the evening. But the rebel Will Fern politely refuses. Lady Bowley complains: 'Who can expect anything but insolence and ingratitude from that class of people?' She and her husband agree that Fern should be punished as a vagrant.

Middle-class People

Money and where it had come from was indelibly associated with class.

Frederick Manning came from a respectable family in trade in Taunton in the West of England; Maria had been a very high-class lady's maid. They belonged to the lower middle class of small manufacturers, shopkeepers, master tailors, innkeepers and commercial travellers, to which was now added a growing array of clerks, schoolteachers and the lower ranks of the professions, together with railway officials and minor civil servants. Such people were either 'in trade' or they provided a paid service, rather than living like 'gentlefolk' on their investments or rents. But they did not live by selling their manual labour either, and this put them firmly among the 'middle' and 'lower' middle classes, who opposed aristocratic idleness, preferring puritan values of 'seriousness', hard work and sobriety.

On 7 July 1849, *Punch*, reflecting middle class disapproval of high-spending Londoners' habits, quotes a fictional 'Mr. Brown', who remarks cuttingly, 'Everybody lives as if he had three or four thousand a year'. 'Everybody' would include Charles Dickens's characters Hamilton and Anastasia Veneering in Dickens's *Our Mutual Friend*, published as a serial in 1864-1865, who live in a 'bran-new house in a bran-new quarter of London' and keep up with their friends by throwing a dinner party which might have cost as much as fifty pounds.

The lower middle class with a regular £80 or £100 a year also feared the poor, the working class, as well as atheists and disreputable agnostics. With little education and little artistic sensitivity, this class prided itself on being 'respectable'. It disapproved of both working-class and upper-class sexual misbehaviour. The lower middle class held itself up as an example to the feckless poor, and preached the doctrine of self-control, especially in the matter of having children. The increasing acceptance of its values gave that class a sense of mission and identity. The responsible, skilled working class, in their view, also deserved encouragement, so Dickens's wealthy merchant Mr Dombey recommends Rob, the son of Mr Toodle, the railway stoker and later engine driver, for a place at the Bluecoat School, fictionalised in *Dombey and Son* as the Grinders.

Although the Mannings' income was insufficient for a middle class way of life, and to allow them to occupy their house without a lodger, Maria certainly had middle class aspirations. The Mannings adopted the middle-class custom of inviting their friend to dinner, even if the real aim of the invitation was sinister. If Frederick had been able to lay off the brandy sufficiently to keep his job at Gover and Company, stationers in Holborn, at a salary of £2 per week and 5 per cent commission, he would have been firmly placed in the lower middle class at about the status of a higher-grade clerk. As an employee, he was probably lower in status than he had been before as a publican, but he no longer had to deal with drunks. He was higher than the class that Dickens, in *Sketches by Boz*, the novelist's observations of London people in the early Victorian age, called 'shabby-genteel'. At a fixed wage he was also in a better position than Mr Micawber in *David Copperfield*, who sold corn on commission only. This was a time when a builder's labourer in the season might be paid £1 per week (much more than he would have received as a Wiltshire or Dorset farm worker), a postman received 22 shillings and a London skilled worker perhaps £1.10s, but might be subject to periodic unemployment. Manning himself had earned only 18s a week when he was a railway guard. Exceptionally, printers, those aristocrats of the skilled working class, had a good wage of £4.4s a week, only a pound less than the reporters for the newspapers they printed.

Charles Dickens, with his outstanding shorthand skills, was employed by the *Morning Chronicle* as a parliamentary reporter at five guineas a week. With the development of his journalistic skills, there was always the chance that he might ascend to the rank of deputy editor of the paper at over £500 a year, if not the editor with his £1,000 a year. An annual income of £500 would allow a man to rent a London suburban villa for £45 a year, plus bedrooms for his children and perhaps two or even three live-in servants.[25]

Most of the lower and 'middle' middle class earned between £100 and £200 a year, though clerks and teachers often got less. The later successful novelist Anthony Trollope started as a clerk at the General Post Office in 1834 at £90 annually, though he was on a rising scale and after seven years was receiving £140, the lowest amount on which it might be considered possible to begin middle class married life. William Guppy, the solicitor's clerk, offers Esther Summerson marriage in Chapter 9 of *Bleak House*. He sees himself as poor when he earns £1,15s a week (though it was the wage of a very well-paid working man), but later, having seen his salary raised to £2 a week and with the promise of a further five shillings in a year's time, he spends money on clothes and wears a flashy ring. He lives in Penton Place, Islington, a good healthy address, at a considerable height above the dirty, smoky City.

As for working hours, the several hundred clerks at the Bank of England, whose employment practices provided a model for City firms, worked from 9am to 3.30pm or until 5pm with an hour and a half for dinner. Nevertheless, the work had to be finished and the daily balance struck before they left in the evening. Most offices closed at six. Below the Bank of England came the clerks who worked in insurance or in the Stock Exchange. They worked six days a week and had no holidays save Christmas Day. In fact, the early nineteenth-century clerk worked harder than his predecessor in the eighteenth, when there had been a much larger number of customary religious holidays.

Tax

When in 1842 Sir Robert Peel reintroduced income tax, abolished after the Napoleonic Wars, on incomes of over £150 a year, a man on an annual £300 would pay sevenpence in the pound on his next £150, a sum of only £4.7.6d. in all. Even on a comfortable £500 a year, on the taxable £350 he would be taxed only £10.4.3d, a sum which would pay the wages, though not the board and clothes, of a female servant. In a sense, though the income tax of the 1840s seems a bagatelle today, it could be judged a burden and was certainly seen so.

The Carlyles' letters and diaries provide quite a full account of their income, expenses and taxation. In 1847 Thomas had earnings from land and writing of £800, but his writing income was irregular and in 1854 his private receipts and his royalties from sales of his books on Oliver Cromwell and on the French Revolution produced only £300. In 1855 inflation caused by the Crimean War had increased the various unavoidable rates and taxes on the house. But the heaviest increase came from taxation. Income tax doubled from 7d to 1/2d in the pound. Jane Carlyle, who managed the household finances, demanded an increase in her quarterly allowance, which Thomas conceded, and in November 1855 she went to the Commissioners of Income Tax in their office in Kensington to protest about their high assessment of her husband's tax obligations. Jane wrote a comic account of the scene, portraying the senior Commissioner as Rhadamanthus, the stern judge of the dead, who asked the undaunted Jane if she expected him to believe that the Carlyles lived on the £150 a year that Thomas had declared as his average income from writing. No, of course not, retorted Jane, adding coldly that her husband had no obligation to give the Commissioners any account of his other income, which came from land and was not subject to tax. 'Take off a hundred pounds,' said the chairman.

Jane was a tough woman to deal with. In 1858 a builder sent in an invoice for £5.7.6d for putting a new grate into Thomas's study. Jane refused to pay more than £3.10s, and got away with it.[26]

The Workhouse

Very few people enjoyed pensionable employment. In Dickens's *Great Expectations* the bill collector John Wemmick looks after his father, whom he calls 'Aged Parent', but if one did not have children to look to for support or had not been able to save sufficiently for one's old age, the workhouse was the grim solution. On Sunday, 5 May 1850 Dickens visited the Marylebone workhouse, and wrote up his visit on 25 May in a piece in *Household Words*, his twopenny weekly magazine.[27] The institution had 1,715 inmates, as well as a further 345 in the infirmary, including 45 lunatics and those in the 'itch' ward. Most of the young inmates were fatherless children, the sort who might have been farmed out to cruel moneymakers such as Bartholomew Drouet of the Tooting Pauper Baby Farm which had been ravaged by cholera the previous year. Others were widows without support. In his article, Dickens wrote:

> Aged people were there, in every variety. Mumbling, blear-eyed, stupid, deaf, lame; vacantly winking in the gleams of sun that now and then crept in through the open doors, from the paved yard ... There were weird old women, all skeleton within, all bonnet and cloak without, continually wiping their eyes with dirty dusters of pocket-handkerchiefs, and there were ugly old crones, both male and female, with a ghastly kind of contentment on them which was not at all comforting to see

Servants in particular, if they had lived long enough to be retired and had worked for employers who did not see it as their obligation or were not able to provide for their old age, took refuge in the workhouse. Illness could also lead to the workhouse. Dickens saw a young woman, pretty and well-mannered, who had been brought there because she was subject to epileptic fits and had no friends who could take her in. It is difficult to know what the elderly middle class did if they could no longer pay the rent, but Dickens underlines that the young woman in question was 'by no means of the same stuff, or the same breeding, or the same experience as those by whom she was surrounded', so it would seem that the workhouse was largely restricted to the aged poor, orphans, and the unfortunate, ignorant and feckless.

The Marylebone Workhouse that Dickens visited was well run, in contrast to the fictional one under the harsh rule of Mr and Mrs Bumble, which he describes in *Oliver Twist*. The paupers were treated kindly, but there was no stimulus for the mind. Dickens, however, says nothing about the separation of husbands from wives in different wards, the fate which the elderly poor most dreaded. Furthermore, he visited the workhouse on a fine spring day. The windows and doors were probably open, which may be why Dickens wrote nothing about the smell.

The permanent smokiness of London, together with the filthy state of the streets, the repellent drains, and the putrescent mud and dung, created the smell or miasma which worried doctors so much. But people smelled as well. The Baths and Wash-houses Act of 1847 allowed some amelioration of the body odour of manual workers who, unwashed, reeking of sour sweat, stale tobacco and beer, their jackets and trousers, shirts, socks and underwear infrequently changed, carried with them the odours of their work: paint, turpentine, coal and glue. On 11 December 1849, the opening of the public baths in Marylebone gave occasion for the socially-concerned middle-class inhabitants of the parish to congratulate themselves on facilitating the cleanliness of the common people. They did this at what the press described as 'an elegant déjeuner', laid out for the occasion.

The working class not only smelled differently; in London, they also spoke a different language. If written records are to be trusted, one of Henry Mayhew's contacts among the common folk of London revealed, perhaps for the first time, the characteristics of Cockney rhyming slang:

> Suppose I want to ask a pal to come and have a glass of rum
> and smoke a pipe of tobacco and have a game of cards with
> some blokes at home with me. I should say, if there were any
> flats present, 'Splodger, will you have a Jack surpass of finger-
> and-thumb and blow your yard of tripe of nosey-me-knacker,
> and have a touch of the broads with me and the other heap of
> coke at my drum?

'Flats' were 'flatfoots' or police, whom the speaker wanted to deceive; 'nosey-me-knacker' was 'tobacco, pronounced 'terbacker', while 'broads' were cards, pronounced 'cords'. Drum leads to 'bass', which is rhyming slang for 'place'.[28]

Chapter 6

Learning, Literature and Liturgy

Widely Diffused Ignorance

The Victorian passion for elaborate and precise statistics allowed the novelist and journalist Charles Dickens to conclude from the Metropolitan Police figures that, of the 20,500 London women convicted of offences in 1847, 9,000 were totally illiterate and 11,000 could read and write only imperfectly. Only fourteen of those women could read and write well. They probably belonged to the middle class or had been superior servants As for the men, only 150 out of 41,000 could read and write well.[1] The rest, where they could read, could do no more than, in Dickens's pathos-inducing words, 'blunder over a book like a little child'. In any case, the standard for measuring literacy was very low, perhaps no more than being able to stumble through an elementary reading book. Dickens linked women's illiteracy with their incapacity to do basic household tasks or simple sewing, and he allied these deficiencies to the general fecklessness of such women's lives. He took the view, and he may be assumed to represent a great deal of progressive opinion at the time, that education had to have a practical and moral end, and, in his words to be 'immediately applicable to the duties and business of life, directly conducive to order, cleanliness, punctuality and economy'. The Scriptures, which were often used as a basic text, were not supposed to be used as a reading primer (in Dickens's words ' a dog-eared spelling book'); they had a moral purpose as well.[2]

In the next issue of *The Examiner*, Dickens used his fluent and compelling pen to launch an attack on the schools of the National Society for the Education of the Poor in the Principles of the Church of England in England and Wales, known for short as the National Schools. A London servant girl, Susan Grant, had recently been tricked out of her savings by a fortune-teller who claimed to be able, for money, to change the influence of the planets on Susan's future life. When the fortune-teller was had up in court, the magistrate expressed surprise that Susan had been so credulous. Dickens used her example to lambast the teaching of the National Schools. Susan Grant could perhaps parrot her catechism without much idea of what it meant, but her so-called education had not taught her that for a pious person the planets were controlled by the Divine will and thus could not be affected by crossing someone's palm with silver.

There were also non-sectarian schools run by the British and Foreign School Society. However, in Dickens's view, their severe utilitarianism would have crushed the sense of wonder of any child who mused 'Twinkle, twinkle, little star, how I wonder what you are'.Dickens wrote about the same jingle in Chapter 3 of his 1854 novel *Hard Times*, where he attacks the harshness of a utilitarian education restricted to bare facts. No little Gradgrind, the name of a family in the novel, 'had ever known wonder on the subject [of the stars], each little Gradgrind having at five years dissected the Great Bear'.

Although Susan Grant appears to have been simple whatever the deficiencies of her education, the fact was that, in 1834, of 130,000 couples who married, one-third of the bridegrooms and half of the brides could not even manage to sign their own names in the register.[3] Later, the 1851 Census showed similar figures: 30.7 per cent of the grooms and 45.2 per cent of the brides could not sign the marriage register.[4] These figures hid an even greater proportion of the population who were illiterate for all practical purposes, even if they could manage to scrawl their names.

In 1840 the Treasury grant for elementary education was a mere £50,000. Although there would be increases, the grant remained below a very inadequate £200,000 throughout the next decade. Tens of thousands of London children never went to school at all, or attended for only a short time or irregularly. Elementary education taught only religion, together with reading, writing and arithmetic (the three R's). It was based on the monitorial system, by which the teacher taught pupils who in turn taught sections of huge classes of up to one hundred children.

SQUEERS: That's our system, Nickleby. What do you think of it?

NICHOLAS: It's a very useful one, at any rate.

(*NICHOLAS NICKLEBY*, Chapter 8)

Middle-class children were educated in private schools. There were 30,000 of these in England and Wales, teaching 700,000 children. They varied greatly. Some were 'dame' schools, costing fourpence or sixpence per week, a sum which was beyond working- and lower middle-class pockets, especially if several children had to be educated. Even the grammar schools, with their humane traditions, which catered for the children of the higher classes if they did not attend one of the great 'public' schools such as Eton, Harrow and Rugby, interpreted their foundation statutes in a way which had hardly changed their practices since they had been founded, often centuries earlier.

However, the major scandal, attacked specifically by Dickens, was that, for not too great a sum, guardians who wished to get rid of inconvenient children could board them out permanently for twenty guineas (£21) a year in places like Wackford Squeers's institution Dotheboys Hall, which Dickens based on a true instance. Squeers's educational system is truly utilitarian in theory, though not of much use in practice. In Chapter 8 of *Nicholas Nickleby*, after learning that 'window' is a 'noun substantive', a boy is ordered to clean the casement in question. Unfortunately, the practicality of the education is marred because Mr Squeers thinks that 'window' is spelt 'winder', and assures his class that 'botany' is written 'bottiney'.

Self-help

After leaving a private, British or National School, or no school at all, a person was not completely abandoned to brutish ignorance, but immense efforts had to be made to use one's scant leisure profitably. Henry Brougham, a distinguished polymath and statesman who became Lord Chancellor in 1830, was one of the founders in 1828 of University College London, the precursor of London University. It was known as 'the Godless Institution of Gower Street' because, unlike Oxford and Cambridge, it did not impose religious tests for entry. Brougham also founded the Society for the Diffusion of Useful Knowledge, which set up Mechanics' Institutes. These were places where the working man who wanted to get on, improving his mind or his skills, could attend lectures and borrow books, They encouraged respectability, keeping men out of gin palaces and pubs, while giving them peaceful rather than violent amusement. By 1850 there were 610 Mechanics' Institutes in England alone with 102 thousand members, including the London Mechanics' Institute, now Birkbeck College, a part of London University where classes are still held at night. This institution offered a wide range of lectures on subjects including literature, the topography of the British Isles and history.

'Pulling oneself up by one's own bootstraps' was an article of faith for early Victorian Utilitarians, who judged everything by its usefulness. While Utilitarians often expressed progressive views, questioning among other things privileges which seemed to have no justification or usefulness, they also tended to take a hostile attitude towards pleasure, amusement, art and beauty. Weekday Utilitarians were often Sunday Evangelicals, Christians of the most 'serious' persuasion. Both believed in the value of serious literature which conveyed the immutable truths of religion and economics. Evangelicals and Utilitarians alike were profoundly convinced of the value of self-help. For both, reading had a purpose, and it was not frivolous amusement. Classes in self-help groups and Mechanics' Institutes were by definition utilitarian. How to read and write a business letter, how to estimate builders' quantities, together with some factual information about geography and history, were in most cases their limits.

Always got his Nose stuck in a Book

In 1849, Karl Marx, the political refugee and author of *The Communist Manifesto*, came to London to join the leisured and the studious and to read some of the hundreds of thousands of books in the British Museum. Before Panizzi's great circular reading room was constructed readers sat in the King's Library. No lights were allowed for fear of fire. The rolling autumn and winter fogs of London often sent readers home early.

Most people owned few, if any, books. The Mannings were typical in this respect. The few books they had were all Maria's.[5] She probably brought most of them with her when she came to England from Switzerland. She owned a volume in French called *Souvenirs Historiques* ('Historical Memories', perhaps the Baron de Méneval's recently published work about Napoleon and Marie-Louise Bonaparte), the Psalms (also in French), a French-English dictionary and a useful guide called *Cook's Letter Writer*.

Most literature, however, whether in the form of books, pamphlets or newspapers, was being read by a growing number of people who had acquired the habit from publications which had been written for their pleasure as much as for their improvement.

An expansion was taking place in newspaper, magazine and book publishing, and consequently in the reading public. Two popular weeklies, the *London Journal* and the *Family Herald*, enjoyed combined sales of over 750 thousand in the mid-nineteenth century. Each had sixteen pages closely printed with adventure stories, general fiction, answers to readers' questions, serious essays and household hints.[6] The Stamp Act of 1818 had not taxed papers which published serials, so Charles Dickens remembered that when he was a boy he used to buy a magazine called *The Terrific Register* for a penny. Every number had an illustration with pools of blood and at least one body.[7] People read sensational thrillers, ballads and broadsides sold in the streets. In London, most of these were published by James Catnach in the slum district of Seven Dials. In 1849, the Catnach press would sell two and a half million broadsides about the Manning murder.

A smaller number took advantage of the limited but growing availability of better literature. From 1827 onwards, Brougham's Society for the Diffusion of Useful Knowledge issued a series of volumes called, appropriately, the *Library of Useful Knowledge*. The booklets were published in parts at two-week intervals, each costing sixpence, which bought thirty-two closely printed pages. The *Library of Useful Knowledge* was followed by the less forbidding *Library of Entertaining Knowledge*. 'Useful knowledge' explained, among other topics, differential calculus and the art of brewing. 'Entertaining knowledge' discussed subjects such as the Elgin Marbles, which were on show at the recently completed British Museum building in Bloomsbury. Rather intriguing, perhaps, was the issue describing 'Secret Societies of the Middle Ages'. Even cheaper enlightening literature was available. The Society for the Diffusion of Useful Knowledge also published the *Penny Magazine* and the *Penny Cyclopaedia*, while the well-known publishers Cassell's *Popular Educator* came out in 1852. This last was produced in a more appealing style and might have attracted people who remained untouched by the offerings of its predecessors. By 1862, in the mid-Victorian age, Cassell's, the publishers, founded in 1848, would be selling 25 to 30 million copies of its penny publications annually.

During the early part of Victoria's reign books fell in price because of cheap reprints and the expansion of publication in weekly, fortnightly or monthly parts. Other changes favoured newspaper publication and reading. In 1836 Stamp Duty on newspapers was reduced to a penny. In 1853 duty on advertisements was abolished, which allowed a further cheapening of newspapers.

The long-lasting *News of the World* began publication of its titillating sex and crime stories in 1843 with a piece headed 'Extraordinary case of drugging and violation'.[8] It would still be flourishing when it was forced in July 2011 to close by a phone-hacking scandal. John Julius Reuter set up his press agency in London in 1851, probably because the British capital provided the richest source of the commercial and financial information which was Reuter's main interest and also perhaps because the abundant British press was the best customer for his information. One early example of the instant and phenomenal success of a serial publication, appearing in 1837, was Charles Dickens's *Pickwick Papers*. An early biographer of Dickens wrote that he visited a locksmith and 'I found him reading *Pickwick* to an audience of twenty persons, literally men, women and children. They had clubbed together to borrow it for twopence from a circulating library because the shilling that the number cost was beyond them.'[9]

Another remarkable genre of popular literature was the 'Penny Dreadful', of which the most famous was George William McArthur Reynolds's *Mysteries of London* of 1847 and his *Mysteries of the Court of London*, which was published in penny numbers from 1849 until 1856. Thirty or forty thousand of these eight-page booklets with their 7,500 words of close printed and double-columned prose, enlivened with occasional woodcuts, were sold every week. Reynolds also edited a family magazine called *Reynolds' Miscellany of Romance, Literature, Science and Art*, and he wrote novels prolifically. In March 1848, Reynolds, a man of progressive ideas, chaired the great revolutionary assemblies of the Chartist movement in Trafalgar Square and on Kennington Common. He also edited a newspaper called *Reynolds' Weekly*, which played an important part in forming radical thought and which survived, under different names, until January 1967. Reynolds's lurid episodes in the *Mysteries of London* contained populist politics, moving social comment, together with dramatic and even voyeuristic illustrations of depravity in high and low places. They were not, of course, meant to be 'improving'. Even today, the reader finds Reynolds's text vigorous, though some parts of it are hard-going. Perhaps language such as in the following extract was expected and appreciated, even by those to whom the *Mysteries of the Court of London* had to be read aloud:

> Indiscreet, my sweet girl! cried her lover.'Oh! How could you suppose that I would entertain a harsh feeling with regard to that goodness on your part which doubtless instigated you to afford me the happiness of this meeting[10]

Melodramatic serials like Reynolds's *Mysteries* had their sensational equivalents in the threepenny weekly newspapers such as *The Weekly Times*, which exposed upper-class corruption and immorality. They also reported crimes and disasters with a wealth of detail.

Henry Mayhew's influential articles, which became the famous *London Labour and the London Poor*, were announced in the *Morning Post* on 18 October 1849. In a piece on 'The literature of costermongers', one of his favourite subjects, Mayhew reported that Reynolds's *Mysteries* was their

Above: **Anti-Catholicism**, 'No Popery' Exeter Hall, 1850 Richard Doyle, *Manners and Customs of ye Englyshe*, 1849.

Right: **Arsenic**: Fatal Facility. Poisons for the asking. *Wellcome Collection, after John Leech*

FATAL FACILITY; OR, POISONS FOR THE ASKING.

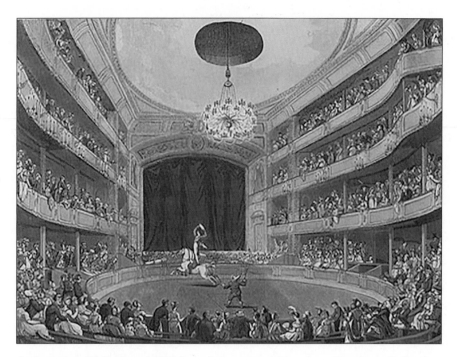

Astley's Amphitheatre, 1808, from *Microcosm of London, Houghton Collection, Harvard University, public domain*

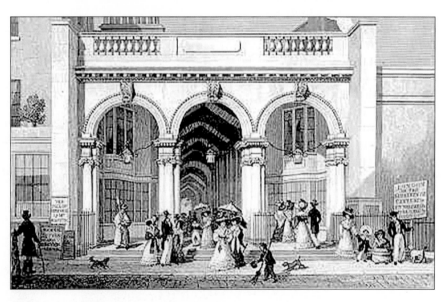

Burlington Arcade 1827-1828, by Thomas Hosmer Shepherd.

The Chamber of Horrors. Richard Doyle, *Manners and Customs of Ye Englyshe* (1849) *Wikicommons. Gutenberg*

Chartist Demonstration on Kennington Common, 1848, E.Walford (d.1897). *Old and New London*

Left: **Cholera**, Broadsheet warning, 1831. *Wellcome Licence. Attribution 4.0 International (CCRY 4.0)*

Below: **Clerks eat out**, Dickens, *Bleak House*. Drawing by 'Phiz' (K.Hablot Brown) (d.1882)

The Colosseum, 1827, E. Walford (d.1897) *Old London*

Cremorne Gardens, The Dancing Platform, 1864. By Phoebus Levin (d.1908)

The Egyptian Hall. *Wikipedia Creative Commons*

Euston Station 1837 showing wrought-iron roof. *Wikipedia.*

Euston Station Arch or Propyleum. *Wikipedia Creative Commons*

Exeter Hall, 1846, the meeting of the Anti Corn Law League. *Wikipedia Commons*

Above left: **Inspector Field.** *Illustrated London News 1855 p/d Wikipedia Commons*

Above right: **King Cholera.** *Wellcome Collection*

Crowds trying to see **Jenny Lind,** from Richard Doyle, *Manners and Customs of Ye Englyshe* (1849). *Wikicommons. Gutenberg*

Lola Montes by Thomas Easterly. *Missouri History Museum, Open Access*

London & Greenwich Railway, 1837. *Illustrated London News*

London, traffic on Ludgate Hill, 1882, by G. Doré (d.1883)

Mannings, Maria and Frederick, from Huish (see bibliography), 1849, originally from the popular press.

Mannings, the Police discover the corpse, from Huish.

NO. 3, MINIVER-PLACE.

Above: **Mannings, their house,** 3, Minver Place, Bermondsey, from Huish.

Right: **Their victim, Patrick O'Connor** from Huish.

PATRICK O'CONNOR.

From the likeness at Madame Tussaud's Exhibition.

Nelson's Column under construction, 1844 *Fox-Talbot photograph, from New York, Metropolitan Museum of Art, open access*

Pepper's Ghost, 1862.

Above: '**A Prospect of a Fashionable Haberdashr Hys Shoppe**', from Doyle, *Manners and Customs of Ye Englyshee,* 1849. (see The Chamber of Horrors above)

Right: **Postal Regulations** 7 January 1840. *Wikipedia*

POST OFFICE REGULATIONS.

On and after the 10th January, a Letter not exceeding HALF AN OUNCE IN WEIGHT, may be sent from any part of the United Kingdom, to any other part, for One Penny, if paid when posted, or for Two Pence if paid when delivered.

THE SCALE OF RATES,

If paid when posted, is as follows, for all Letters, whether sent by the General or by any Local Post,

Not exceeding ½ Ounce	**One Penny.**
Exceeding ½ Ounce, but not exceeding 1 Ounce	**Twopence.**
Ditto 1 Ounce .... 2 Ounces	**Fourpence.**
Ditto 2 Ounces .... 3 Ounces	**Sixpence.**

and so on; an additional Two-pence for every additional Ounce. With but few exceptions, the Weight is limited to Sixteen Ounces.

If not paid when posted, double the above Rates are charged on Inland Letters.

COLONIAL LETTERS.

If sent by Packet Twelve Times, if by Private Ship Eight Times, the above Rates.

FOREIGN LETTERS.

The Packet Rates which vary, will be seen at the Post Office. The Ship Rates are the same as the Ship Rates for Colonial Letters.

As regards Foreign and Colonial Letters, there is no limitation as to weight. All sent outwards, with a few exceptions, which may be learnt at the Post Office, must be paid when posted as heretofore.

Letters intended to go by Private Ship must be marked "*Ship Letter.*"

Some arrangements of minor importance, which are omitted in this Notice, may be seen in that placarded at the Post Office.

No Articles should be transmitted by Post which are liable to *injury* by being stamped, or by being crushed in the Bags.

It is particularly requested that all Letters may be *fully* and *legibly addressed,* and *posted as early* as convenient.

January 7th, 1840.

By Authority : –J. Hartnell, London.

The Quadrant, Regent Street, 1837, from *The History of London*, J. Woofs after J.F. Salmon (d.1886) p/d.

A Scene in St. Giles's.

Theatrical Reflection.
or a Peep at the Looking Glass Curtain at the Royal Coburg Theatre.

Above: **Rookery 1850, 'A scene in St. Giles'.** *Wikicommons p/d from Beames, T.B. The Rookeries of London, Past, Present and Prospective*

Left: **The Royal Coburg (later Royal Victoria and Old Vic) theatre**, 1822. *Wikicommons*

Shillibeer's Omnibus, author unknown, from Moore, H.G. *Omnibuses and Cabs, 1902 p/d*

Vauxhall Gardens, Thomas Rowlandson, 1785. *Wikicommons*

'Water, water everwhere and not a drop to drink'.
Wellcome collection, open access

Wentworth Street, Whitechapel
(Old Clothes), G. Doré (d.1883).
Wellcome Collection, open access

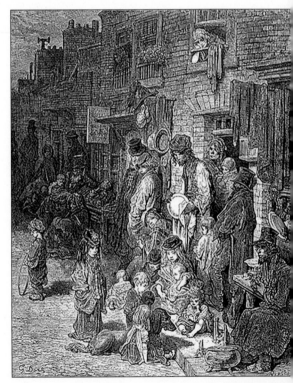

preferred reading material. A literate costermonger read it to groups who could not do so for themselves, and the reading was interrupted by queries and comments. Reynolds's *Mysteries* and similar works might well be sneered at by the better-educated, some of whom must have been tempted by the racy style and the occasional bit of titillation. Yet such popular publications possessed, without realising it, a true vocational function in increasing vocabulary and expression among their readers. Abel Heywood, a Manchester bookseller, reported in 1851 that the *Mysteries of the Court of London* was selling 1,500 copies a week even in the provinces, Penny fiction, he said, was read by 'a *spreeing* (*sic*), sort of young man, the type who visits taverns and puts cigars into their mouth in a flourishing way as well as by many women'.[11]

So, despite the low level of literacy, many factors, especially in a great city such as London, stimulated the urge to read, not the least of which were the cheapening of printed matter and the rise of popular journalism. As in so many things, the early Victorians lived on the brink of a new age. The reductions and removal of tax from paper, newspapers and advertisements allowed the *Daily Telegraph* to halve its price from twopence to one penny. Moreover, there had also been a technical revolution, especially in newspaper production. By 1848, state-of-the-art machines could print both sides of four thousand sheets in an hour. By 1854, the circulation of *The Times* had reached 55,000 copies a day.

High quality and expensive magazine journalism of a surprisingly modern kind, but beyond most people's purses, appeared in the *Illustrated London News* and in the humorous and socially-critical *Punch*, both of which date from the 1840s. Charles Dickens's *Household Words*, which he began to publish in March 1850, was a rival to the *Mysteries*. Competent and professional, this journal did not patronise its readers, and its cover price was modest. It was well-designed to appeal to a wide public. Dickens wrote also in *The Examiner*, founded in 1808 and converted from 1830 onwards by Albany Fontblanque, renowned as the wittiest writer of his day, into a serious but easily read publication, and one that a modern critic has called 'A mixture of the *New Statesman*, *The Times*, and *The News of the World*'.[12]

Reprints of books could now be bought for between one and six shillings. In the early Victorian years, John Murray, the publisher, was issuing his *Home and Colonial Library*, which included George Borrow's *The Bible in Spain,* arguably one of the best travel books ever written, while novels by Fenimore Cooper and Captain Marryat came out in Bentley's series of *Standard Novels.*

Has Mudie's box come?

In the spring and summer of 1849, a House of Commons committee was meeting to discuss the question of free libraries. In France, there were public *cabinets de lecture* or reading-rooms, 198 in Paris alone in 1845, although one had to pay a monthly subscription to read in them.[13] A bill was proposed that would allow one halfpenny in the pound of local rates to be spent on local libraries. Naturally, there was opposition, but the Bill became law on 14 August 1850. Few London parishes, however, adopted the Act. Prosperous people continued to borrow their books as they had before, from private circulating libraries such as Mudie's.

Charles Edward Mudie was a hymn writer and lay preacher who set up a circulating library in Southampton Row in Central London in 1842. Ten years later, he moved to New Oxford Street, just south of the British Museum. Mudie's was not wound up until 1937 when the famous London department store, Harrod's, which also ran a subscribers' circulating library, bought up its stock.

Mudie's was big business. From London, it sent boxes down by rail to all parts of the country and even abroad. It bought close on one million volumes a year. Mudie's purchasing power enabled it to buy books at a large discount. With many copies of the same popular work, it could satisfy the demand stimulated by its large number of members who paid no more than one guinea a year, thus heavily undercutting its competitors. The firm took 2,400 copies of volumes three and four of Macaulay's *History of England* and two thousand of George Eliot's novel *The Mill on the Floss*. Given that a novel, usually published in three volumes, cost £1.11. 6d, a substantial sum even for a person with an income of three or four hundred pounds a year, Mudie's mere one guinea a year subscription was a bargain.

Long railway journeys also stimulated the reading market. A traveller would buy a book at W.H. Smith's bookstall, opened in 1848 at Euston Square Station in London, to while away the long hours of the journey to Scotland. It would certainly be nothing even mildly salacious. Smith came from a strict Methodist background and acquired the nickname of the 'North-Western Missionary'.[14]

At Paddington Station, there was a lending library with a thousand volumes, mainly of fiction, which passengers could browse through as they waited for their trains. A slight charge allowed them to borrow the book and take it with them to read on their journey. They would give the book in at the bookstall at their destination. It was not long before special editions for railway journeys were being published. George Routledge launched his *Railway Library* with its 'yellowback' book series and John Murray his *Literature for the Rail*.[15] Serious, particularly religious, literature was also much in demand at railway stations, for some readers feared to meet their Maker if a fatal railway accident caught them with a frivolous work of fiction in their greatcoat pocket or lady's reticule.

Apart from the Penny Dreadfuls and the under-the-counter erotica sold in Holywell Street, just north of the Strand, popular literature was decorous. Nevertheless, even the highly successful *Pickwick Papers* was judged by the *Eclectic Review* as being somewhat near-the-knuckle, while Anne Brontë's *The Tenant of Wildfell Hall*, her sister Charlotte's novels *Jane Eyre*, *Villette* and *Shirley*, and Emily Brontë's *Wuthering Heights*, were all criticised for coarseness and indelicacy.[16]

The late 1840s were halcyon years for the English novel. Between 1846 and 1848 Dickens was publishing *Dombey and Son* in parts. From May to November 1849 he was issuing *David Copperfield*. At the same time, Thackeray was bringing out his *Pendennis*. Nothing, however, would equal the triumph of *Uncle Tom's Cabin* when it appeared in 1852. In a single fortnight in October of that year, at least ten editions of the American Harriet Beecher Stowe's anti-slavery novel came out in Britain. Six months after publication, the book had sold 150,000 copies, and within a year, according to one account, the total sales in England and the colonies had reached a million and a half.[17] Other great publishing successes of the early Victorian age included the first two volumes of Macaulay's *History of England from the Accession of James II*. These sold like a novel. From their publication in November 1848, the bookshops ran through five printings in six months. Twenty-two thousand copies were sold within a year at the high price of £1,12s. The next two volumes produced £20,000 in royalties for their author within eleven months of their publication. Had authors been protected against American pirate publishers, Macaulay would have done even better.

Nevertheless, for large sections of the reading public, novels were out of the question on principle. Many people considered novels a waste of time during the utilitarian week, and sinful on the evangelical Sunday, when only improving religious literature was thought appropriate.

Do you believe in...?

Fiction, drama, poetry and science all together scarcely equalled the amount of religious literature among the 45,260 titles which appeared during the years 1816 to 1851, at a rate of about 1,300 new works per year. The artisan, shop assistant or servant could neither find the time nor afford to read a newspaper every day. The pious alternative to the sensational serial novel or paper, which came out on Saturday and would be read in the leisure hours of Sunday, were the tracts which the Religious Tract Society, founded in 1799, distributed in their millions in the streets of London. People would be bothered by the unsolicited visits of representatives of the British and Foreign Bible Society and other such hawkers of religious literature, as they tried to place the books, pamphlets and tracts that were printed in their millions. One indefatigable young man was reported to have made 18,727 calls in a year, selling 3,795 pious items.[18]

In many families, these were required reading, even for children. In the third chapter of Dickens's *Little Dorrit*, Arthur Clennan sits in a London coffee house on a gloomy Sunday evening listening to the church bells. They remind him of:

> the dreary Sunday of his childhood, when he sat with his hands before him, scared out of his senses by a horrible tract which commenced business with the poor child by asking him in its title, why he was going to Perdition ... and which, for the further attraction of his infant mind, had a parenthesis in every other line with some such hiccupping reference as 2 Ep. Thess.c.iii.v.6 and 7.

Religion was almost an obsession among the middle classes. However, some questioning of religious belief was already evident among intellectuals. Sir Charles Lyell's *Principles of Geology*, whose three parts were published in the 1830s, offered a different view of the age of the Earth from that of the biblical account. Robert Chambers's *Vestiges of the Natural History of Creation* of 1844 was a popularisation of recent thought about evolution, defending the theory that nature, not a force outside it, was responsible for change, while in 1846 Mary Ann Evans, who would later write novels under the pseudonym of George Eliot, translated David Strauss's critical account of the life of Jesus from the German *Das Leben Jesu*, Nevertheless, until Charles Darwin published his *Origin of Species* in 1859 and Bishop Colenso began to issue his *The Pentateuch ... Critically Examined* in 1862, there was little to be read on the question of the truth of the biblical narrative.

Today, nearly two centuries later, when indifference is widespread, it is hard to imagine the emotions aroused in Victorian times by the doctrinal aspects of religious faith, as well as by its public manifestations. The House of Commons no longer argues about whether or not there should be candles on the altars of Anglican churches, or whether priests of the Church of England should wear vestments and hear confessions. In the twenty-first century, *The Times* does not often express a view on the restoration of the images of saints in Anglican churches. But in the early Victorian age, people would have been well aware of the importance of such questions as they discussed the progress of Christian life in Britain.

Hi, Mass! Lo! Church!

The majority of the people of England belonged to the Anglican Church, some to the 'High' version, which meant tending to favour the ceremonies – the 'bells and smells' as they were sneered at by their enemies – of the Catholic Church. Others adhered to the 'Low' Church, meaning that they leaned towards the starkness of the Nonconformist or Dissenting Churches. The American Unitarian minister Henry Colman, on his visit to London, noted that the Church of England, as integral a part of the Establishment as the House of Commons, was very formal in contrast to the 'naked simplicity' of the churches of his home town of Boston, Massachusetts. In New England, churches, in the footsteps of the Pilgrim Fathers of 1620, were by definition and history dissenting from the Church of England. Some of their English equivalents were old, going back to the seventeenth century, such as the Congregationalists, the Baptists and the Quakers, but New Dissent, arising from eighteenth-century Methodism, was growing. In the little Bethels, Mount Zion or Ebenezer chapels, sometimes made of corrugated iron, and located in dim alleys, many people in the grim industrial cities and in London found comfort in their toilsome lives.

Ventura de la Vega, a Spanish dramatist who visited London mid-century, was impressed by the devoutness of the worshippers in Westminster Abbey. He noticed that they did not indulge in the habit of looking up to see who was there, how they were dressed and how they behaved, as was common in Spain where church attendance was as much a social or even political act as a religious one.

Never on Sunday

Ventura de la Vega was struck also by the closed shops and the sepulchral silence of the London Sunday, enlivened only by church bells, so different from the animated Sundays of Spain.[19] The Lord's Day Observance Society was founded in 1831 to keep Sunday free of most recreation, shopping and travelling. This restriction bore heaviest on the poor, whose only day free from work and available for amusement was Sunday. Public entertainment on the Sabbath was seen by many as devilish, with the exception perhaps of the wholesomeness of Jenny Lind, the 'Swedish Nightingale', who was in 1849 conducting her third triumphal tour in Britain. While the sacred oratorios in which she sang might just about be tolerated on the Sabbath, even though many had to work in order to allow them to be staged, the public house was of course out of the question for a Sabbatarian. Thus the reading of improving religious literature flourished during the endless Sunday hours spent at home. There was nothing else to do.

Benjamin Disraeli, a future Conservative Prime Minister, who although of Jewish parentage had been baptised in his youth, took a train one Sunday in 1849 from his country home to London. On receiving an admonition from his local vicar to set a better example, Disraeli replied that only public urgency compelled him to travel on the Sabbath. In any case, and more pointedly, he retorted that when he attended Divine Service he did so to worship his Maker, not so that others should emulate him.[20] Although the Bishop of London failed to stop trains running on Sundays, he was nevertheless successful in banning the opening of museums, picture galleries and the zoo, as well as in silencing military bands in parks.[21] On 30 May 1850, the powerful Sabbatarian lobby persuaded the House of Commons to end Sunday collections and deliveries of letters. Charles Dickens, a noted enemy of the Sabbatarians, thundered against them in the leading article of *Household Words* on 22 June, quoting the words 'The Sabbath was made for Man and not Man for the Sabbath'. More pointedly, Dickens asked whether Lord Ashley, the proposer of the parliamentary motion to stop Sunday postal services, did not require his servants to work on Sundays. And what about the police? Were citizens not to have their protection and did criminals observe the Sabbath? The unpleasant Noah Claypole, who bullies the young Oliver Twist in the eponymous Dickens novel, ends up as an *agent provocateur*, tempting publicans to provide brandy for a fainting person and then reporting them for doing so during church time. The Sabbatarians succeeded in forcing the Great Exhibition of 1851 to close on Sundays, thus preventing large numbers of people visiting it on their only free day. In 1856 Sabbatarian opposition again defeated proposals to open the British Museum and the National Gallery on Sunday afternoons.

The Sabbatarians did not have everything their own way, however. At a demonstration on Sunday, 30 September 1855 in London's Hyde Park against a proposal to limit Sunday trading in the capital, a move which would bear hardest on the poor, the demonstrators hissed the splendid equipages of the swaggering aristocrats in Rotten Row, shouting 'Go to church!' Band concerts were later permitted to provide orderly and civilised entertainment on Sundays in London parks. Sunday work at the Post Office was eventually permitted to continue.

London Sundays remained gloomy, however, as Dickens described in Chapter 3 of *Little Dorrit*.

> It was a Sunday evening in London, gloomy, close and stale. Maddening church bells of all degrees of dissonance, sharp and flat, cracked and clear, fast and slow, made the brick and mortar echoes hideous. Melancholy streets in a penitential garb of soot, steeped the souls of the people who were condemned to look at them out of windows in dire despondency. In every thoroughfare, up almost every alley, and down almost every turning some doleful bell was throbbing, jerking, tolling, as if the Plague were in the city and the dead-carts were going round. Everything was bolted and barred that could by possibility furnish relief to an overworked people. No pictures, no unfamiliar animals, nor rare plants or flowers, no natural or artificial wonders of the ancient world- all taboo with that enlightened strictness that the ugly South Sea gods in the British Museum might have supposed themselves at home again. Nothing to see but streets, streets, streets. Nothing to breathe but streets, streets, streets. Nothing to change the brooding mind or to raise it up. Nothing for the spent toiler to do, but to compare the monotony of his six days, think what a weary life he led, and make the best of it

George Augustus Sala offered a balanced view when he pointed out that people like himself might claim that the 'serious' (that is, pious) world was 'an amalgam of bigotry, hypocrisy and selfishness', but at the same time there were millions of sober and solid citizens who, he wrote, 'are honestly persuaded of the sinfulness of many things which we consider harmless recreations'.[22]

Not for the Likes of Us

Victorian London had a low level of Church attendance.[23] In 1851 a census was taken of congregations at places of worship on Easter Sunday, 30 March. The result shocked many out of their complacency. Large numbers did not attend any place of Christian worship at all. A quarter of the population worshipped at Anglican churches on that day. Another quarter attended churches of other denominations, but half of London's two and a half million went nowhere at all.[24]

It was easy to see that London's proletariat had turned its back on the established Church to which most of them nominally belonged, and this was despite the probability that most of them had at some time or other in their childhood attended day or Sunday schools run by the Church of England. Commentators on the apparent abandon of the Church claimed that the charges for pews, the general boring nature of Church services together with the upper-class voices and views of Anglican clergy, led working people to feel that going to Church was not for them. One study in 1849 wrote that 'the poor man is made to feel that he is a poor man; the rich reminded that he is very rich'.[25] In his account of mid-century London costermongers, Henry Mayhew repeated the words of one who had 'heerd a little about our Saviour'. 'They seem to say,' added Mayhew, ' "he were a goodish sort of man, but if he says as how a cove's to forgive a feller as hits you, I should say he'd know nothing about it".' In 1848, Charles Kingsley, the novel-writing Anglican vicar, wrote boldly: 'It is our fault. We have used the Bible as if it were a mere special constable's handbook – an opium dose for keeping beasts of burden patient while they are being overloaded.'[26]

Middle-class Christians were not, however, content to allow the situation to remain as it was. Two major movements, Tractarianism and Evangelism, girded their loins and strove to rechristianise society.

Meet The Lord in Exeter Hall

Evangelism was concerned with disciplining sinful people's lives with the aim of fitting them to receive Divine Grace and thus to merit Eternal Salvation. The Evangelical side of Anglicanism linked up with the more introspective and conscience-watching Methodist spirit. Evangelism had a wide meaning and appealed to a spectrum of Christian opinion, from Low Church of England to Dissenters. It could be combined with the harsh spirit of Utilitarianism, provided that the latter's frequently secular attitude was ignored. Evangelism chimed well with the Victorian social ethic of 'God helps those who help themselves' and with the spirit of personal responsibility.

Evangelism spread rapidly, led by Victoria and Albert's Court, which was a model of respectability compared with the Courts of her uncles, George IV and William IV, monarchs who sired only illegitimate children.

From the Court, 'seriousness' spread to the aristocracy, which began to behave as properly as the new rising middle class demanded.

> We must go with the times, my Lord. A virtuous middle class
> shrinks with horror from French actresses: and the Wesleyans –
> the Wesleyans, must be considered

The young Benjamin Disraeli put these words ironically into one of his characters' mouths in 1845.[27] Things had changed since Lord Melbourne, Prime Minister when Victoria came to the throne in 1837, had complained that:

> things have come to a pretty pass when religion is allowed to
> invade the sphere of private life[28]

Evangelism went in for major public events. It had a purpose-built London location in which to do so. Exeter Hall had been opened in the Strand in 1831 as an Evangelical conference centre. It had a massive organ, one auditorium with a thousand seats, another with four thousand and choir space for five hundred singers. Mass Evangelical rallies were held there as well as the annual meetings of several religious, missionary and philanthropic organisations. For Evangelicals, the May meeting of the Lord's Day Observance Society was what the contemporary Royal Academy Exhibition, held at the National Gallery in Trafalgar Square, just under a quarter of a mile westward along the Strand, was for the fashionable set.

Exeter Hall had been financed by a company of rich Evangelicals, including prominent members of the 'Clapham Sect' (also known as the 'Clapham Saints'), who lived in that healthy semi-rural suburb of the capital, and counted among their number the historian Macaulay and the humanitarian William Wilberforce, who led the campaign to free slaves in the British Empire. In novels of the time, however, Exeter Hall symbolised sanctimoniousness and virtue-signalling. Godfrey Ablewhite in Wilkie Collins's *The Moonstone* of 1868 orates in Exeter Hall in defence of good morals and on behalf of many philanthropic causes, but he turns out to be a hypocrite and a swindler. Dickens's Luke Honeythunder in his unfinished *Edwin Drood* of 1870 presides at Exeter Hall over meetings of the 'Convened Chief Composite Committee of Central and District Philanthropists', a target of the novelist's dislike of a particular variety of do-gooders.[29] Philanthropy and social concern were, however, thought to be essential if England were to avoid the threat to the very foundations of society implicit in the two great revolutions that had taken place in France within human memory: the Revolution of 1789-1792 and the uprising of 1830 which had overthrown the restored Bourbon monarchy. Another took place in 1848, was accompanied by convulsions in many European capitals and aroused considerable apprehension in London.

Can I interest you in a tract?

The decline in the religious spirit, which the 'religious census' of 1851 demonstrated so alarmingly, especially in the poorer parts of London, was energetically tackled. Evangelism's target was social improvement by making the better-off classes more responsive to their Christian consciences. Another movement, Tractarianism, in contrast, urged a more devout attitude towards the liturgy, to religious ceremonial, to the pious observance of the holy days of the Christian Calendar, and to the role of the Church in general.

In one sense, both Evangelism and Tractarianism began as protest movements. Tractarianism, also known as the Oxford Movement, rebelled against the feared subjection of the Church to the State. Close ties with the State had been appropriate when the House of Commons had been an Anglican institution. But now the reformed House included Roman Catholics and Dissenters. Even worse, Tractarians saw the Commons as peopled in part by secularists and Utilitarian Liberals. Such men were fundamentally hostile to the Church of England and its historic privileges. Consequently, asked the Tractarians, why should the Church of England be a department of the State. Why should Anglican bishops be nominated by a Prime Minister who might be an unbeliever? Moreover, the Marriage Act of 1836 had introduced civil marriages. By an Act of 1837 Dissenters had been granted the scandalous, in Tractarian eyes, right to celebrate legal marriages and baptisms in their own places of worship. In addition and, in the Tractarian view, by unjustified interference, the Government was reforming the scandals of the Anglican Church: nepotism, pluralism, absentee vicars and sinecures such as the one that the Reverend Mr Harding enjoyed in Anthony Trollope's novel *The Warden* of 1855. To retain its independence, claimed the Tractarians, the Church needed to break away from the State.

Tractarianism was so-called because its doctrines were expressed in ninety *Tracts for the Times*. The series was launched when the Professor of Poetry at Oxford, John Keble, who, like all Oxbridge dons, was an ordained clergyman of the Church of England, preached a sermon in July 1833 on the subject of 'National Apostasy'. He advocated returning religious authority to the bishops and reinforcing discipline by reducing the Protestant tendency towards emphasis on the individual's personal understanding of the Scriptures. John Henry Newman, a leader of the Tractarian movement, author of the famous hymn 'Lead, Kindly Light' ('And look where it led him,' sneered his detractors, referring to his conversion to Catholicism), and vicar of St Mary's, Oxford, was at the time insisting that the Anglican Church, though not Roman, was still the Catholic Church.

Tractarianism's principal effect on ordinary people, however, was to excite traditional English anti-Catholicism. In London, in the early years of Queen Victoria's reign, elderly people could still recall the Gordon Riots of 1780. Younger ones could read about those disturbances in Charles Dickens's novel *Barnaby Rudge* of 1841. Tractarians were accused of 'Popery' and the new offence of 'Ritualism'. Ritual, that is candles, gorgeous vestments and the rich odours of incense, was probably the Tractarian movement's most visible outward sign. Riots broke out in 1850 and 1851 in the London suburb of Pimlico following the opening of St. Barnabas's Church, with its ornate liturgical practices, its candles and its clouds of incense. One of its enthusiastic young curates paid choirboys to throw rotten eggs at a sandwich-board man who had been paid to walk around with anti-ritualistic slogans on his back.[30]

Evangelicals, and Tractarians, so long as they did not go over to Rome and convert to Catholicism, were two sides of the same Anglican coin. Methodists and other Nonconformists or Dissenters might be seen as over-enthusiastic, disrespectful of the proper ordering of English society and even vulgar, but Roman Catholics were a different matter altogether.

Chapter 7

Outsiders

'The Pope and his cardinals have learnt nothing from adversity'

Catholics had the taint of the foreign about them. Not the old pre-Reformation families, some of whom were aristocrats, but the poverty-stricken Irish and particularly some high-profile Tractarians who 'went over to Rome', that is converted to Catholicism.

Anti-Catholicism was part of being English. Foxe's *Book of Martyrs*, with its gruesome details of the torture and burning of heretics by the Catholic Queen 'Bloody' Mary in the 1550s, was regular Sunday afternoon reading in many households and had only recently been reissued in a fine new edition.[1] People who had the taste for it could go to Exeter Hall and hear a clergyman rant for an hour and a half against Catholicism. One Essex curate even claimed in his sermon that there was a connection between 'the advance of Popery' and the cholera epidemic.[2]

Nothing, save her foreignness, indicated that Maria Manning, the murderess, was a Catholic. On the contrary, her father's position as postmaster in Protestant Geneva suggests the opposite. Nevertheless, Robert Huish's lengthy and imaginative account of her early life claims that she had a Catholic convent education and suggests that this was the origin of her murderous character. Frederick Manning told the prison chaplain, the Reverend Rowe, that his wife was an atheist, although this could have been in connection with his attempt to throw the blame for the murder entirely on her. After the execution of the Mannings, a letter in *The Times* signed by 'Northumberland Rector' enquired whether the Reverend Rowe had administered the Sacrament to Maria. The letter would have appalled readers of *The Times* in today's ecumenical age because it commented that a Catholic priest would have been satisfied with a cursory expression of regret for the sin of murder. Mr Rowe replied that he had administered the Sacrament, but insisted that he had 'gravely exhorted' the couple to receive it in a true spirit of remorse. To its credit, the newspaper published a retort from a Catholic priest. Neither he, nor any colleague of his, he insisted, would have given the Mannings communion without being convinced that their repentance was genuine.

Hostility towards Catholics explains the petition with over one million signatures against Sir Robert Peel's proposal in 1845 to make a substantial increase in the annual grant to Maynooth College for the training of Irish priests. The protests were short-sighted, however, because Maynooth had been founded in 1795 precisely to remove the need for seminarists to study on the Continent and be imbued there with what was considered the politically reactionary stance of Continental European Catholicism.

In Britain, however, it was evident that opinion was changing in a more tolerant and politically wise direction, The old repressive or 'penal' laws against Catholics had been repealed in 1829. Catholics could now hold State and municipal office. Furthermore Tractarianism, also called the 'Oxford Movement' encouraged a significant number of the socially and intellectually distinguished to go further and convert to Catholicism.[3]

Recognising the Catholic revival, on 19 September 1850 the Pope restored the Catholic hierarchy in England, officially appointing bishops rather than the administrators who had supervised dioceses up till then. The Spanish-born Nicholas Wiseman was appointed Cardinal Archbishop of London. Popular animosity towards Catholicism surged. 'The Pope and his Cardinals have learnt nothing from the lessons of adversity', commented the *Illustrated London News*. Primitive fears of the alien allied to historical wariness of Jesuit plots against Protestant England were revived. 'Papal Aggression' became a vogue phrase. Lord John Russell, the Prime Minister, wrote to the Anglican Bishop of Durham in terms which echoed the emotions of an earlier age when the Spanish Armada and Guy Fawkes were in recent memory:

> No foreign prince ... will be at liberty to fasten his fetters upon
> a nation which has so long and so nobly vindicated its right to
> freedom of opinion ... a nation which looks with contempt on
> the mummeries of superstition[4]

In August 1851, almost in a panic, Parliament passed the Ecclesiastical Titles Act, which forbade Catholic bishops to adopt the same place names in their titles as their Anglican equivalents. The law, however, was never enforced and repealed twenty years later.

Charles Dickens reacted to 'Papal Aggression' in his characteristically fierce and vivid style. On 23 November 1850 he published an attack on the Anglican Bishop of London, the Reverend Charles James Blomfield, for his pro-Tractarian instructions to the clergy under his direction. Dickens's essay took the form of a story about Mr and Mrs Bull, representing England. They reprove Master C. J. London (Bishop Blomfield) for his tolerance of vicars who introduced 'Catholic' or 'Romish' practices:

> Hadn't you had warning for playing about with candles and candlesticks? You were told often enough that ... when they got to candlesticks, they'd get to candles; and when they got to candles, they'd get to lighting 'em; and when they began to put their shirts on outside, and to play at monks and friars, it was as natural that Master Wiseman should be encouraged to put on a pair of red stockings, and a red hat, and to commit I don't know what other Tom-fooleries and make a perfect Guy Fawkes of himself ... Is it because you are a Bull, that you are not to be roused till they shake the scarlet close to your very eyes?

This last sentence was clever, linking 'John Bull' with the bullfights of ultra-Catholic Spain, England's traditional enemy since Elizabethan times, and the scarlet of the bullfighter's cape with the colour of Cardinals' robes and hat.

Mr and Mrs Bull are the English, while what Dickens calls 'the Bulls of Rome', meaning the Catholic Church, 'perpetuate misery, oppression, darkness and ignorance'. This can be seen, Dickens continues, in the 'horrible condition of Mrs. Bull's Catholic sister, Miss Eringobragh, (the slogan meaning 'Ireland till the end of time'), who 'presented a most lamentable spectacle of disease, dirt, rags, superstition and degradation'.[5]

'The Wail of Distress' (*Illustrated London News*, 4 August 1849)

The most numerous and noticeable Catholics in London were indeed the very poor Irish immigrants. Patrick O'Connor, the Mannings' victim, belonged in contrast to the Irish middle class. Rumour said that he had obtained his undemanding and well-paid job in the Customs through some influential people who thought he would be able to proselytise among Irish Catholic dockers and turn them away from Rome. The story comes from Robert Huish's imaginative account of the Manning case, but Huish names O'Connor's patrons, among them the Bishop of Llandaff, so the story may be true. If it is, it may explain why O'Connor obtained his job independently of his patron, the well-known defender of Catholic causes, the Irish barrister Robert Sheil.

It was evictions from their farms and the terrible famine caused by the potato blight of 1846-1847 which brought so many people across the sea from Ireland. Earlier, by 1841 there were already 74,000 Irish-born inhabitants of London. By 1851, however, the Irish-born population was 108,548. The census, however, recorded only the place of birth, and while many Irish-born inhabitants may have been Protestants, or even English born in Ireland, there was an increasing number of Catholic Irish who had been born in England. The Catholic Irish population of London was thus probably larger than the census suggested. Furthermore, given the transient and rough-living nature of many Irish labourers' lives, some, particularly the 'navvies', away 'on the tramp' in search of work, may have been missed by the enumerators.

Poor Irish people lived in the rookery of St Giles or off Commercial Road in London's East End. They worked on building sites, laying railway tracks, or at the docks. Irish dockers in London were among the lowest paid labourers in the capital. They were reputed to live on a daily plate of mashed potatoes and a herring, to occupy one room with their families and to be paid a miserable 3d or 4d an hour, not in cash but in vouchers redeemable only in their employer's 'tommy-shop'.[6] Their improvidence and their hard drinking were encouraged by the lowest quality of housing which they occupied, and the concomitant high death rates. A diarist of the times, Charles Greville, commenting on the spread of cholera among the Irish dockers, wrote:

> the lowest and most wretched classes [are] chiefly Irish, and a
> more lamentable exhibition of human misery than that given
> by the medical men ... yesterday, I never heard. They are in the
> most abject state of poverty, without beds to lie on. The men
> live by casual labour, are employed by the hour, and often get
> no more than four or five hours of employment in the course of
> the week. They are huddled and crowded together by families
> in the same room, not as permanent lodgers, but procuring a
> temporary shelter; in short, in the most abject state of physical
> privation and moral degradation that can be imagined[7]

'The worst quarters of all the large towns are inhabited by Irishmen', wrote Friedrich Engels, the factory owner who subsidised Karl Marx.[8] Many Irishwomen had no domestic skills at all. They could not work in the needle trades or in domestic service. Selling fruit from stalls or walking the streets with a heavy basket of vegetables was a typical occupation of Irish women. They bought oranges, lemons, walnuts and chestnuts, or greens according to the season, in Covent Garden or in Duke's Place market close by Aldgate, and sold them, as one of them told an investigative journalist 'for a ha'pinny the three apples which cost a farruthin', either from door to door or in the poorer markets. The profits were very low: five shillings a week at the most, from which a room had to be rented. But even the meanest room could not cost less than two shillings. One woman to whom Henry Mayhew spoke gathered old walnuts, dried them and used them for fuel. She and her children had no bedspread; just a flock bed in a corner of a room on the floor, with a sheet, blanket and quilt. This was absolutely insufficient for the winter. The room had neither chair nor table; just a stool with two pieces of board for a table and a narrow tea canister to hold a stump of candle. Yet the Irish women were known to be chaste; the adolescent girls were not allowed to attend the cheap and vulgar theatres known as 'Penny Gaffs', and the children were brought up to be pious.[9]

The arrival of immigrants who occupy scarce housing among the native working class, and who also work for lower wages, is often a cause of social tension which may explode into violence. The Camden Town riot in the summer of 1846 is an example.

On Monday afternoon 9 August that year, a mile along the railway line out of Euston, where Chalk Farm Road is now, a fight broke out between a large group of Irish navvies and the English labourers working inside the gate at the entrance to the building site of the Round House, where the engines were turned around. Shovels, pick-handles and brickbats were freely used as weapons. After an hour the fighting had spread all over the wide expanse of railway-owned land at Camden Town. Even large forces of police brought in from local stations were unable to stop the conflict until the equivalent of modern 'snatch squads' managed to arrest about twenty men and take them to the nearby Albany Street police station. The next day, the leaders of the Irish navvies tried to explain to the magistrate that they had been provoked, that the English labourers swore foully at them and refused to allow them to enter the building site to begin work.[10]

The large Catholic Irish immigration would in time be a great source of strength for the Catholic Church, but at the time created grave problems for it, given that in 1840 there were only 26 Catholic churches in the whole of London. Henry Mayhew vividly describes the powerful influence of the Catholic priest as he walked through the slums in which his parishioners lived, and the respect in which he was held even by drunken wife-beaters.

From his appointment in 1850, Cardinal Archbishop Wiseman strove to meet the needs, both religious and material, of the poor Irish arrivals. In the coming years, many more churches, religious houses, fee-charging and free schools and orphanages would be established.[11]

England ... The only safe Refuge (*Illustrated London News*, 8 September 1849)

The Irish were not, of course, foreign, but London had always had a small population of foreigners. They lived near Leicester Square, in Soho or, if they were poor, in the slums of St. Giles or the East End. There were Italians fleeing from the earlier failure of the *Risorgimento* in the 1820s and 1830s, including the distinguished Giuseppe Mazzini, who arrived in January 1837, returned to Italy in 1848 and sought refuge once more in London after the overthrow of the Roman Republic. Poles came to London fleeing the Russian repression of their independence movement in 1831. Another small group were the Liberal Spaniards, who fled their country when the reactionary Ferdinand VII was restored to his throne after the Duke of Wellington had defeated the French in the Peninsular War in 1813. They were recalled by the historian Thomas Carlyle in 1851:

> In those years a visible section of the London population ... was a small knot of Spaniards who had sought shelter here as political refugees ... Six and twenty years ago when I first saw London, I remember those Spaniards among the new phenomena. Daily in the cold spring air, under skies so unlike their own, you could see a group of fifty to one hundred stately figures in proud threadbare cloaks perambulating ... Euston Square and the region around St. Pancras New Church[12]

By the later 1840s, however, most of the Spaniards had left for home, with the exception of a few who had become domiciled and found prosperity or academic appointments teaching Spanish at the new University and King's Colleges in London.

Perhaps the only foreigners that most people were likely to see in the streets were the ubiquitous Italian street entertainers. London's Italian colony lived in Hatton Garden, Leather Lane, Saffron Hill and the streets leading north off Holborn. This area, known as 'Little Italy' was one of dilapidated lodging houses. It had probably attracted the Italians because of its closeness to Clerkenwell, where the long-established clock and instrument trades interrelated with the repair of the barrel-organs or 'hurdy-gurdies' which the Italians played in the street. St Peter's church was built in 1864 in the heart of the district, in order to protect the Catholic Italians from the missionary campaigns of evangelical Protestants.[13]

The Italians seen in London's streets were mainly organ-grinders or street vendors of plaster statuettes, looking glasses and picture frames. Among the street entertainers competing for the pennies of passers-by was an Italian man who had dolls which he made dance by a string attached to his knee as he played the pipe and the drum.[14] Other Italian men and boys entertained the passing throng with dancing dogs and mechanical figures. Italian boys exhibiting white mice aroused pathos, especially since one boy was murdered in 1831.[15]Organ-grinders, however, were so frequently to be heard that banning or protecting them became a significant point of political difference. Members of the House of Lords, cocooned in their gated estates and living behind long gardens, could escape from the noise of London's streets, so they were tolerant, but the upper middle class of the capital's more prosperous terraces were exasperated in the summer by the endless din of street organs.[16]

An Italian name, incidentally, had its uses in certain fields, particularly millinery and dressmaking. In Chapter 10 of *Nicholas Nickleby*, Dickens's character Muntle (perhaps 'mantle' in northern English pronunciation) has changed his and his wife's name to Mantalini:

> the lady rightly considering that an English appellation would
> be of serious injury to the business

London sheltered political refugees, among them Continental European lawyers and military officers of liberal views, republicans and socialists. Karl Marx, the French Socialist Louis Blanc, the Russian intellectual Alexander Herzen, the deposed French king Louis Philippe and Louis Napoleon, nephew of Napoleon Bonaparte, soon to be President and then Emperor of France, all sought shelter in the British capital. London also had a foreign artistic population. The wealth of the city could support a number of French artists, hairdressers, actors, singers and chefs, Italian musicians and German nursemaids. Greek merchants had settled in Finsbury; German bakers and Swiss watchmakers in Clerkenwell. The centre of London's foreign district was an island bounded by Soho Square, Leicester Square and Golden Square. Its streets were dreary, with multi-occupied houses. When Charles Dickens, who knew London intimately, places Ralph Nickleby's office in Golden Square, in the Soho district, he remarks that:

It is a great resort of foreigners ... On a summer's night, windows
are thrown open, and groups of swarthy moustachioed men
are seen by the passer-by lounging at casements and smoking
fearfully[17]

Darkness of complexion, beards and moustaches, and smoking characterised
foreigners in British eyes.

The British attitude to foreigners, while officially tolerant, was
notoriously unfriendly and superior. Two marine engineers from Bombay,
Nowrojee and Merwangee, who spent a long time studying in London's
dockyards, advised foreign theatregoers to avoid the rowdiness of the
gallery and pit. They concluded that:

The majority of the lower orders in England are very rude ...
towards strangers, whom they do not like to see in their own
country[18]

Political refugees, however, were tolerated, often welcomed and sometimes
lionised, especially if they were anti-Catholic, as was the case with some
Italian ex-priests who arrived after the failed revolutions of 1848-1849.[19]
Lajos Kossuth, the Hungarian revolutionary against Austrian domination,
reached London in 1851, to be acclaimed at a public reception at the
Guildhall, while in contrast the Austrian General Baron von Haynau,
staying at Morley's Hotel in Trafalgar Square, who had ordered women
revolutionaries to be flogged, was chased out of Barclay and Perkins'
brewery on Bankside in September 1850 by draymen flourishing their
cartwhips and mispronouncing his name as they shouted 'Hyena'. Haynau
was chased down the Borough High Street and forced to take refuge in the
George Inn. Finally, he was rescued by policemen who rowed him to the
other side of the Thames. A meeting was held later in the Farringdon Hall
on Snow Hill congratulating the draymen.[20]

Land of Freedom

Restrictions on immigrants entering Britain, first imposed in 1793 during
the Napoleonic Wars, came to a delayed end in 1826. From that year until
the Aliens Act of 1905, nobody was refused entry or expelled from Britain
on political grounds. The 1851 census revealed that there were only 50,289
foreign-born people in England and Wales, although in London there were

25,500 out of the total population of 2,362,000. It was, nevertheless, a percentage of only 1.79. The percentage was probably even smaller because some foreigners, particularly seamen, were in London only on the day the census was taken.

The main intention of Lord Palmerston, Foreign Secretary from 1846 to 1851, was to avoid major European war. The revolutions of 1848 in Paris, Berlin, Vienna, Budapest, Prague, Milan, Naples and Rome created a potentially explosive situation. However, the government of the French Republican regime of 1848, which replaced King Louis Philippe, assured London that it envisaged no changes to the international peace settlement of 1815. The suppression by Austria of revolution in Piedmont restored the status quo. When the Hungarian aristocracy rebelled against Austrian domination, Lord Palmerston approved of Russian intervention to crush the revolt. Only after the situation had returned to what it had been, did Palmerston protest against Russian and Austrian severity. He lectured Continental autocrats about their tyranny but believed in maintaining the international balance of power undisturbed.

In 1848 Chancellor Metternich of Austria arrived in London, in hurried flight from revolutionaries. Louis-Philippe of France (under the alias of 'Mr Smith') also arrived. For safe, self-confident Britain, of course, what those excitable foreigners got up to was rather funny. *Punch*, as usual, caught the mood. On 25 March 1848 it published a poem by Thackeray about the fleeing French monarch, who was reputed to have arrived with only the clothes he stood up in:

> A veteran gent, just stepped out of a boat,
> In a tattered old hat and a ragged pea-coat

The poet suggested that the deposed monarch should get himself outfitted by E. Moses and Son as soon as he could.

Revolutions on the Continent were seen as the usual state of things, so much so that, in its *Almanack* for 1849, *Punch* suggested that:

> If any complaint is made [about overstaying leave of absence
> from work], you have a capital excuse, by declaring that you
> were stopt [sic] by a revolution on the Continent

In 1848 about 7,000 French, Austrian, Polish, Hungarian, Italian and German refugees entered Britain. The largest individual numbers were Germans, Poles, French and Hungarians.[21] An echo of today is heard in the complaint from the Channel port of Dover to the Home Secretary on 18 July 1849 when a shipload of refugees applied for relief, which had caused 'a great burthern' on the rates of the town.[22]

Most of the fugitives lived in financial straits, earning their living by teaching their own language or any other skill, such as music, which they possessed. For most of them London was a dirty, cold and unwelcoming place. They were overcharged for rent and swindled by dishonest money-changers. Many had no employment and, though in general the refugees were law-abiding, some went in for petty crime. The important political exiles usually had enough money and friends to live in modest comfort. One rotten apple, such as the swindler who called himself 'Colonel Count Sarcie Dumbiski'[23] who begged money as a political refugee and lived in high style between spells in gaol in 1849 and 1850, led people to consider all the refugees as scroungers. Foreign fugitives were associated with immorality, atheism and not paying their rent. Perhaps this was because they were frequently bearded, or perhaps beards were associated with such improper behaviour because foreigners wore them.

Their nightly gatherings in London 'cafés' – a new word – were seen by the journalist George Augustus Sala as exotic:

> rings of fantastic fashion, marvellous gestures, Babel-like tongues ... the smoke as of a thousand brick-kilns; the clatter as of a thousand spoons[24]

Refugees, dressed in what was, in English eyes, outlandish and picturesque style, met in political clubs, smoke-filled rooms over a Soho café or perhaps in a hired schoolroom where they listened to a lecture, had a discussion or often a row about principles, personalities or money. Whatever came to the ears of the authorities about the activities of foreigners would have underlined that they were intensely schismatic and thus unlikely to prove a threat to the stability of Her Majesty's Government. At the time of the Great Exhibition of 1851, Prince Albert wrote to the King of Prussia that the political refugees understood that London was not a good place to conspire and that, consequently:

> we have no fear here either of an uprising or an assassination[25]

Foreign governments of course protested about the tolerance shown to revolutionaries in England, but lordly British conceit led public opinion to take a superior attitude towards their fears. Let other regimes govern properly and they would have nothing to fear. The foreigners should behave themselves properly while they were guests in this country, of course, but State interference was so disliked that spying on them was thought to be unacceptable. Britain's lack of a centralised and expensive State police machinery and army of secret agents snooping on the populace, in comparison with Continental Europe, was a favourite subject for self-congratulation. The agents of the Austrian government, in particular, were suspected of watching the refugees, so much so that Jane Carlyle wrote to one of her correspondents that a particularly nosey maidservant whom she had caught reading the family letters was like 'an Austrian spy'.[26]

Chartists

In England, while political refugees were accepted, people tended to fear the ideals of the French Revolution. Some even thought that advocating democracy and votes for all was treasonable, and many were out of sympathy with revolutionary ideals. In his novel *Barnaby Rudge* of 1841, Charles Dickens, who, for all his liberal sentiments, feared the mob and disdained demagoguery, described with scorn the Gordon riots of London in 1780 with their anti-Catholic raging and pillaging, which were still in the common memory sixty years later. More recently, the fifteen years after Waterloo had seen an epoch of extreme reaction in England, typified by the 'Peterloo massacre' of 1819, when troops ran down a protesting crowd in Manchester, hitting out left and right with their sabres.

Now, the ebb of reaction was changing into a swelling drive for progress. Parliament had been reformed in 1832 by the Reform Act. The Tolpuddle Martyrs, a group of Wiltshire agricultural labourers transported to Australia for swearing illegal oaths but in reality for forming a trade union to raise their wages, had been given a free pardon and brought back to England in 1837. Factory Acts to protect children working with machinery had been passed in 1833 and 1844. The Corn Laws had been repealed to bring down the price of bread. It was not surprising that these reforms and movements of the 1830s and 1840s led to demands for even greater improvements. Socialism, the extension of the suffrage to most men, greater protection for workers and many more issues were in the air, especially in the 1840s, called the 'Hungry Forties', because most of the decade had seen economic depression, unemployment and bad harvests. The decade would end in 1849 London with cholera.

The Chartist movement, so-called because it advocated *The People's Charter*, was a sustained progressive campaign. Its demands for all men to have the right to vote in a secret ballot, that Members of Parliament should receive a salary so that they did not have to enjoy a private income before they could represent a constituency, equal-size electoral districts, and annual Parliaments, were all rejected by Parliament in 1839,1842 and 1848.

Chartism was not, however, focused. It consisted of a variety of radical groups presenting a range of grievances, including the unemployment and short time caused by the introduction of machines, together with the harshness of the Poor Law. These were working-class complaints, but demands for the abolition of property qualifications for Members of Parliament came from property-less members of the middle class.

The poor harvests of 1846 and 1847, the bad winter which followed with its toll of deaths from influenza, bronchitis, pneumonia, measles and typhus, and the examples of the fall of the French monarchy, the humiliation of Chancellor Metternich, forced to escape Vienna in a laundry basket, the Hungarian uprising and the other rebellions on the Continent, all encouraged the advocates of the *Charter* to try again.

In February 1848 rumour spread that a republic was soon to be declared in France. There was much rejoicing in Soho and around Leicester Square. The audience in the pit and the gallery of Sadler's Wells theatre in London sang the *Marseillaise*, which was still a revolutionary rather than a national anthem. On 6 March 1848, a meeting of well-dressed people in Trafalgar Square, called to protest about the income tax, was taken over by G.W.M. Reynolds, taking valuable time from his composition of several thousand weekly words for the *Mysteries of London*. Since Parliament was sitting, the police told the assembly of ten thousand people that their meeting was illegal. Refusing to disperse, the accompanying mob tore down the railings around the still incomplete Nelson's Column. Shouts of '*Vive la République!* were heard, coming either from Frenchmen or from Englishmen pretending to know how to shout the fashionable slogan (or perhaps reported falsely by newspapers spreading the rumour that revolutionaries from over the Channel were making trouble in London). The police managed with difficulty to disperse the crowd, but later that day a mob smashed lamps and windows, and looted shops. The Queen and the Government were alarmed.

The authorities were preoccupied by the fear that foreign revolutionaries might make common cause with home-grown ones. Despite their small number, the concentration and high visibility of foreign people suggested that there was a large number of them. 'We need only walk from Temple Bar to Charing Cross' (about three-quarters of a mile or a kilometre and a half along the Strand, a main road though Central London),' to satisfy ourselves that London contains an unusual number of citizens from a powerful military republic within sight of these shores', wrote *The Times* coyly on 4 April 1848. Did this mean that the few thousand French people here were the vanguard of an invasion? Apprehension that foreigners would cooperate with native revolutionaries led to the Aliens Act of 1848, which allowed deportation. In the event, it was not found necessary to deport anybody. It had been feared that foreigners would play a leading part in the Chartist demonstration on 10 April. They did not, as *The Times* congratulated itself on 15 April. This was probably fortunate, as police constables had orders to beat up bearded rioters, assumed to be foreign, in particular.[27]

The mass Chartist demonstration at Kennington, south of the river, was to be followed by a march from there to Westminster and a presentation of a petition to Parliament. The plan was that, if the Commons rejected the petition, the meeting would elect a national assembly and call on the Queen to dissolve Parliament. The assembly would remain in permanent session until the Government agreed to accept the Charter. Alarm ran through the London middle class. Was the British capital about to experience a Continental-style revolution?

Emergency measures were swiftly taken. Waterloo Station was cordoned off by troops while Queen Victoria left for the Isle of Wight off Britain's south coast. However, there was concern. What if the military were ordered to fire on revolutionaries advancing on Parliament? Would they obey their orders or would they fire over people's heads? It was feared that the revolutionaries might board a warship in the naval base of Portsmouth, sail it into the Solent and fire on Osborne House, the Queen's place of refuge on the Isle of Wight.

The Duke of Wellington, victor of Waterloo, was appointed to oversee the capital's defence. He had at his disposal 7,122 infantry and cavalry. As many as 85,000 special constables were sworn in to back up the 4,000 police, as well as 1,231 Chelsea Pensioners, who were brought out of their retirement to put their old soldiers' training to use. Government offices, the General Post Office, the British Museum, Buckingham Palace, the Customs House, the Guildhall and the Bank of England were barricaded with sandbags and provided with loopholes and the occasional cannon, while students at University and King's Colleges were armed with staves.

The Chartist convention assembled at 9.00am as planned in John Street, just north of the City. The procession marched down Gray's Inn Road, then along Holborn to Farringdon Street, over Blackfriars Bridge, and thence to Kennington Common, which they reached by 11.30. Other groups marched from Stepney Green in East London and another from Russell Square.[28] Figures vary, but they were far below the half-million feared by the authorities and hoped for by the Chartists The leaders decided not to resist when the police refused them permission to cross north over Westminster Bridge and to approach the Houses of Parliament. The Chartist petition was taken by cab over Blackfriars Bridge and through the back streets to Westminster. Reputedly containing five million signatures, it bore just under two million, but many were either forgeries or facetious, such as 'Queen Victoria', 'Old Cheese', and 'Punch'.[29] It was again rejected.

The Chartist movement was not violent. The troops who had been put on alert were not called in; the police remained armed with no more than their truncheons. Neither Bronterre O'Brien nor Feargus O'Connor, the Chartist leaders, wanted to risk the consequences of violence. In the spring rain, O'Connor shook hands with the Commissioner of Police and by early afternoon the great day was over.

Nevertheless, there was still life in the revolutionary movement. On 29 May 1848, 80,000 people marched silently through the City. On 4 June the Home Office ordered the police to disperse meetings of Chartists in the East End. A day of protest was planned for 12 June, but it was prevented by the arrest of the Chartist leaders. An uprising was also planned for 15 August. Its leadership was penetrated by agents and arrested by armed police at the Orange Tree pub in Orange Street, off the Haymarket. The 'rebels' were 'armed' with a few pikes and swords. A Continental-style barricade was feared when a man was seen to prise up a cobblestone in the semi-criminal district of Seven Dials, but the police warned off the participants. About a thousand Chartists who had used violence were arrested and sentenced to long terms of imprisonment.

On 3 July 1849, the Prime Minister, Lord John Russell, announced in the Commons that he could not support the Chartist demands, given 'the state of France and the results congruent upon universal suffrage there'. It was obvious that the aims of the Chartists would not be achieved by purely working-class agitation. Middle-class supporters were, however, rare. Conservative-minded citizens in the 1840s feared the paraphernalia of Continental-style revolution: the Phrygian cap stuck on a pole and waved beneath the windows of magistrates and manufacturers, anticlericalism, violent rhetoric at torchlit meetings, marches, banners and chanted slogans. In any case, London's population was too vast to be efficiently organised. Its complicated social structure and the large variety of occupations meant that no single sustained effort would be able to concentrate on a particular end. London's size (it was twice the size of Paris), its inertia and its efficient police contrasted with the provocative use of troops elsewhere. London was not ripe for revolution.

As it collapsed, however, Chartism left in its wake over a hundred working-men's clubs.[30] More importantly, perhaps, the radical tailor Francis Place called a meeting on 29 January 1849 to form the National Association for Parliamentary and Financial Reform. His aim was to try to unite radicals and moderate Chartists. The Association proposed a 'Little Charter', to demand suffrage for all male householders, the secret ballot, parliamentary elections every three years and a more equal distribution of seats. But the impossibility at the time of combining a working-class with a middle-class movement led to the Association's dissolution in 1855. Its leader, the Chartist Bronterre O'Brien, went on to form the National Reform League, which would meet at 18, Denmark Street in London's Soho, for another twenty-four years. A crowded meeting on 16 March 1850 demanded the reform of the Poor Law in a humane direction, that the Government purchase land to occupy the unemployed, and sweeping nationalisation. Land, the meeting proclaimed, should not be owned by individuals. There should be a national credit system, and shops to sell essential items at cost price. These demands, of course, had no chance of even being considered.

English reform would move in the direction of trade unions rather than revolutionary movements. Early Victorian London was on the cusp of the appearance of skilled workers' unions in the modern sense, concerned with protecting their conditions of work, wages and sectional interests. The Amalgamated Society of Engineers was established in 1851. Its members paid the high fee – possible only for skilled men in regular employment – of one shilling a week, and the Union had salaried officials and a London headquarters.[31]

'Ol' Clo!'

The Irish were the largest identifiable minority in London, followed perhaps by the Continental Europeans. The third group were the Jews, who totalled perhaps 20,000 out of the 35,000 who lived in the country as a whole.[32] Jews were neither feared like Catholics nor thought to be revolutionary like foreigners.

In better-off parts of London, bearded Jews with sacks on their shoulders and wearing several hats on their heads to keep their shape, might be seen tramping the streets shouting 'Ol' Clo'!' They bought used and unwanted clothing, which was later cleaned, altered and resold, until the spread of firms such as the also Jewish E. Moses and Son enabled ordinary people to buy new clothes rather than wear others' cast-offs.

Most Jews were born in England. Yet they were seen as a foreign element, not really because of their religion, which concerned hardly anybody except the well-meaning but resented groups who had appointed themselves to try to convert Jews to Christianity, but rather because of what was considered their clannishness. As a consequence, although most of the 'sweaters' in the needle trades were not Jewish, Charles Kingsley's pamphlet 'Cheap Clothes and Nasty' describing the starvation wages of the sweaters' victims, indulged in an anti-Jewish diatribe. In *Oliver Twist*, Charles Dickens depicts the Jew Fagin as keeping a team of boys at work pickpocketing, because there were in fact such people earning a living by fencing stolen articles, though it is doubtful if Jews ever ran schools for juvenile thieves. Dickens, however, never suggests that Fagin's criminality is racially or religiously determined. Indeed, Fagin is kind to Oliver and not a murderous thug like Bill Sikes. This was the upshot of Dickens's reply to a protest about Fagin which he received from a Jewish correspondent. To redress the balance, he introduced a group of Jews into *Our Mutual Friend*, one of whom is the gentle Mr Riah, who is in the harsh hands of a Gentile moneylender. Most London Jews were in fact poor; some very much so. At the end of the 1840s, one-third of the capital's 20,000 Jews were receiving poor relief from the better-off members of their own community.[33]

Down the Lane

Living in Houndsditch, the Minories, Aldgate and off Brick Lane, just outside the boundaries of the City of London, Jews roamed all over central London hawking walking sticks, jewellery, 'fancy goods' such as pencils, sealing wax, penknives, looking glasses and razors, although the coming of the railway had put an end to their market among travellers leaving by coach from La Belle Sauvage Inn on Ludgate Hill or the Saracen's Head on Snow Hill. In Duke's Place, near Aldgate, they had run the orange, lemon and nut business until the Irish had undercut them. There were 'superior' Jewish fruiterers in Covent Garden, Cheapside and the West End. Mayhew describes Jewish fried fish vendors whose product was more expensive but had a better flavour because the Jews used salad oil rather than lard and dipped the fish in egg. Alexis Soyer, the French cook who became a celebrated chef in Victorian England, included a recipe for 'Fried Fish, Jewish Fashion' in the first edition of his 1845 cookbook *A Shilling Cookery for the People*. Soyer's recipe backs the investigative journalist Mayhew's observation that the Jews used oil as the frying medium.[34]

'The Lane' that is in Middlesex Street, known as 'Petticoat Lane', and in the streets leading off it was the Jewish area, Mayhew wrote about it :

> Gowns of every shade and every pattern are hanging up, but none, perhaps, look either bright or white; it is a vista of dinginess, but many-coloured dinginess as regards female attire. Dress coats, frock coats, great coats, livery and gamekeepers' coats, paletots, tunics, trousers, knee breeches, waistcoats, capes, pilot coats, working jackets, plaids, hats, dressing gowns, shirts, Guernsey frocks ... present a scene which cannot be beheld in any other part of the greatest city of the world[35]

On a winter's night, with flaring gaslights, a multiplicity of shadows was cast over the Lane, causing the clothes swinging in the wind to assume ghostly forms and, 'if the wind be high, as they are blown to and fro, look more mysterious still'.[36] Mayhew considered that the Jews in Petticoat Lane gave the best value, as did those who bought old clothes at upper-class Gentile back doors. He writes also that the Jewish men were in general good husbands and fathers and that the girls were chaste.[37]

Most of the opposition to giving Jews the civil rights that Nonconformists and Catholics had received was based on the view that to excuse Jews who were elected to Parliament, for instance, from swearing the oath 'on the true faith of a Christian' was tantamount to removing the Christian basis of English life. One did not hear fears expressed, as on the Continent, of the mysterious powers of the Jews, that they were both extremely rich and, contradictorily, planning to overthrow bourgeois capitalist society. References to Jews were often joking, contemptuous even, but not vicious and rarely reasoned. Does Mr Caudle, for instance, in Douglas Jerrold's *Mrs Caudle's Curtain Lectures*, object to having Lazarus Goldman as a godfather to the latest addition to his family because Goldman is 'a usurer and a hunks [slang for a miser]', as he claims, rather than for the reason, which would have surely been valid in this case, that Goldman must have been Jewish? 'Actually', says Mrs Caudle, 'I'm sure it's well there's some people in the world who save money, seeing the stupid creatures who throw it away.' As she says this, one can imagine her glancing meaningfully at her spendthrift husband if they were not in bed in the dark. As for the newborn infant's Christian name, since it was apparently the custom to give the child the same name as that of the godparent, she concedes that Lazarus is not a 'genteel' name but, after all, she says, the little boy can always call himself Laurence later.[38]

Until 1832, Jews were not allowed to engage in retail trade in the City of London. Until 1835 they might be challenged to swear an oath 'on the true faith of a Christian' if they tried to vote in local elections. Nevertheless, by the late 1830s prominent Jews had held the office of Sheriff in the City. At the same time Lionel de Rothschild, repeatedly elected Member of Parliament for the City, was being refused permission to take his seat because he would not take the oath in the prescribed form. Sir David Salomons, elected for Greenwich and later the first Jewish Lord Mayor of London, was expelled after taking his seat, because he had not taken the oath with the words required. While the Commons had voted year after year to change the oath, the Lords had not consented. Finally, in 1859 a compromise was reached: each House would determine its own form of the oath. Jewish members at last took their seats in the Commons, but not in the Lords until a Rothschild was granted a peerage in 1885.

Chapter 8

Communications

Cab!

> You cannot conceive, if 'tis not pointed out,
> How quickly in London you travel about...
> So I'll tell you, all fabulous narratives scorning,
> The various places we saw in one morning.

So wrote a young lady in 1842 to her friend who lived in the provinces.[1]

The really fast method of getting around London, the Metropolitan underground railway, the first of its kind in the world, would not draw crowds into its smoky tunnels and stations for another twenty-one years. The only way the young lady could travel so rapidly around London was by cab. The rich could buy or hire broughams, barouches and phaetons, with varying degrees of comfort and stylishness, but when others needed urgent transport they made do with a hansom cab, named after Joseph Aloysius Hansom, who patented his vehicle in 1834. The hansom kept out bad weather and allowed the passenger to speak to the driver through a trap in the roof. The light and fast hansom was very successful and was used in London until motor transport came in during the early 1900s. The hansom was drawn by just one horse and could be steered around the notorious traffic jams of the city. It was more manoeuvrable than the old-style hackney coach. This was usually a shabby and lumbering carriage which had been sold off by a noble family and was propelled by a foul-mouthed and well wrapped-up coachman. Young Pip in Chapter 20 of Charles Dickens's *Great Expectations*, published in 1861 but set in the 1820s, arrives from the country at the Cross Keys coaching inn in Cheapside and takes a hackney carriage to Mr Jaggers's office near Smithfield.[2]

> a hackney-coachman, who seemed to have as many capes to
> his greasy great-coat as he was years old, packed (sic) me up
> in his coach ... His getting on his box, which I remember to
> have been decorated with an old weather-stained pea-green

116

[cloth], moth-eaten into rags, was quite a work of time. It was a wonderful equipage, with six great coronets outside, and ragged things behind for I don't know how many footmen to hold on by, and a harrow behind them to prevent amateur footmen from yielding to the temptation. I had scarcely had time to enjoy the coach and to think how like a straw-yard it was, and yet how like a rag-shop ... when I observed the coachman beginning to get down...

The fare was a shilling. This was a substantial sum, although the carriage could take four people. In Pip's case, the coachman does not dare to demand any more, confessing that he does not want any trouble from the lawyer Jaggers, who would know that the correct fare was indeed one shilling for the first mile and then sixpence per half-mile or under. The hackney could also be hired by the clock, which would make it cheaper for long distances along less busy roads. A shilling would buy thirty minutes, which suggests that the full mile in London would take half an hour. Hackney carriages had to have a licence plate issued by the Excise Office at Somerset House in the Strand, so that annoyed passengers would know where to direct their complaints.

If one wanted to travel further afield, there were short-stage coaches which were not allowed to infringe the monopoly of the London cabs by plying for hire in the central streets. These short-stage coaches would take prosperous City men out to semi-rural suburbs such as Paddington, Clapham, Clapton, or Hammersmith, and as far as Richmond upon Thames, which was nearly ten miles from Charing Cross. Really wealthy people, with incomes of £1,500 a year or more, who needed to get around London comfortably and in style, would usually own a carriage, but they could save themselves the expense of the groom and the horse by hiring a complete equipage for a couple of pounds a day, or even commute the hire for £300 a year. A very convenient arrangement for those who liked to get out of town at weekends was to arrange to have a coach and driver at their disposal every Sunday for £60 a year.

Hurry along there, please!

Since 4 July 1829, however, getting around London had been revolutionised by the omnibus, very soon known and spelt as the 'buss'. George Shillibeer, a coachbuilder who took the word for the vehicle from the French and Latin *voiture omnibus* or 'carriage for all', words which described vehicles which were already running on the streets of Paris, pioneered a route which went from the Yorkshire Stingo pub, which was not far from where its namesake stands today next to Edgware Road Bakerloo Line tube station, along the New Road, later the Marylebone and Euston Roads, and then via Pentonville and City Roads to the Bank of England. All the passengers sat inside and there was a conductor to take the fares, described in the advertising as 'a person of great respectability' dressed in a uniform resembling that of a Navy midshipman.[3] The omnibus left Paddington Green at 9am, noon, 3pm, 6pm and 8pm, returning from the Bank at 10am, 1pm, 4pm, 7pm and 9pm. It cost a shilling to go all the way, but if you wanted to go only as far as Islington it was 6d. It was at the start of this route that 'Pretty little Polly Perkins of Paddington Green' lived, in Harry Clifton's song, published in 1863. Polly Perkins was 'as proud as a queen', and turned down the simple milkman, who loved her, in the unreal hope of marrying a wealthy man or even an aristocrat, but in the end she had to settle for 'the bow-legged conductor of a tuppenny bus'. 2d was all it cost once competition had brought fares down by the time Polly Perkins came on the scene, but until late 2005, London's buses still employed conductors who collected the fares, issued the tickets and stood bow-legged as the bus stopped, started, bumped and jerked along the city's often ill-surfaced streets.

At first, Shillibeer's omnibuses ran outside the area of the cab monopoly, so he was allowed to set down and pick up passengers anywhere along his route. There were no regular bus stops and no regulation to prevent the driver from turning his horses in response to a hand summons from the other side of the road.

Cab drivers were faced with competition when omnibuses were allowed into central London in 1832 and when the tax on them, originally the same as that paid by cabs, was reduced. Shillibeer could now run his omnibuses through profitable Oxford Street. Fares halved; it now cost sixpence 'all the way', or threepence for half the route.

Omnibuses did not run until 9am, so they were of no use and in any case far too expensive for labouring men who had to be on the spot at 6 in the morning to compete for whatever work was going. The omnibus was for taking ladies to the shops, while the first journey from Paddington to the Bank carried prosperous senior officials, businessmen, chief clerks and other men who did not have to be at their offices promptly at 9 in the morning.

The very word *omnibus* brought back memories of schooldays to the gentlemen who rode on it, and encouraged the quotation of Latin tags which played heavy-handedly on the meaning of the word *omnibus*, that is 'for everyone'. Two of the best known were '*Impendet omnibus periculum*' or 'danger hangs over all of us', and '*Mors omnibus es communis*' or 'Death is common to all of us'. The joke went on into the twentieth century. When motor buses were introduced to Oxford, the Latin orator of the historic University and humorous poet A.D. Godley composed a rhyme which began 'What is it that roareth thus? Can it be a motor bus?' It continued by declining '*motor bus*', as if it were two Latin words, in its various Latin cases, concluding with the heartfelt appeal to the Almighty to defend us against 'these motor buses' (in the accusative plural case):

> Domine, defende nos
> Contra hos motores bos[4]

Omnibus might well mean 'for all', but the vehicle was not only expensive but slow. So, though Maria Manning must have been in a hurry to get to Patrick O'Connor's lodgings in Mile End to take his money and share certificates after she and her husband murdered him, she probably walked the two miles from Bermondsey rather than take the omnibus which would have had to negotiate the blocked traffic crossing London Bridge. Then she would have had to wait for another going east through Aldgate and Whitechapel towards Mile End. And in Chapter 1 of Wilkie Collins's *The Woman in White,* Walter Hartwright as a matter of course walks three miles uphill from Clement's Inn in the Strand to see his mother and sister who live in Hampstead. Nevertheless, by mid-century, 3,000 omnibuses, each able to carry 22 passengers, were negotiating the narrow and crowded streets of the capital. Their routes were as yet unnumbered, so buses were identified by their different bright colours, according to the companies which ran them: Paragon, Atlas, Waterloo, Camberwell and many others.

The omnibus was basically a rectangular box with windows at the sides and a door with a window at the back. It was upholstered with bright scarlet or green plush cushions, but in order to try to absorb the mud that passengers brought in with them, the crew had to put down straw which soon became dirty. The omnibus, especially in winter, was stuffy and grimy.

Working on the omnibus was a hard job. Drivers were exposed to the weather and conductors were on their feet all the time. The owners treated the crews harshly. They had no free day, just two hours off every second Sunday. They started early enough to get the vehicle and the horses to their starting point by about 8.30. They did not get home until at least 11pm. The long day was broken up by a series of intervals between services, but none long enough to go home and eat a proper meal. Like most working men, they were liable to dismissal without notice or compensation. Drivers were not as easily replaceable as conductors, but they were fined if they did not keep to the timetable. Nevertheless, like many of their equivalents a century later, the conductors were often in high spirits, singing out 'Hurry along there, please!' and banging, probably on the ceiling of the omnibus, to tell the driver to move off.

Bells came in later, but passengers could tug a leather strap, running above their heads and fixed to the driver's arms, one to the left and the other to the right, according to the side of the road where they wanted to get off. There were no fixed stops but at certain places, drivers knew they could pick up passengers and so were in the habit of delaying a long time so that they could fill their buses, much to the irritation of passengers waiting for the bus to move off.

The financial arrangements at first required the conductor to pay a certain amount over to the owner. The conductor shared what was left with the driver. Later the conductor handed in his takings and received a wage, augmented with a commission. There were no tickets, so owners could not check on their conductors' honesty. The latter had to be careful, all the same, because the owners employed a woman known as a 'watcher' or 'ladylike', sometimes even, for better cover, accompanied by a child. The 'watcher' estimated the number of passengers who had been carried. Nevertheless, it was known that she could be bribed, or even, if the conductor recognised her for what she was, handed off the bus straight into a puddle or pile of horse dung. Conversely, owners could sack drivers on mere suspicion of pocketing the fares. Nevertheless, working on the omnibus was a good job. The 24/- a week that the best routes paid conductors was not a wage that could easily be found elsewhere. Drivers could earn up to 34/-.

Some drivers were well-known characters who sported a white top hat, a rose in their buttonhole and a cigar given to them by their favourite passengers, who expected to have the seat next to the driver reserved for them as they drove down, say, from Highgate to the City. These passengers, fantasising perhaps that they were Regency bucks posting down to Brighton in the old days, would show off by tipping the driver generously.

Some of the routes took over from the short-stage coaches. Jane Carlyle liked to take long rides on the upper deck of omnibuses from where she lived in Chelsea to Islington, Hampstead Heath and Richmond.[5] Herman Melville once took a long ride as far as Hampton Court, returning more quickly by train.[6]

When omnibuses with seats on top were introduced, ladies travelled 'inside'. They could not ride 'outside' because it would mean displaying their ankles to loiterers in the street as they climbed the iron rungs up the back of the vehicle. Later, stairs which were easier to climb were built to reach the 'knifeboard' upper deck, where one sat against a backboard facing outward and rested one's feet against a destination board which also served to protect the modesty of the occasional woman who preferred the fresh air 'outside' to the stuffiness, dirty straw and excessive proximity of the people 'inside'. Nevertheless, the wide skirts and especially the crinolines of the 1850s made it hard to climb the stairs and indeed to get into the narrow bus itself.

Soon, complaints began to reach the authorities about the rudeness of bus conductors. Since the fares were collected when the passengers got off, some tried to get away without paying, while others were irritatingly slow to extract the coins from their pockets or purses. Conductors, especially if they were on commission, wanted as many passengers as possible but sometimes ran short of change or were stubborn about providing it. One of Dickens's *Sketches by Boz* describes a conductor, pictured standing on the step at the back door of the omnibus, pulling elderly gentlemen onto the vehicle even if they were not sure that they wanted to travel on it. On 30 June 1849 the clerk at the Mansion House court in the City of London reported that more than 4,000 summonses had been issued in the previous year to bus conductors for rudeness and even for manhandling passengers.[7] The 'cads', as the conductors were called, were fined so often that they got together and collected a fund to help individual conductors. The matter became so serious that one irritated magistrate sent a bus conductor to prison for two months for deliberately delaying his bus in order to collect more passengers and then refusing to give change. 1849 in particular seems to have been a bad year for riding on a London omnibus. *Punch* was running a campaign against the behaviour of the conductors. In one case, where there was a notice posted on the bus to the effect that sixpence was the fare 'ALL THE WAY', but only three pence 'TO CHARING CROSS', an argument arose about whether the conductor had stood intentionally to block people's view of the words 'TO CHARING CROSS' in order to attract passengers to what they thought was a cut-price service for the full distance. In another case, there had been an argument over exactly which point constituted Charing Cross. Still, in defence of the conductors, *Punch* published a letter from one of them (possibly a spoof) complaining about old ladies who took ages to extract a few coppers from their purses.

Complaints aside, omnibuses could be most convenient, as Thackeray's eponymous hero Pendennis finds in Chapter 28 when 'A City omnibus would put him down at the gate'.[8] But sometimes they could be dangerous as well, especially if they were racing to pick up passengers before a competitor. *Punch's Almanack* for 1849 advised readers who found that they had to stand out in the road to attract the driver's attention and to climb into the bus:

> If two omnibuses are racing, never hail the first, unless you
> have a particular fancy to be run over by the second

Heigh Ho, the Wind and the Rain

Rather than squelch through the mud and dung of London streets or squash into a packed and crawling omnibus where the passengers were probably bad-tempered and perhaps damp, one could travel by one of the 69 steamboats whose paddle wheels churned up the malodorous water of the Thames.

Steamboats with fares ranging from a penny to fourpence plied from London Bridge westward, past Southwark, Westminster and Vauxhall, as far as Chelsea, and eastward to Greenwich and Gravesend. Competition led to price-cutting to the bone. It was not surprising that in 1847 the boiler of the *Cricket*, carrying 150 passengers who had just embarked at Hungerford Pier, blew up, killing five people and seriously injuring fifty others. Nevertheless, two years later, the American novelist Herman Melville paid a mere halfpenny to take the steamboat from the Adelphi pier, just south of his lodgings near the Strand, to London Bridge.[9]

In fine weather especially, the river steamboat was a pleasant, if slow, alternative to the train. One could reach Margate in six hours for a fare of eight or nine shillings, or go down river as far as Greenwich on a 'Diamond' line boat for 1/2d in the main cabin or 2/- in the ladies' saloon. There was a boat every half-hour in the winter and every fifteen minutes in summer, leaving from the wharf on the north bank of the river near London Bridge.

Travelling by steamboat was not, however, always pleasant. Sometimes the boat was allowed to become dangerously overfull. In the winter passengers crowded below to find shelter from the wind and the rain. When you reached your destination you still had to walk or find a cab to where you wanted to go. Perhaps this is why the Thames, though it is often declared to be the natural route through London, is not really convenient unless one both lives and works near a landing stage. Indeed, in 1852 when Thomas Carlyle went to Scotland he took the steamboat from where he lived near the river at Chelsea as far as the London Docks and continued his journey to Scotland by ship up the coast. Jane Carlyle, on doctor's orders, went by train. However, when Jane returned from a break at Ryde (Isle of Wight), she left the train at Vauxhall and boarded a steamboat to take her home to Chelsea.[10]

'Away with a shriek, and a roar and a rattle' (Charles Dickens, *Dombey and Son*, Chapter 20)

As early in the railway age as 1844, the artist John Turner exhibited his railway picture *Rain, Steam and Speed* at the Royal Academy. Speed was the dominant characteristic by which people judged the railway. Dickens, as so often, expressed it in a nutshell:

> Whizz! Dust heaps, market gardens and waste grounds. Rattle! New Cross Station. Shock! There we were in Croydon.[11]

By 1845 hundreds of railway lines had been planned and scores of speculative companies had been set up. The speculators would rent an office, put a noble name, sometimes without permission, on a fancy prospectus, and tout shares to the public. In one week of 1845 alone 89 new schemes were seeking £84 million from investors. Lawyers, Members of Parliament and bankers, but also less financially acute clergymen, tradesmen, landladies, widows and even servants and tavern potboys sold shares before they had even paid for them. In his *Yellowplush Correspondence*, Thackeray's character Jeames de la Pluche, really the footman James who wore yellow plush, makes £30,000 in share dealings after starting out with a £20 loan. People who applied for an allocation of shares and sold them at once for a profit before they paid for them were called 'stags'. Thus Dickens chose 'Stagg's Gardens' in *Dombey and Son*, for the name of the slum district which was demolished to make way for Euston Station. 1846 was the peak year of the railway bubble. Parliament authorised the raising of £60 million of railway capital. However, by 1848 only 1,182 miles of new track had been laid. In 1847, the bubble had burst when investors were called on to pay for their shares, many of which were now worthless. In April 1847 the Bank of England raised the discount rate to 5 per cent and in August to 5.5 per cent. Many firms, set up specifically to deal in railway shares, collapsed and thousands of people were ruined in the railway mania. On 28 July 1847, commiserating with anxious parsons and officers on half-pay who had sunk their savings in railway shares, *Punch* wrote, in imitation of Cowper's 'Wreck of the Royal George':

> Toll for a knave!
> A knave whose day is o'er.
> All sunk – with those who gave
> Their cash, till they'd no more.

The 'knave' in this case was George Hudson, who controlled a sizeable proportion of the 5,000 miles of track in the country. He was Chairman of the Eastern Counties Railway, the Midland, the York and North Midland, and the York, Newcastle and Berwick. When the price of railway stock fell in 1848 as a result of Continental revolutions, Hudson did some manoeuvring to keep up the price of his stock, including paying dividends out of capital. Company Law was not yet sufficiently developed to make this illegal. Hudson was never prosecuted although the shareholders of the Newcastle and Berwick Railway tried to sue him for applying £18,204 of the Company's funds to his own use.

Hudson was a semi-literate draper's son from York. While his shares were riding high, elegant society flattered him, inviting him to receptions while from behind their kid gloves and perfumed fans, ladies and gentlemen sneered at his uncouth manners and Yorkshire accent. Mrs Hudson, who is caricatured as 'Mrs Hodge-Podson' in Thackeray's novel *Pendennis*, was jeered at behind her back. She was reputed to have once enquired if a bust of Marcus Aurelius was one of 'the last Markiss', the father of her host the Marquess of Westminster, and to have returned a pair of magnificent globes to the famous James Wyld, exhibitor of the Great Globe in Leicester Square, because they did not match the decor. The Hudsons owned a mansion in Albert Gate, today the French embassy, which they had bought from Thomas Cubitt the builder for £15,000, and on which they had spent another £14,000.[12]

By mid-century, London was well-connected by rail to most parts of the country. One could take a train from the newly opened Waterloo Station to Southampton. One could travel by rail from London to Bristol, Birmingham, Manchester, Liverpool, Leicester, Sheffield, Norwich, Hull, Newcastle and Edinburgh, though not always directly. From where the Mannings lived in Bermondsey, they would have heard and perhaps gone to see the huge 5'6" driving wheels, the bright brass and the green and red paint of the locomotives which since December 1837 had been hauling the trains at fifteen-minute intervals along the viaduct carrying the London, Deptford and Greenwich Railway. For the inaugural journey, a band played at London Bridge Station as the directors of the company took their seats. Cannon fired, church bells rang and the excited crowd of Londoners cheered as the train steamed off. Spa Road, the intermediate station 'was reached with almost the swiftness of a discharged rocket'. There and at Deptford the crowds were enormous.[13] From 1839 the Croydon railway, from 1841 the Brighton line and from 1849 the Gravesend line also brought their trains into London Bridge Station. The fare from London Bridge to Greenwich was cut to 4d in 1844, and as a result, the numbers travelling rose to two million.[14]

Since 1844 one had been able to enjoy a day excursion to Brighton, leaving London Bridge at 8.30am. The first train on Whit Monday of that year, used four engines to haul 45 carriages. At New Cross, six more carriages and yet another engine were hooked onto the serpentine train. This took two thousand passengers to the seaside, which they might never have seen before, and back that day. On the same day, the railway carried 35,000 to Greenwich and back, charging just the single fare. Fares were going down all the time. In 1850 3/6d bought a day trip to Brighton and back, and a mere shilling bought a day excursion ticket to Hampton Court.[15] Travel had changed immensely in little over a decade. It was not just the cheapening of the railway, but the speed and the comfort which had all had changed so quickly. Even youngish people could recall:

> a life which has passed away ... and only lives in fond memory.
> Eight miles an hour for twenty or five and twenty hours ... a
> tight mail coach, a hard seat ... who has not borne these evils
> in the jolly old times.[16]

Railways were modern. The speed at which they had been constructed was breathtaking. In 1830, in the whole of Britain, there were no more than 100 miles of track. By 1852, 6,000 miles were in use. The increase had, however, been very recent. In 1845 there had been only 2,200 miles of railway track. It was the 1845-1848 period that saw the most ambitious programme of track laying in the early Victorian age.

No longer did travellers have to put up with dirty old-style coaching inns from where the long-distance stages left, with their horse dung, flies and untidy ostlers. The London coaching inns, with their outdated accommodation, such as the White Horse Cellars in Piccadilly and the Saracen's Head in Snow Hill, had given way to railway 'termini' with proper hotels.[17]

The railway even changed the concept of time. The guard's watch replaced the sun. In 1845 the Great Western Railway synchronised its clocks with London's 'railway time'. 'Greenwich Mean Time' became the standard in Britain in the 1850s, and when 25 countries agreed to accept Greenwich as the Prime Meridian, British 'railway time' became the standard against which other times were measured.

The Noise ... and the People

Despite the separation of travellers into three classes – and the absence of corridors meant that you had to stay in your own carriage – the cheapening of travel would cause, as Lord de Mowbray in Disraeli's novel *Sybil* feared, 'a most dangerous tendency to equality'.[18] This was somewhat of an exaggeration for, although more people than ever could now travel, entire trains were of one class, and third-class trains were extremely uncomfortable, as Herman Melville discovered when travelling in third class from Canterbury to London in 1845 'exposed to the air – devilish cold riding against the wind'.[19]

The 'Parliamentary' trains, which were obliged to have roofs on the carriages and to run over the whole route at least once a day at a fare of one penny a mile and at a minimum speed of twelve miles per hour, were, if the company could get away with it, scheduled during the most inconvenient times.

In order to avoid contact with people not of one's social class, for quite a long time the wealthy could travel by train yet remain in their own landaus and barouches on a flat wagon. The Argentine-born Spanish dramatist Ventura de la Vega discovered this when he was invited to accompany the Spanish embassy staff to go to Chertsey on 21 June 1853 to see a royal military review.[20]

Perhaps Disraeli's Lord de Mowbray was worried about the tone of 'mutual frankness and civility – so new to the English character' that was noticed among railway passengers by a writer in the *Quarterly Review*.[21] More extreme was the comment of Thomas Arnold, headmaster of Rugby School, who said of the London and Birmingham Railway:

I rejoice to see it, and to think that Feudality is gone for ever[22]

In this case, Arnold seems to have been a prophet before his time. Nevertheless, the railway allowed the upper and middle class to travel much more. There were three times as many railway passengers in 1849 as in 1842. One of them was Maria Manning the murderess, though nobody reported having spoken to *her* on her journey to Scotland.

Brought back by the Police

Five days after she and her husband had murdered Patrick O'Connor, Maria Manning took a short cab ride from where she lived in Bermondsey to London Bridge Station. She deposited a trunk full of clothes in the left-luggage office and continued in the same cab to the Euston Square Station of the London and Birmingham Railway. She stayed overnight in one of the adjacent hotels and began her long journey to Edinburgh at 6.15am on Tuesday, 14 August 1849.

Even someone as blasé as Maria could hardly have failed to gasp at the magnificence of the entrance to Euston, just north of the yet incompletely developed New Road.

Passing through a gateway, wrote the *Penny Magazine*:

> we feel at once that as the mode of conveyance is different, so is the place. We are not within the narrow precincts of an inn-yard jostled by porters and ostlers, and incommoded by luggage; everything is on a large scale ... 'First' and 'Second' class passengers have their different entrances and their separate booking desks; and on passing through the building have to produce their tickets as passports into the covered yard where the trains lie[23]

It was rather like the change that travellers in the next century would experience when they enjoyed air travel for the first time: the sheer 'modernity' of it all. When one's cab, one of a restricted number allowed to drop off and pick up passengers at Euston Square Station, arrived, a porter opened the door, took out the luggage, and invited the passengers to walk at their ease into the station and to find him and their luggage waiting on the platform.

From the outside of Euston, one's eye was drawn to the screen of seven stone blocks (two of which still stand), inscribed with the names of the places to which the railway would swiftly take you, linked by iron railings. In the middle stood the immense Euston Arch, more properly the Propylaeum. Behind the portico was the station yard, and at its end, Maria entered the just completed outer vestibule with its mosaic pavement, and passed through one of the five entrances to the Grand Hall. This was 'a regal apartment in its style and size', proclaimed the *Illustrated London News* on 15 September 1849. It was 125 feet (38 metres) long and a towering 62 feet (19 metres) high, lit by high windows. A grand double staircase led to a central flight of steps to an even longer vestibule, and thence to the Shareholders' Room. At the foot of the staircase stood a statue of the railway pioneer George Stephenson. Eight bas-reliefs depicted the towns one could reach by train. Passing through glass doors Maria reached the booking offices where, never one to economise, she paid £3.17.6d for a first-class ticket to Edinburgh. She could hardly have been expected to travel third-class, on a hard seat, exposed to the rain and getting covered by smuts from the engine.

After seeing that her baggage was properly stowed in the luggage van, and paying the extra charge for its huge volume, Maria settled in one of the three comfortably upholstered seats on either side of her first-class compartment. There was no corridor and no lavatory facility, so she may be assumed to have made some precautionary arrangement. However, the first stop was not too far: Tring in Hertfordshire, which the train reached in just under an hour.

The London and Birmingham, which was by now part of the thousand miles of track of the London and North-Western Railway, together with the Grand Junction, the Manchester and Birmingham and the Liverpool and Manchester, was probably the largest public work ever to be undertaken in human history, save the Great Wall of China. It had been finished in a record five years, by 20,000 'navvies', and had cost over £6 million. New techniques of surveying and engineering and particularly management had been required.

For the first few years, the carriages were hauled up the incline outside Euston by cable for about a mile until the ground levelled at Camden, where there was a goods station with a warehouse of colossal dimensions, equipped with steam cranes and capstans to deal with thousands of tons of goods daily. Then the traveller would have felt the bump as an engine was connected to the train after chuffing over from the turntable in the Round House, still there on the east side of the tracks at Primrose Hill. The train steamed off, descending into the Primrose Hill Tunnel and emerging at speed to rush past the few houses being built at the three-mile post around the recently-opened commuter station at Kilburn. A few trains stopped there every day, but railways were not used much by commuters. For example, at Waterloo in 1849 only 1,500 season tickets were issued.[24]

Richard Doyle drew the pictures and Percival Leigh wrote the text of *Manners and Customs of ye Englyshe: Mr Pips hys Diary*, a comic version of Samuel Pepys's seventeenth-century diary. When Mr Pips and his wife travelled to Bath they had to use their elbows to get to the bar at Swindon Station. Mrs Pips spilt the scalding soup over her dress and her husband had managed to finish only half his glass of stout before he had to run with her to the train carrying his half-eaten ham and veal pie.[25]

Maria had to change at Birmingham, 112 miles from London, and again at Newcastle, to trains belonging to other companies, and she did not arrive in Edinburgh until the next day. Still, twenty-four hours was a fraction of the time it would have taken by coach.

She came back to London, under arrest, at 4.45am on 22 August, accompanied by Superintendent Moxey of the Edinburgh police. In the summer dawn, the passengers yawned, stretched and prepared to leave the train after their all-night journey. By now, the last few hundred yards as the train coasted down the incline to Euston Square Station were no longer as they had been in the late 1830s when in Chapter 6 of *Dombey and Son* Charles Dickens described the area during the construction of the approach to London:

> Houses were knocked down: streets broken through and stopped; deep pits and trenches dug in the ground; enormous heaps of earth and clay thrown up ... here a chaos of carts , overthrown and jumbled together ... Everywhere were bridges that led nowhere, wildly mingled out of their places, upside down, burrowing in the earth ... thoroughfares that were wholly impassable

But, by the time the railway was built, in Chapter 15:

> There was no such place as Staggs's Gardens. It had vanished from the earth. Where the old rotten summer houses once had stood, palaces now reared their heads, and granite columns of gigantic girth opened a vista to the Railway world beyond. The miserable waste grounds where the refuse-matter had been heaped of yore, was swallowed up and gone; and in its frowsty stead were tiers of warehouses, crammed with rich goods and costly merchandise. The old by-streets now swarmed with passengers and vehicles of every kind; the new streets that had stopped disheartened in the mud and waggon-ruts, formed

towns within themselves ... Bridges that had led to nothing led
to villas, gardens, churches

At Euston terminus, four minutes after the train had been authorised by
electric telegraph to descend the gradient from Camden, a guard listening
for its approach waved a flag. Porters hastened to their allotted posts and a
few seconds later the train was to be seen emerging from the tunnel 'like
a serpent from its hole'.[26] Slowly, the puffing engine slowed, stopped and
released jets of steam as the porters hastened to open the doors and help the
passengers with their luggage.

The Electric Spark

Semaphores, with their multi-armed posts, were quickly outdated when
Euston Square railway terminus was connected in 1837 by electric telegraph
to Camden, a mile and a quarter down the line. At first, the telegraph
was used as a device to warn of the approach of a train, but this new and
immediate mode of communication was soon used for another purpose.

In January 1845, John Tawell committed a murder in the Buckinghamshire
town of Slough, twenty-two miles west of London. He was seen to board
a train. The station master at Slough telegraphed to London, where police
were waiting when Tawell's train arrived.

In 1849 the telegraph played a part in the arrest of Maria Manning, Once
she was known to have taken the train to Scotland, Inspector Haynes of
Scotland Yard 'wired' her description to the Edinburgh police. On Tuesday,
21 August 1849 Superintendent Moxey telegraphed London that he had
arrested Maria only one hour after receiving Haynes's message. It was
a stunning result, though *Punch*'s reaction to the news was somewhat
overwrought:

> the inexorable lightning ... the electric pulse – thrills in the
> wires – and in a moment Idiot murder stammers and grows
> white in the face of Justice[27]

Within three years, 1,800 miles of track had been lined with telegraph poles.
People went to the railway station to 'send a wire', as they said. However,
by the 1850s telegraph companies had offices, often employing women, in
several parts of London, and the streets were beginning to be festooned with
cables which, together with the later telephone wires, would be backdrops

as characteristic of London streets as mobile telephone masts and dish television aerials are today.

It was expensive to send a telegram, as the telegraphic message came to be called: eight or nine shillings to send twenty words from London to Manchester, and fourteen shillings to Glasgow.[28] The telegraph was used primarily by the railways in their running operations, and by businessmen. It was a useful tool also for stockbrokers and for bookmakers, who needed immediate information about changes in share prices and horse racing odds.

Postman's Knock

What a wonderful man the postman is,
As he hastens from door to door.
What a medley of news his hands contain
For high, low, rich and poor;
In many a face he joy doth trace,
In as many he grief can see,
As the door is ope'd to his loud rat-tat,
And his quick delivery.
Ev'ry morn, as true as the clock,
Somebody hears the postman's knock.

Although this song was chanted by street urchins and ground out by every barrel organ in London, its composer, L.M. Thornton, sold his copyright to music publishers for a mere one guinea and died a pauper in the workhouse.[29]

After a polemical debate about the new system, during which 40,000 copies of a favourable pamphlet were sewn into the twelfth instalment of Dickens's *Nicholas Nickleby* in March 1839, the new Penny Post was approved by Parliament.

The railway, in its turn, facilitated the circulation of the vast increase in letters, parcels and books. Beginning on 10 January 1840, after a few years letters and packets were carried entirely by the railway at twice the speed of the old mail coaches. This made the greatest difference to the lives of literally millions in the early part of Victoria's reign by enabling them to communicate with their families if they were away from home or, if they were in trade, with their salesmen, suppliers and customers.

An enormous change occurred on 10 January 1840 when the cost of sending a letter – one sheet folded and sealed with a wax 'wafer' and with the address written on the outside – from London to Edinburgh fell from

1/1d to a single penny, one-thirteenth of the previous fee, but paid for by the sender. It was as revolutionary as the introduction of electronic mail at the end of the twentieth century. Previously the envelope had been charged for as well as each sheet enclosed, and many a woman might have had to do without news of her absent husband or son because she could not pay the fee. Now the envelope was free. Whatever it contained, if it weighed under half an ounce, went anywhere in the United Kingdom for a penny. Six hundred thousand of the famous 'Penny Black' stamps were bought at once and the volume of post doubled in a year to 169 million letters. Six deliveries came to one's door daily, rising later to twelve, so when, in Chapter 44 of Dickens's *David Copperfield*, the eponymous hero meets his friend Traddles in town he can post a note to his wife Dora to say that he will bring Traddles home to dinner that evening and expect his message to arrive well in time.

Like today's emails and mobile phones, the early Victorian years witnessed a need to communicate that had not been evident previously. So great was the volume of London post that the capital was divided into twelve districts to aid sorting. On some old street name plates in London, the letters indicating the district can still be seen on a plate to which a metal disc bearing a number was added when the districts were subdivided during the 1914-1918 war because the temporary postmen and postwomen who were recruited did not know the streets as well as the older sorters, and because of the vast increase in mail from men in the armed services.

The postman, still known in early Victorian days as the 'letter carrier' wore a scarlet uniform with blue lapels and cuffs, and a blue waistcoat. He rapped twice on the door. Now that the postage had been paid by the sender, there was no need for the postman to collect any money, so people were encouraged to have a slit opened in their front doors so that the postman could insert the letters without knocking and waiting. The elaborate frames around the slits had hinged covers incorporated in them so that the noise of the letters being delivered could be heard from inside. But perhaps in a big house you would not hear your letters coming through the slit and falling on the floor. An enterprising businessman found the solution to telling residents that they had mail. This was *Dean's Postal Alarum and Letter Box*, which not only told you that post had arrived but also caught it neatly in a metal basket together with other items which came through the door. 'Without it' warned the advertisement, 'communications of the utmost importance often remain for hours unnoticed'.[30] Was this an example of a product sold to solve a non-existent problem?

In 1843 Henry Cole, a civil servant who played an important part in developing the postal service and would go on to be instrumental in the success of the Great Exhibition of 1851, introduced Christmas cards. The first of these depicted three generations of an ideal family (actually the Coles themselves) eating their Christmas dinner. Tens of thousands of these were soon being posted every year.

Moreover, letters came from abroad surprisingly quickly. On 18 June 1853, Ventura de la Vega, the Spanish visitor to London, received a letter sent from Madrid a week earlier. He commented that it usually took only five days.[31]

The postman brought letters, but if you wanted to send one you went to the Post Office. In the early days, 'bellmen' walked around the busy parts of London ringing a bell and holding a bag with a slit in it into which you could put your letter. Letter boxes appeared in 1852 when the first one was placed in Jersey, recommended by the novelist and employee of the Post Office Anthony Trollope, who had seen post boxes in France. In London, the first letter or pillar box was placed on the corner of Fleet Street and Farringdon Street in 1855.[32]

Omnibuses in London, trains all over the country, letters anywhere in the United Kingdom for a penny, and the telegraph, were ubiquitous by the end of the early Victorian age. The Underground railway, the electric tram and the telephone would come later.

Chapter 9

'A burst of applause which made the building ring'

London Amusements

Getting Away

That hot Thursday afternoon 9 August 1849, as Patrick O'Connor walked over London Bridge on his way to dine – and be murdered – at the Mannings' house in Bermondsey, he might well have glanced at the landing stage below him and thought that on the Sunday he might take the steamboat leaving at 8am for Margate. Or he might even spend the weekend at Gravesend. This town, close enough to London for men who did not want to be too far away from business, was a pleasure resort with dancing and fireworks in the evening, a promenade, a yacht club, gardens at Rosherville and villas on Windmill Hill. However, Margate and further away, Ramsgate, were proper holiday resorts, or so Mrs Caudle nags her husband in Douglas Jerrold's enormously successful series *Mrs Caudle's Curtain Lectures*, first published in *Punch* in 1845 and often reprinted, in which Mr Caudle endures a lecture from his wife night after night in bed as he tries to get to sleep.

In the end, Mr Caudle gives in and they go to Herne Bay, on the North Kent coast. One day they venture across the Channel to Boulogne. Despite Mrs Caudle's insistence on going, she dislikes France, beginning with her outraged objections to being searched by a woman in the French customs shed, even though she herself is not above smuggling lace, velvet and silk stockings when they return to England. She is also shocked by the bare legs of the Boulogne fisher-girls and perhaps would have preferred to take what she calls a 'really genteel' cottage at Brixton, Balham, Clapham, Hornsey or Muswell Hill, suburbs of London today but semi-rural in the early Victorian period.

On the Beer

Mrs Caudle is endlessly scathing about her husband's visits to the public house and his 'drinking friends'. She would have turned her face in scorn as she passed a rowdy pub; not for her the words of a prostitute recounted by an officer of the Salvation Army: 'the drink drowns all feelings of sorrow and shame, deadens the conscience, and hundreds could not live the life they do were it not for the excitement of alcohol'.[1] A working man, earning his fifteen shillings to a pound a week in 1841, drank a mere pint of beer a day, but even this cost one shilling and twopence a week. Some families spent over 20 per cent of their income on drink.[2]

That was at home, but the pub was warm and cheerful when home was probably dark and the family comprised a worn-out wife doing the washing by candlelight amid a crowd of quarrelling children. For London's 2.3 million inhabitants there were about 7,000 retailers of alcohol, one for every 333 people, and an outlet could be found on average every one hundred yards.[3] The annual consumption of beer in England and Wales was 19.4 gallons a head in 1849, or about three pints a week for every man, woman and child. However, given the substantial number of teetotallers in the Methodist and Evangelical movements, the average was deceptive. Many people drank much more alcohol than the average, not just in the traditional pub but in the newer gin palaces with their brilliant gas lighting reflected in abundant mirrors. Dickens wrote a piece about what he calls a 'gin-shop', towards the southern end of Tottenham Court Road, in a part of London 'of filthy and miserable appearance'. The gin-shop is however 'all light and brilliancy' with 'a bar of French-polished mahogany'. The saloon is 'lofty and spacious' and the gin is dispensed by' two showily-dressed damsels'. Near the bar are two washerwomen drinking glasses of gin and peppermint.[4]

Nevertheless, drinking beer and spirits apart, London, an enormous and incomparable city, offered a wide range of public entertainment, depending on the consumers' pockets, their inclinations and the company they wished to keep.

Much entertainment was as traditional as it had always been. The stage offered a wide variety, but other entertainment was new: promenade concerts, musical shows and circus-type spectacles, such as the trained horses in Astley's Amphitheatre. Something really new, however, was the panorama.

Panoramas, Dioramas and Cosmoramas

The growth of scientific knowledge and its application to mechanical devices overflowed into the world of entertainment. The panorama in particular was all the rage in the early Victorian era, when John and Robert Burford were displaying one on the east side of Leicester Square. There one could marvel at immense circular pictures of the Alps, the Himalayas, Naples by moonlight or the oriental mystery of Cairo, as well as the Arctic and the search for Sir John Franklin, whose expedition was lost in the frozen North in 1845. This panorama did not move, however, unlike what was probably the best-known one to be seen in London.

This was the New Yorker John Banvard's Moving Panorama with its 36 scenes taking the spectator on a thrilling 3,000 mile trip down the Mississippi River from its source in northern Minnesota to New Orleans. Banvard invited Charles Dickens to a private showing of the spectacle. The novelist, who had completed part of the trip in real life, guaranteed the accuracy of the spectacle that Banvard offered to the spectators.

> an indisputably true and faithful representation of a wonderful region– wood and water, river and prairie, lonely log hut and clustered city rising in the forest – is replete with interest throughout[5]

Banvard's Panorama could be seen at the Egyptian Hall, an exhibition space fronted by sphinxes and built in 1811-1812 on the site of the present numbers 170-173 Piccadilly. This building, located opposite the fashionable Burlington Arcade. is called Egyptian House today in memory of its original name.

Banvard's Panorama created a sensation at once. The canvas unrolled for two entire hours before the spectators as they gazed open-mouthed at the bluffs, the lonely cabins, the prairies with their vast herds of bison, the Red Indian wigwams and the wagon trains of new arrivals from Europe as they made their slow way westwards, the swamps and the alligators, the riverboats and the levees of the South with slaves picking cotton and cutting sugar-cane. Banvard accompanied his show with a witty commentary, which some found to be the height of Yankee vulgarity but which others found amusing. His Panorama was a huge success, crowned by the honour of an invitation to Buckingham Palace.

As with the silent film half a century later, it helped to have music as an accompaniment. Banvard himself played the piano and a sort of harmonium called a seraphine. Spin-offs were also profitable. Banvard sold sheet music, probably including Stephen Foster's immensely popular 'Oh, Susannah!'

To see one of the greatest shows of London, a short omnibus ride along the New Road or up Regent Street and Portland Place would bring a spectator to within a few minutes' walk of the Royal Colosseum, built in 1825 on a site where the Royal College of Physicians now stands beside Regent's Park. The Colosseum was a multi-sided structure behind a classical portico. On entering, one passed through a rotunda hung with silk and lined with classical statuary, while behind the Colosseum was a garden with reproductions of ruins such as the Arch of Titus, the Temple of Vesta and the Parthenon. In the centre stood the Salon of the Arts, with paintings, sculptures and casts of famous works. The principal entertainment consisted of moving panoramas, called dioramas or cycloramas, including 'Paris by Night' as seen from a balloon suspended and hovering over the city. Along one side of the Colosseum was a luxurious minor auditorium which recreated for the spectators, as if they were floating down the river Tagus, the great Lisbon earthquake of 1775 with spectacular lighting effects. Sound was provided by an enormous organ called the Great Apollonicon, which thundered out the descent-into-hell music from Mozart's opera Don Giovanni. The main exhibit of the Colosseum was a massive panorama with 46,000 square feet of canvas, depicting twenty miles around London, as seen from the dome of St Paul's Cathedral, but without its usual mantle of cloud, smoke and fog. To see it one was hoisted high into the dome by the first hydraulic passenger lift in London, called the 'ascending room'.

Slightly to the south of the Colosseum, at Numbers 9 and 10 Park East, in one of John Nash's new and fashionable terraces, stood a building which housed Daguerre's Diorama. The inventiveness of the early Victorian age with gaslight, mirrors and sound allowed the creation of illusion on a massive scale for people who had never seen any sort of moving picture and for whom the photograph was new and unfamiliar. Here there was an ingenious system of lighting which could at once change a gentle landscape into a stormy sea, or give an illusion of depth to a flat picture. The circular viewing area held two hundred spectators, who entered through a dimly-lit corridor, groping their way or led by an usher (an experience would be reproduced many years later in the cinema). The auditorium moved through an arc of 73 degrees, but the spectator received the impression that the scene itself was moving. By the use of an intricate system of lights and prisms, shutters and pulleys, the pictures dissolved into each other with such variation that the viewer saw them with an almost cinematic effect. The diorama was highly effective at producing the impressions of light and clouds, sunshine and shadow. Among other sights, there was on offer a thrilling depiction of an eruption of Mount Etna:

> first beheld at evening in moonlight, then in sun, then night.
> Flashes of light from the mountain; clouds over the summit,
> changing colours from burning lava, streams of liquid fire rush
> down[6]

Dioramas and panoramas offered what newspapers, magazines and finally the cinema would do later when pictures could be better reproduced and made to move. They offered fidelity to fact. One could see what one had read about in the newspapers. Like the later screen newsreel, the panorama was 'first with the news'. Only a week after the Houses of Commons had burned down on 16 October 1834, a panorama of their destruction was on show.

These shows reflected and to some extent satisfied British curiosity about foreign parts. In two hours and for a shilling or two, a sum large enough to retain an upper middle-class audience, one could see glamorous places such as Lake Maggiore, the Rhine, the Alhambra at Granada, St Petersburg, Cairo, Venice, Niagara Falls and the Swiss Alps.

The craze for panoramas stimulated the production of large canvases with a multiplicity of scenes. They contributed to the popularity of William Frith's famous mid-century paintings of the 'Railway Station', 'Derby Day' and 'Ramsgate Sands'. Access to paintings came when the National Gallery in Trafalgar Square, free to the public, opened in 1838. In the 1840s the number of visitors to its rooms doubled even though *Punch* complained unceasingly about its poor lighting. One Sunday the American novelist Herman Melville took an omnibus in Fleet Street all the way through South London and out as far as Dulwich Village, where he admired the art collection in the oldest purpose-built public gallery in England.[7]

Nothing Half So Good

Mechanical and scientific curiosity could be satisfied at the Royal Polytechnic Institution at the top of Regent Street:

> We have given a very long account of the visits we paid to
> the Royal Polytechnic Institution because we saw nothing in
> London – nothing in England – half so good[8]

So wrote two Indian students of naval architecture who spent two and a half years in London. The Polytechnic, founded in 1838 in newly-completed Regent Street, added 'Royal' to its title in 1841 on receiving the patronage of Prince Albert, and is today the main building of the University of Westminster. It was a place to visit which was indeed unlike anywhere else. It popularised science and technology. It gave free space to inventions and offered a programme of lectures and demonstrations for laypeople. For a shilling, one could visit the Polytechnic for several hours during the day and late into the evening. A band played as visitors toured its thirty rooms and particularly the Great Hall, which was over a hundred feet long and had miniature canals dotted with models of locks and dockyards, printing presses and other highly intricate and specialised machines. Among its greatest attractions were a three-ton diving bell, inside which members of the public could descend, and a diver who walked around the bottom of a tank of water and collected coins thrown by the spectators. Along the gallery of the Great Hall were models of all sorts of inventions, which fascinated the two Bombay students. Experts lectured on coal gas, the adulteration of food, electricity and chemistry, or demonstrated microscopes, particularly one which revealed the rich animal life of the Thames water which Londoners drank. On the roof stood one of the earliest photographic studios in the world, Under the Great Hall could be found an Aladdin's Cave, 'an infinite variety of ingenious models', wrote Dickens in his magazine *Household Words*.[9]

In 1847 John Pepper was appointed Lecturer in Chemistry at the Royal Polytechnic. In 1852 he became that institution's Honorary Director and Professor of Chemistry. Pepper set up regular classes in Drawing, French, German, Maths, Chemistry and Physics, and he used his skill with mirrors to produce the illusion known as 'Pepper's Ghost'. This was first displayed at a performance of Dickens's *The Haunted Man* at the Polytechnic on Christmas Eve 1862. A quarter of a million people were said to have come to see it in the first fifteen months, among them the Queen's eldest son, the future Edward VII.

There was something similar to the Polytechnic, but perhaps a little less earnest, called the National Gallery of Practical Science, at the Adelaide Gallery, located at the north end of Lowther Arcade, a passage off the Strand. The Adelaide was a long, narrow room on two levels. The lower floor had a miniature canal containing 6,000 gallons of water on which sailed a number of model steamboats. The new photograph, the Daguerreotype, was exhibited there from 1839, taking views from the roof, which were developed in-house. Nitrous Oxide, or 'Laughing Gas' whose anaesthetic properties were only later put to use, was demonstrated there, more for curiosity than anything else. The most striking exhibit was a steam-powered machine gun, which gave extremely noisy demonstrations of firing a thousand shots a minute into an iron plate. But, compared with the Royal Polytechnic, the Adelaide Gallery was already going downhill. By 1846 the scientific exhibits had been dispersed and the Adelaide soon became a dance hall.[10]

Some mechanical amusements could be bought and enjoyed at home. Among them were Sir Charles Wheatstone's Stereoscope of 1838, which enabled right eye and left eye views to be merged, thus producing a three-dimensional effect, while the Zoescope, invented in 1834 by the mathematician William George Horner, was a drum pierced with a succession of slits. When the drum was spun around at speed, it showed a succession of images, placed opposite the slits within the drum, as one moving image.

'Benighted heathens'

Since May 1848 the newspapers had been publishing articles and pictures of the brilliantly-painted, three-masted Chinese junk, the *Keying*, built of teak, moored in the East India Docks near Blackwall pier where the river steamboats tied up. The junk, which had sailed from China around the Cape of Good Hope, and had visited New York, was the first to have been seen in the West. It had a mixed Chinese and British crew. One could go aboard and be received by a mandarin of the first class. Queen Victoria and the Royal Family visited it.

More conveniently situated near Hyde Park Corner stood a Chinese pagoda, containing a collection of chinoiserie. It was a conspicuous landmark for years, with two storeys and a green roof supported on vermilion-painted columns. Finally, it was moved to Victoria Park, in Hackney, where it remained for over a century.

China apart, in London there was much interest in the exotic. From 1810, the massive-buttocked 'Hottentot Venus', a member of the Khoikhoi people, brought from South Africa and whose Afrikaans name was Saartje Baartman, was exhibited publicly. Unsuccessful attempts under the anti-slavery legislation were made in court to stop her exposure. Saartje, a woman in her twenties, died later while on exhibition in Paris.

George Catlin, an American who had travelled widely among the native American peoples and produced many paintings of them, exhibited a group of American Indians for five years in London's Egyptian Hall. They performed war dances, buffalo hunts, and pipe of peace ceremonies, and demonstrated feats of archery and ball games. Queen Victoria invited them to Windsor Castle for a command performance.

These exotic and 'savage' exhibits both provoked the spectators' curiosity and encouraged their sense of racial and cultural superiority. While Catlin's 'Red Indians' were still in the mould of the 'noble savage', untouched by the evil traits of European civilisation, by the 1840s the theorists of race had stereotyped other peoples as inferior. In 1847 Bushmen from Southern Africa were exposed on a stage with an African backcloth. *The Times* saw them as 'benighted heathens', little superior to monkeys. Yet the interest shown in such unfamiliar peoples would soon change into a climate of intense and sentimental sympathy, reflected in the enormous success of *Uncle Tom's Cabin*, Harriet Beecher Stowe's novel of American slavery.

The Egyptian Hall, one of London's greatest exhibition venues, had opened its premises in 1812, catering to the vogue stimulated by Napoleon's expedition to Egypt. In addition to housing Banvard's Moving Panorama, the Hall contained models of the Sphinx, together with stones inscribed with hieroglyphics, and innumerable curiosities from many other exotic places. There were models of giraffes, rhinoceroses and elephants set among African and Indian plants and curios, while Laplanders, Egyptian mummies and veiled models of Bedouin competed for space. The Egyptian Hall also hired out a room where one could present one's own exhibition of 'freaks', such as a multi-limbed male child, the Siamese twins Chang and Eng, and a woman with no limbs, as well as a six-year-old pianist, a group of Indian dancing girls and the Strongman advertised as 'The Modern Samson, the Wonderful Fistic Stone-Breaker', who could lift a weight of five hundred pounds between his teeth. Specialised museums in the modern sense were not yet on the scene, so the Egyptian Hall exhibited at one time or other in the 1840s clairvoyants and the Burmese State Coach, together with John Sainsbury's massive collection of Napoleonic relics. The famous 'General Tom Thumb', a midget, was exhibited in 1844 and 1846 by P.T. Barnum, the legendary American showman, together with sundry other dwarfs, giants and the inevitable bearded lady. Tom Thumb's pièce de résistance was to stand on a chair and perform his imitation of Napoleon Bonaparte. This brought the house down at the Egyptian Hall and led to an invitation to appear at Windsor Castle, where Queen Victoria was reported to have been much amused.[11]

'Freaks' were there to be shown off for money. Political correctness had only just reached the stage of making people ashamed of going for amusement to see the lunatics at Bethlehem Hospital, a place so disorderly that it gave the English language the word 'bedlam'. But how else could the freaks live? It would have been thought absurd to say that the exhibitors exploited them if Barnum and others took responsibility for their welfare and treated them well.

Chamber of Horrors

Londoners who could afford the shilling entrance fee could also visit the waxworks that Madame Tussaud was exhibiting in her premises in Baker Street, including the room known as the Chamber of Horrors, costing an extra sixpence, where one of the attractions around which spectators gathered was that of Burke and Hare, murderers who provided bodies for surgeons to dissect. Here, in 1849, Madame Tussaud was showing a newly-made model of James Rush, the Norfolk farmer who had shot and killed his landlord, together with the latter's son, and wounded his victim's wife and her female servant. These multiple shootings with their irrational ferocity had horrified and fascinated the sensation-hungry public. At his trial, Rush acted as his own counsel, and had subjected his mistress Emily Sandford to rigorous interrogation to try to prove that he was with her and not at the scene of the murders. Although the killings had been sparked off by prosaic tensions about mortgages, loans and leases, the press suggested that Rush had been inspired by revolutionary agitators, and this increased the anxious interest of the public.

Maria and Frederick Manning gave themselves a treat one day and went and stared at Rush's wax replica in the Chamber of Horrors. Frederick asked William Massey, the medical student who lodged with them, whether he thought a murderer would go to Heaven after death, as well as about the effects of poison. This would be interesting evidence at the Mannings' trial for murder. The dramatic irony of the event is that Frederick and Maria would themselves be exhibits at Madame Tussaud's not so long afterwards.

Queen Victoria's coronation in 1837 was on permanent show at the waxworks as was Napoleon's carriage, captured at the battle of Waterloo and presented to the Prince Regent, who later gave it to the Egyptian Hall from which Madame Tussaud bought it. She was always up-to-date with her models and tableaux and, before photography, she gave people the most accurate and lifelike reproductions (perhaps better than photography because her models were coloured) of the politicians of the time such as Sir Robert Peel, Lord John Russell and Lord Palmerston, as well as of stars of the stage such as the actor William Macready and the singer Jenny Lind.

Madame Tussaud maintained very high-quality premises with brilliant gas lighting, mirrors, sofas and even an orchestra. Nevertheless, some of Napoleon's personal relics that she exhibited were activated by internal mechanisms, and in this she indulged the passion for clever tricks by which the showmen of London sought to attract the capital's growing audience for the spectacular and the curious. In one case, at the so-called Anatomical Waxworks in the Strand, one could see a female body being dissected. According to the leaflet which described the show, the body was that of the Venus de Milo. Of course, the spectacle dared not suggest its major purpose, which was to titillate the sexually curious, but insisted that its aim was to display 'the order and beauty created by God'. Private showings could be arranged for modest ladies, claimed the publicity disingenuously.[12]

'No, they don't move'

A somewhat more suggestive spectacle was available for gentlemen. On the principle that anything French was daringly sexy, a certain Mrs Wharton and a 'Professor' Keller (this title was often affected and should not be taken to suggest a connection with a university) put on *Tableaux Vivants* with *Poses Plastiques*, that is nude scenes from history, scripture and mythology. As at London's Windmill Theatre a century later, the participants in these scenes did not move. In the 1840s their nudity was faked by the use of skin-tight pink 'fleshings'. The journalist George Augustus Sala saw such a performance at Saville House in Leicester Square, the centre of London's more tawdry entertainment world. The man representing Adam in the Garden of Eden scene was suddenly arrested as a deserter from the army and marched off with a greatcoat over his fleshings.[13]

Spangles and Sawdust

Astley's Amphitheatre in Westminster Bridge Road was one of the great permanent shows of London. Dickens captured the atmosphere of a visit to Astley's in his novel *The Old Curiosity Shop*:

> what a place it looked, that Astley's; with all the paint, gilding and looking glass; the vague smell of horses suggestive of coming wonders; the curtain that held such glorious mysteries; the clear white sawdust in the circus; the company coming

in and taking their places; the fiddlers looking carelessly up at them while they tuned their instruments. What feverish excitement when the little bell rang and the music began in good earnest

There were clowns, acrobats and conjurors, but the real spectacle was horsemanship. Horses were trained to feign dropping dead, to rise from stage traps and to descend into them, and to sit and eat a meal. The famous exhibition rider Andrew Ducrow often played the horseback hero. His great act was 'Mazeppa's Ride' in which he was bound flat on the horse's back. The most popular performance was 'The Battle of Waterloo', but 'The Burning of Moscow', 'The Crusaders of Jerusalem' and 'The Conquest of Mexico' were among Ducrow's other dramatic compositions. In the summer of 1849, he put on his 'New Grand Equestrian Military Spectacle', subtitled 'Mooltan and Goojerat', or the 'Conquest of the Sikhs', which allowed the audience to share vicariously in that recent victory of British arms. If the depiction was not as accurate as it might have been in a panorama or diorama, the bugle calls and cannon fire at Astley's Amphitheatre made up for it and gave the children, especially, a thrilling treat.

'An increasingly notorious haunt'

In the summer, Vauxhall Gardens and Cremorne Gardens were the places to go. Just behind today's Albert Embankment, Vauxhall's groves, bosky paths, statuary and coloured lanterns, its fireworks on warm nights, its cascades and its balloon ascents were widely mentioned in Victorian fiction. When Thackeray's *Vanity Fair* first appeared in monthly parts in 1847, older readers would indulge in nostalgia as they enjoyed the description of an evening spent there over thirty years earlier by a group of characters in the novel. Its refreshment booths served slices of ham whose thinness was one of the oldest jokes in town. In the 1830s Dickens evoked Vauxhall's magic by night:

> The temples and saloons and cosmoramas and fountains glittered and sparkled before our eyes; the beauty of the lady singers and the elegant deportment of the gentlemen captivated our hearts; a few hundred thousand additional lamps dazzled our senses; a bowl or two of punch addled our brains; and we were happy[14]

Vauxhall had a theatre where one could hear the renowned contralto Madame Vestris, scandalous for having donned breeches in some of her roles, and the famous tenor John Braham sing 'Cherry Ripe', as well as a supper room, an ice house and a remarkable construction known, unpronounceably, as a 'heptaplasiesoptron', which displayed the passion of the age for optical illusions, for it consisted of revolving glass plates reflecting pillars, palm trees, models of serpents and a fountain. In mid-summer Vauxhall put on its 'Waterloo Fête', illuminating the name 'Wellington' with a ducal coronet and laurels. The orchestra played military marches; there was a 21-gun salute and lastly another illumination, this time of the Duke's head in a star surrounded by martial trophies.[15]

Vauxhall Gardens was, however, beginning to be seen as a little tacky. In his novel *Pendennis*, which followed close on *Vanity Fair*, Thackeray gave a more harshly realistic picture of Vauxhall Gardens:

> How dingy the pleasure garden has grown, how tattered the gardens look[16]

Women might be accosted, and there were 'goings-on' in the bushes. Vauxhall Gardens was forced to halve its admission charge. It was certainly going down market, despite its flashy attractions. It had become a magnet for the yob clientele and for young men on the prowl for girls who were happy to be whirled around shrieking in the disreputable new dance, the polka, in which the man, disgracefully, in the eyes of many, held his female partner around her waist. Vauxhall was now described as 'the increasingly notorious haunt of London lowlife'.[17] Complaints multiplied about its vulgarity and the rowdiness of the customers, the high cab fare to get there and the toll charged to cross the bridge, not to speak of the infamously poor quality of the refreshments on sale. Closed finally in 1859, Vauxhall Gardens are recalled today only by Jonathan and Tyers Streets, which bear the name of a manager of the venue in its halcyon eighteenth-century days.

Vauxhall's rival was Cremorne Gardens, just west of Battersea Bridge on the north side of the Thames, which opened in the 1840s. Hundreds came there by riverboat in the summer and paid the one shilling entrance fee. Cremorne boasted a theatre, a bowling saloon and an orchestra. There were wooded paths, delightful bowers and a dancing platform, as well as the ubiquitous pagodas, kiosks, temples and Swiss chalets. Cremorne put on an original show, the Aquatic Tournament, on its lake. This was described by one of the rare Spanish visitors to London, the playwright Ventura de la Vega, who visited Cremorne one evening in 1853. He noted that the lake was ringed with false mountains and there was a harbour and ships. Suddenly the orchestra stopped playing, ships emerged from between the mountains firing rockets and shells. Finally the ships exploded in a multicoloured and patterned conflagration.[18]

When dusk fell late in summer you could buy a half-crown supper in the long banqueting hall and eat it as you admired the firework display and Madame Saqui walking on a sixty-foot high tightrope.[19] During the day there were balloon ascents by Charles Green, billed as the 'aeronautist', whose brightly coloured balloon soared over the capital, sometimes even with an acrobat twirling and swinging from a trapeze suspended beneath the gondola. In the gardens, a certain Herr von Joel yodelled peripatetically.

Cremorne put on a tournament with horses hired from Astley's Amphitheatre and the band of the Life Guards. There were also concerts and a ballet, whose title *L'Amour et la Folie* suggested that it was a little *risqué*. Cremorne was slightly flashy, but it did not decline until much later in the Victorian century when the behaviour of the customers began to provoke complaints from the neighbouring inhabitants. In 1877, having been refused a licence, Cremorne closed down. Lots Road power station stands on its site.

In the Street

Horse-drawn omnibuses were slow, cabs were expensive and traffic jams were monumental, so most people still made their journeys through London on foot. There was a great deal to be seen as one walked. Even though playing football in the streets, prize-fighting and cock-fighting had been prohibited by Acts of Parliament, street shows could be seen everywhere. Men made their living from the pennies which they hoped to collect from spectators as they displayed their menageries of cats, mice and birds living amicably in the same cage, a show called 'Happy Families'. There were five different shows of this nature to be seen in the capital in 1849, the largest with 534 birds and animals in one cage, which was exhibited at a spot near the south end of Waterloo Bridge.

In the street, there were acrobats, jugglers, musicians who could play several instruments at once, the Punch and Judy show, the strongmen, conjurors and fire eaters, and the hawkers of popular poetry about current events, such as, for example, the vast number of sheets of verses about Maria Manning which were offered for sale in the streets while she awaited justice in the summer and autumn of 1849.

All the Fun of the Fair

Greenwich Fair was the best-known of the popular places near London where one could have a good time. With its showgirls in spangly and short dresses, its clowns, its dancing at night, including the intriguingly-titled 'French Chin and Shoulder Dance', its stalls which sold food and cheap toys, the 'raree shows' with their strange exhibits, tin trumpets blasting one's ears, and Richardson's Show, which gave the impatient spectator a tragedy, a pantomime and a comic song all in thirty minutes, you could have a good time if you liked that sort of thing. The German novelist and poet Theodore Fontane noted that Greenwich was rowdy and girls ran about making noise with rattles.[20] In the end, Greenwich was degraded by the stench of cheap liquor, by drunks, and the menacing, swearing and violent London rough.

For the nineteenth-century middle class, Greenwich was where one's servants went. Dickens describes how David Copperfield has to dismiss a maid who went off to Greenwich wearing Mrs Copperfield's bonnet. From central London, Hampstead Heath, which also had a fair, was nearer. Karl Marx, living at 28, Dean Street, Soho, in the 1850s, went there on summer Sundays with his family, and bought ginger beer and cheese at the pub known as Jack Straw's Castle near the Round Pond.

'Well, I come from Alabama with a banjo on my knee'

Another very popular amusement seems, in today's age, distant and distasteful. Yet 'Black and White Minstrels' survived well into the age of television. The first to appear in London were Dan Emmett's Virginia Minstrels, who played to packed audiences at the Adelphi Theatre in the Strand in 1843. They were followed by the Ethiopian Serenaders in 1846 with their songs, dances and jokes and the Banjo and Mr Bones characters.[21] In the streets the buskers who imitated them blacked up, singing 'Old Mr Coon', and 'Buffalo Gals', and rarely omitting the famous 'Oh, Susannah!'

'Hallelujah'

Not all London entertainment was either spectacular or vulgar. A mania for sheet singing swept over the country in the 1840s, started by Joseph Mainzer who came over from Germany in 1841 and devised a catchphrase which sounds as if it belongs to the mid-twentieth century rather than the early part of Queen Victoria's reign: 'Singing for the Millions'. One of the biggest halls for mass singing, also used for political and religious meetings, and those of the temperance and anti-slavery campaigns, was Exeter Hall in the Strand, on the site of the present Strand Palace Hotel.

Public singing was intended to wean the lower classes from drink and to encourage them to be patriotic and industrious. Like the Mechanics' Institutes at which the working man could make up for some of the education that he had not enjoyed in his childhood, it was allied to the contemporary impulse to 'improve the industrious classes'. Yet it seems unlikely that habitual gin or beer drinkers would be attracted to public singing any more than they would be to the Exeter Hall to hear revivalist preachers or sit among the audience of three thousand who listened to Handel's *Messiah* there at Christmas 1848, or Mendelssohn's *Elijah* a year earlier, performed by the Sacred Harmonic Society before the Queen and Prince Albert with a chorus and orchestra of five hundred. The 1840s saw a flood of oratorio performances; Handel and Mendelssohn being the most popular composers. Oratorio was respectable 'the opera of the serious-minded middle classes,' wrote George Augustus Sala.[22]

Concerts with immense orchestras were very popular by mid-century. The moustachioed and white-waistcoated Monsieur Louis-Antoine Jullien, one of the best-known names on the London music scene, was conducting orchestras with between three and four hundred instrumentalists at the Surrey Gardens, a venue which could hold 12,000 people. These concerts were held on summer evenings, ending at dusk, when fireworks were let off. Yet even the most spectacular firework display could not match Jullien's 400-piece orchestra, his three military bands, his three choirs and his Roman march led by twenty trumpeters blowing into instruments three yards long.[23] In the winter, Jullien put on his concerts at Drury Lane Theatre, where the crowd stood or, if there was room, walked about in the pit, hence the name 'promenade' concerts. Herman Melville, who seems rarely to have stayed in of an evening, went to one of these 'Proms' on 6 November 1849, paying a shilling.

'The Management reserves the right ...'

Sophisticated audiences went to the Italian Opera House at Her Majesty's Theatre, on the corner of the Haymarket and Pall Mall. On 4 May 1847 Jenny Lind, 'the Swedish nightingale' made her British début in Meyerbeer's *Robert Le Diable* and was received with acclaim. Her private life was blameless and her voice matchless. Long queues formed to pay the high prices demanded for tickets. Stars like Jenny Lind could command vast fees, but Nowrangee and Merwangee, the Bombay Parsees who wrote an account of their stay in London, thought the English absurd to pay the ballerina Madame Taglioni 150 guineas a night for what they called 'jumping about'.[24]

The Covent Garden theatre was redesigned in 1847 as the Royal Italian Opera House, and opened with Rossini's *Semiramide*, Its reputation was, however, shady, because its bar was frequented by prostitutes. The Theatre Royal, Drury Lane was also notorious for the prostitutes who paraded around its Grand Saloon until the actor William Macready put a stop to their activities when he became the manager in 1841. Both Covent Garden and Drury Lane were very large venues, lacking the intimacy of the smaller houses. Refreshments were on sale during the performances at Drury Lane, which in itself caused disorder. Its pit was furnished with unreserved hard benches. Women roamed around selling apples, oranges, nuts and ginger beer from large baskets, just like Nell Gwyn in the days of Charles II nearly two centuries earlier.

However, behaviour in theatres was changing as were the audiences. In some, conduct was still unrestrained; the audience let off steam by shouting at the actors. Charles Dickens had found the spectators 'ruffianly', swearing, blaspheming and fighting, when he visited Sadler's Wells Theatre in 1841. Later, however, this theatre came under the very firm hand of Samuel Phelps, who strove to make the audience sit and listen to Shakespeare as if they were in church. Sadler's Wells was at the height of its Shakespearian fame in the latter half of the 1840s, *Hamlet* alone being performed repeatedly as well as most of the other plays. The famous actor William Macready was playing the lead in *King Lear* in 1849. The highly-impressed Dickens wrote in *The Examiner* of 27 October that '[the audience] rose in a mass to greet him with a burst of applause that made the building ring'.[25]

Until 1843 Covent Garden and Drury Lane had enjoyed a monopoly of theatre plays. Other halls were allowed to 'give musical performances of a dramatic nature'. They put on operettas and burlettas – musical plays, usually in rhyme – where the speeches grew longer and the musical pieces shorter – but provided there was some music they were not considered to be trespassing on the monopoly enjoyed by the two big theatres. After 1843 when Parliament ended the monopoly the twenty or more other theatres in London could put on plays without music.

Theatre managements responded with superb new halls, and disciplined their audiences into a more subdued mood. A Victorian husband could take his wife to see Douglas Jerrold's play *Black-eyed Susan*, a popular melodrama about a sailor's last-minute reprieve from execution after he strikes an officer in defence of his wife's honour. This was put on at the Marylebone Theatre in Church Street, Paddington, which was by then a well-conducted house. 'The audience laughed and wept with all their hearts', wrote Dickens in *The Examiner* on 12 May 1849, and continued: 'It is a pleasant duty to point out the desserts of this theatre as it is now conducted, and to recommend it.'[26]

'Unhand me, Sir!'

Drury Lane, Covent Garden and the West End Theatres were expensive, but plenty of places would provide a play for sixpence or even less. In 1850, Dickens visited the Royal Victoria Theatre in Lambeth on the south side of the Thames, called since then the 'Old Vic'. He saw a melodrama called *May Morning or the Mystery of 1715, and the Murder*! 'May Morning' turned out to be the name of the main character. In the play the heroine swooned, the heroes were noble and the villains dastardly. The pit cost 6d and the gallery 3d. The house was full. Some of the audience, reported Dickens, were none too clean, but the novelist observed some good-humoured working men with their wives. They had brought their babies too, as well as cold fried fish and stone bottles of drink. Solemn behaviour could hardly be expected of them. People whistled, booed and shouted their way through the evening's entertainment. They would not put up with delays and instructed the scenery-shifters loudly in their duties.[27]

At a somewhat lower level, Dickens also visited the Britannia Saloon in Hoxton, called thus because the only way into the theatre was through the saloon bar of the pub itself. Whole families were enjoying a night out to see the melodrama. Dickens noted that the common people were in the pit and the play was directed at them. They were not shut away in the gallery as in most theatres. Everybody was attentive, despite the ham sandwiches and other comestibles being hawked around the closely-packed and not very sweet-smelling audience.[28]

Herman Melville, the American author, saw Madame Vestris and her husband Charles Mathews on the stage at the Royal Lyceum Theatre in the Strand. He sat in the gallery for a shilling, noting with apparent surprise that the people there were quite well-behaved, although a man went around with a pot and mugs offering 'porter, gents, porter' (the popular beer, later called 'stout'). On the following day, he went to the Princess's Theatre in Oxford Street where he sat in the pit for a shilling.

The 'Penny Gaff'

Those who could not afford even as little as threepence and wanted some entertainment went to the 'Penny Gaff', as it was called. This was a room, sometimes an empty shop front, where bawdy songs and pantomimes were put on every evening. The Penny Gaffs suited the crowds of adolescents who thronged the streets rather than go back to the one or two squalid rooms where their parents quarrelled and a horde of younger children squalled. There were three Penny Gaffs in South London's New Cut alone, putting on shows from 6pm until 11pm. James Grant, who published his book *Sketches in London* in 1838, calculated that 24,000 people attended Penny Gaffs each night.[29] Just like the early cinema, the Penny Gaffs received the blame for juvenile crime. With bare brick walls and wooden joists, a candle-lit stage close to the audience, a crudely-painted backcloth, a couple of fiddlers, and actors who were unable to get any better parts and to whom the owner paid a pittance, the Penny Gaffs put on melodramas with titles such as 'The Red-Nosed Monster and the Tyrant of the Mountains', 'Sweeny Todd the Demon Barber' and 'Maria Marten and the Red Barn'. However, they also staged performances of cut-down versions of Shakespeare's *Hamlet*. This would take a bare half-hour, and was followed by a singsong. *Othello* and *Macbeth* were also favourites. It was the blood and gore that mattered. Like the early Music Halls of which the Penny Gaffs were the predecessors, the actors and the audience exchanged witticisms, obscene insults and the occasional bottle, either shared or thrown.

'Ladies and Gentlemen, at en-o-ormous expense...!'

Towards the end of the early Victorian years, the first Music Halls were opening in South London, which had always been the centre of popular entertainment. The first was the Surrey, later called the Winchester, in Southwark Bridge Road. In 1848 the Canterbury Music Hall opened at 143 Westminster Bridge Road. This was luxuriously fitted out and had a master of ceremonies who announced the 'turns', all of whom were announced as having been engaged 'at eno-o-ormous expense'. The Canterbury heralded a new age, with its Scottish 'Hieland Laddies' and its ribald and buxom female singers. The manager of the Canterbury, the enterprising Charles Morton, introduced Musical Saturday Nights. The entertainment was free but the customers spent so much on food and drink that Morton soon enlarged the hall to accommodate 1,500 spectators, who now paid 6d to sit at tables or 9d in a gallery. It was Morton who later engaged Geoffrey Leybourne to sing his famous ballad 'Champagne Charlie is me name'.[30]

'Damn your eyes'

Husbands, tired of crying children and complaining wives, might go out on their own and spend an extravagant two shillings on the show and supper at the famous Cyder Cellars near Covent Garden. This was one of the song and supper rooms – the Coal-Hole was another and the slightly up-market Evans's a third – open from 10pm to 2am. Only men went. Poached eggs and roast potatoes were the favourite meal. The audience ate, smoked and sang. Percival Leigh's Mr Pips, whose comic journal was published in *Punch*, went to the Cyder Cellars on 10 March 1849. He consumed kidneys and stout, followed by brandy and a cigar. He listened to G.W. Ross perform the famous macabre tale of Sam Hall the Chimney Sweep, with his soot-blackened face, wearing a battered hat, smoking a short clay pipe and leaning over a chair as if over the side of a tumbril taking him to be hanged, cursing the audience:

> I'll see yer all in 'ell
> And I 'opes yer frizzle well,
> Damn yer eyes.

At the Coal-Hole, the German dramatist Theodor Fontane saw a parody of a law court, called *Judge and Jury*. He wrote with considerable penetration:

> The whole business is extremely interesting. Its importance
> lies in the fact that England can tolerate such a parody of its
> highest authorities and its oldest institutions[31]

Improving One's Mind

Upwardly aspiring London people would have made a point of improving their minds by taking advantage of the policies of the administrations of the early Victorian age, which wanted to make public monuments such as St. Paul's Cathedral, Westminster Abbey and the British Museum more accessible to ordinary people. The crowd's behaviour at public events had much improved of late, according to *Punch* and the press. The evangelical or 'serious' mechanic out for the afternoon would avoid the tawdry delights of Greenwich Fair, preferring to admire the contents of the glass cabinets of the British Museum, where several new galleries opened in 1847. As a result, the following year visitors totalled 897,985, compared with 81,228 who had visited the exhibits twenty years earlier.[32]

In Hackney, Victoria Park, lungs for the serried houses of the East End, had opened, while the zoo in Regent's Park had been open since 1828. The manager, David Mitchell, reduced the entrance charge to 6d on Mondays, and had added to the zoo's popularity by acquiring numerous new and fearsome reptiles. The Reverend Greatorex noted in his diary that on 23 July 1855 he went to the zoo and saw a newly-arrived hippopotamus and the new parrot-house. On 2 January that year, he had skated on the Round Pond in Kensington Gardens. And even American bowling was on offer in a place in the Strand.

Journalists like Henry Mayhew, Charles Dickens and George Augustus Sala, reveal that Londoners of all sorts had ample opportunities to amuse themselves, and that the level of entertainment was steadily improving. Nevertheless, it was sharply divided in its appeal to different classes of society. Entertainments were heavily contrasted in the cost of access and attracted very different classes of people. A Penny Gaff cost one penny, while a visit to a panorama or the Royal Polytechnic Institution cost a shilling, that is twelve times as much, and the West End theatre very much more.

However, popular literature and theatre centred on crime and particularly murder. This fascinated the Victorian public and in the first part of the Victorian age, its most notorious example in London was the murder of Patrick O'Connor by Maria and Frederick Manning.

Chapter 10

Crime, Police, Detectives and the Manning Murder

Insufficient policing of the vast and increasing size of the urban area, added to mass migration into London, the shortage of suitable housing, and extreme poverty, led to the growth of a universe of crime in the capital.

Burglary and housebreaking were common. Affrays and violent street robbery were frequent, but most crime consisted of petty theft. Pickpocketing of watches and wallets was common, as was shoplifting, aided by women's voluminous clothing. Even children were at risk of becoming the prey of thieves called 'child skinners'. 'Good Mrs Brown' in Chapter Six of Dickens's *Dombey and Son* strips young Florence Dombey. 'I want that pretty frock, Miss Dombey,' says she, 'and that little bonnet, and a petticoat or two, and anything else you can spare. Come! Take 'em off.' At the same time, a large proportion of London's criminals were themselves children. Orphaned, abandoned and neglected, some of them became skilled pickers of pockets, like Dickens's 'Artful Dodger'.

Middle-class people thought it wise to arm themselves. When the Carlyles' house was burgled in 1852, the police told Mrs Carlyle that they could not catch the thieves, who would have sold the stolen articles at once. After that, whenever her husband was away, Jane Carlyle slept with a pair of loaded pistols beside her.[1]

When Robert Peel became Home Secretary in 1822, murder and other criminal and often violent behaviour had reached so dangerous a level that it was decided to establish a police force This was despite the widespread opposition to authority by those who were convinced that freedom to do what they liked was their birthright, and that the creation of a police force on Continental European models would inevitably lead to arbitrary arrest, the end of freedom of speech and of trial by jury. Those who were hostile to the new institution also claimed to be satisfied with the existing corrupt and inefficient system of parish watchmen, and with the 'Bow Street Runners' who, like a detective agency, pursued malefactors on behalf of the magistrates but also acted privately for individuals. The Bow Street Runners were often accused of neglecting their duty to the public and associating with the criminal world.[2]

Peel's contrary view was that a civilian police force, though disciplined and uniformed, would obviate the need to call out armed troops to restore the peace, and at the same time would be more efficient than the existing systems for catching criminals. Despite the opposition, the Bill to establish the Metropolitan Police Force was approved on 19 June 1829.[3] Often known as the 'new police', the 'Met' as it came to be known, was to be run by two 'Commissioners', retired Colonel Charles Rowan and Richard Mayne, a barrister. Importantly, the police were to be unarmed and their purpose was the prevention of crime, the security of persons and property and the tranquillity of the streets. They were certainly not to be quasi-military and not to wear anything like an army uniform, but rather a dark-blue civilian coat with tails and a black top hat which was strengthened both to protect the wearer and, it was rumoured, to provide something to stand on when the policeman needed to look over walls.[4] The behaviour of the constables was to be polite, unmilitary, quiet and determined, in such a manner as to attract the support of bystanders if needed.

Peel's vision of a civilian police force was successful. When the German writer Theodor Fontane visited London in 1848, by which time there were police forces over almost all of the country, he noted that the British police were: 'not so intolerably abusive as in the land of gendarmes ... they don't clatter about with a four-foot sword'.[5] Presumably he was thinking of police in France and Germany. A Spanish visitor to the British capital in 1853 was amazed by the absence of soldiers in the capital's streets. He was struck to see, in contrast to Madrid, that policemen were unarmed and that there were no bureaucratic controls requiring visitors to register with the authorities or display their passports. No official asked you your business. He realised that there was certainly a downside to such freedoms, namely that criminals could not easily be traced, but he thought – perhaps naively – that London held few malefactors and that they were soon captured.[6]

The first five divisions of the 'Met' went on duty at 6pm on Tuesday, 29 September 1829. Known affectionately as 'bobbies' or 'peelers', after their founder, Sir Robert Peel, the neutral word for them was and still is 'coppers', possibly because they 'copped' or caught criminals. Those who disliked them called the constables 'bluebottles', because of their uniform, while Londoners' backward slang reversed the word 'police' and pronounced it 'ecilop' or 'slop', a word still around in the 1860s as the educational pioneer Quintin Hogg recalled many years later. He had tried to recruit a couple of adolescent crossing sweepers to teach them to read. Spotting a policeman, the boys shouted 'kool ecilop' and ran away.[7]

The Met was independent of the local parish vestries. It was the only body that covered London under the direct authority of the Home Office for seven miles around Charing Cross, extended in 1837 to fifteen miles. Perhaps the nature of the complaints which were now being made about the police reflected just how much they were valued. Rather than accusing them of being the authoritarian arm of a tyrannical government, the complaint now was that the police were not doing their job of crime prevention properly. On 27 January 1849 *Punch* grumbled that the police were never to be seen when they were needed because they were courting servant girls down in the areas in front of houses. They ought, wrote the anonymous wit, to put a sign on the railings with an arrow to say that 'Police Constable B96 is here'. 'What adds to the audacity of this crime,' pronounced the *Illustrated London News* of 4 August 1849, 'is that it was committed within a stone's throw of the police station of this district.' After a series of crimes in South London, *The Times* of 28 October of the same year asked 'Where are the police in Lambeth?'

Promotion in the London police was to be from the ranks. Salary was only a guinea (£1.1s.) for the six twelve-hour days per week that a constable would be on duty. If he worked hard he might become a sergeant at a few shillings more, but even an inspector's salary was only £100 per year, which did not provide for more than a very lower middle-class lifestyle. This was, nevertheless, a regular wage and policemen would in due course receive a pension. However, they risked injury and even death in London's rough areas. A copper was strictly disciplined, wore an uncomfortable uniform, and was at risk from every violent criminal in the capital, or a thug like Dickens's Bill Sikes, capable of murder if it would help him avoid a long prison sentence breaking stones on Dartmoor or transportation as a convict to Australia.

Detectives

Keeping public order was one thing: detecting and arresting criminals was another. In the early years of the police service, detective work was carried out by police constables in plain clothes. In 1842 Daniel Good murdered his wife at Putney, just over six miles from central London. He fled and for a couple of weeks until his arrest he seemed to be always one step ahead of the police, which led to acerbic remarks in the press. Consequently, a detective department was set up in the capital with two inspectors and two sergeants. Its office was in Scotland Yard, which gave rise to the world-famous title of the Metropolitan Police's criminal investigation department or C.I.D. Chamber's *Journal* noted:

> Intelligent men have been recently selected to form a body called "the detective police"... at times the detective policeman attires himself in the dress of ordinary individual[8]

An aura of efficiency and admiration for the detective branch was created by the Manning murder case, which would occupy public attention almost to the exclusion of everything else in the late summer and autumn of 1849.

''Orrible Murder in Bermondsey!'

Turning right off Tooley Street, which runs along the south side of the Thames, brings one into Bermondsey, a typical inner part of London. Once, children played in the streets, which were lined with stalls and loud with the rattling of wheels on the cobblestones, the cries of the coalman, the milkman and street vendors. At night, especially in winter, the streets were dark. Shopfronts and house windows were shuttered. The few gas lamps cast a dim, yellowish light. But the gin palaces and public houses brought a riot of sudden noise and light when their doors opened and their carousing customers poured out, bidding each other loud farewells before dispersing to their cold, dark homes.

Nearly two centuries later, the streets are eerily silent. There are no stalls; nobody bawls his wares. Children play elsewhere. The old pubs have been replaced by expensive restaurants, and the people lunching in them wear smart clothes, speak into mobile phones, and park expensive cars in the gutter where in early Victorian times shabby men and worn-out women offered cheap goods for sale. The area has been colonised by the public relations consultants, the lawyers and the property men, while the older inhabitants have been corralled away into public housing estates. They do their shopping in distant malls. The little shops no longer exist, while the fancy offerings of the local markets suit neither their taste nor their pockets.

Continuing, one comes to what was, before the bombing of the 1939-1945 war, the centre of the Bermondsey leather trade. In 1849, close to the corner of Guy Street, stood a row of newly-built two-storey villas. The terrace was called Miniver Place.

In early Victorian London people usually rented their homes. Maria and Frederick Manning, who had been married for two years, took a year's tenancy of No.3, Miniver Place. Frederick was about 30 and Maria 28. The rent was not mentioned at their trial but for a house of that type, it would have been about £22 per year plus the extra charges called the Poor Rate and the Church Rate. It came to a total that they could not afford. Frederick, whose previous business attempts had failed, largely because of his addiction to brandy, had a job as a salesman for a stationery firm in Holborn, which paid him £2 a week plus 5 per cent commission. They needed to find a sub-tenant, so they invited Patrick O'Connor, a tall Irishman of about fifty, who had been Maria's lover before her marriage and was suspected to have maintained relations with her afterwards, to occupy part of the house. He agreed and then went back on his word, so the Mannings had to ask William Massey, a medical student at the nearby Guy's Hospital, to take his place.

The Mannings had some capital, but their income was insufficient for even a middle class standard of living. O'Connor, in contrast, was a well-salaried official in the Customs and Excise Service, as well as a moneylender who owned railway shares. Maria bore a grudge against him for not marrying her and also suspected that he was having affairs with other women.

The Mannings conspired to murder the Irishman and to rob him of his cash and shares. On 25 July 1849 Frederick bought a crowbar; the next day the couple ordered a bushel of quicklime. On the 28th they told their sub-tenant to leave, saying that they intended to spend some time out of London. On the morning of Thursday, 9 August, Maria bought a spade.

The Mannings invited O'Connor to dine that same evening at half past five. Somewhat earlier, two of his acquaintances saw him walking across London Bridge on his way to No. 3, Miniver Place. Only his murderers saw him alive after that.

The afternoon was still hot when O'Connor arrived. Maria suggested that he might like to have a cooling wash in the basement kitchen. She led him over a hole where the Mannings had lifted a flagstone to dig a pit for his corpse, telling him that it had been excavated for some work which was needed on the drains. As he bent over the sink to cool his head and neck, one of the Mannings, very probably Maria, shot him through the back of his head with a pistol which Frederick had recently bought at a gunsmith's. O'Connor fell, According to the confession which Frederick made later in the death cell, the Irishman was still breathing stertorously, Frederick, now able at last to discharge the hatred he felt towards his wife's lover, raised the crowbar (in his confession in the death cell, he said it was a ripping chisel but the weapon, described as a crowbar, was discovered some time afterwards at Lewes railway station, where it had been left to be collected by a 'Mrs. Smith') high above his head, and finished the dying man off in a paroxysm of anger.[9] The police surgeon estimated that O'Connor had suffered seventeen savage blows to the head. Then the Mannings tied the legs of their victim up behind him, bound them to his trunk with strong twine and manhandled his corpse into the pit under the stone-flagged floor, pouring over it the quicklime which at once began to eat O'Connor's body away. Some journalists later wrote imaginatively that the couple then sat down calmly to eat the goose that Maria had cooked, ostensibly for the three of them to enjoy.

Later that evening, Maria went to O'Connor's lodgings in Mile End, where the Irishman rented a bedroom and a sitting room over a shop on the corner of Greenwood Street. O'Connor's landlady told the court that her tenant had instructed her to allow Maria into his rooms even when he was not there. Maria rifled his possessions, taking all the cash she could find and a number of share certificates,

Strangely enough, the Mannings were in no great hurry to flee, nor do they seem to have laid their plans with care. O'Connor's workmates reported him as missing when he did not appear at work the next and the following day. Since he had been seen crossing London Bridge, apparently on his way to dine at the Mannings, his colleagues reported this to the police. The police asked Mrs Manning if she knew where he was. Maria could not say. No, he had not eaten a meal with them, she said, which was strange because he had been seen on the way. On the following Monday, 13 August, a policeman again visited the house. Maria, he reported, seemed nervous. She confirmed that she had invited O'Connor for a meal, so he might well have been seen on London Bridge on his way over the river to Bermondsey, but she said that he often changed his mind at the last moment.

O'Connor's friend, William Flynn, was a persistent man. On the Monday he visited the Irishman's lodgings in Mile End and discovered that Maria had been there and that the cashbox had been emptied. Then he went to 3, Miniver Place and learned that, earlier on that same Monday, Maria had left in a cab with several large boxes and trunks. Flynn returned the next day, gained entrance to the house and found it unoccupied. On the next morning a second-hand furniture dealer, Mr Bainbridge, came round to collect the furniture which Frederick Manning had sold him for £13. Bainbridge told Flynn that Frederick Manning had been staying with him and had just left.

As yet there was no suspicion of foul play. No dead body had been found. O'Connor might have left his lodgings hurriedly and arranged to meet the Mannings, or perhaps only Maria, somewhere else. But by the Friday, 17 August, already eight days after the murder, and with no trace of the Mannings nor of O'Connor, the police began to make serious enquiries.

That's a toe!

Friday, 17 August 1849 was a sultry day. Police Constables Henry Barnes and James Burton, who had been sent to search the house thoroughly, had removed their uncomfortable, if protective, reinforced hats, their heavy brass-buttoned, stiff-collared blue coats in whose tails they kept their truncheons, and their black-varnished belts, on which hung their bull's eye lamps for the night patrols and the rattle which they 'sprang' to call for aid.

They dug fruitlessly in the garden, and then sought shelter indoors from the sun. It was Barnes who spotted that the basement kitchen was exceptionally clean and scrubbed, and that the mortar around one of the flagstones was new and still soft when they dug into it with a pocket knife. The policemen borrowed tools from some nearby labourers, and lifted the flagstone. Under it were layers of damp mortar and of hurriedly spread earth. Soon a human toe appeared and then the rest of the gruesome corpse, almost unrecognisable after more than a week under a coat of quicklime. A local surgeon, closely observed by an eager journalist, lifted away the skull and found several fractures in it. Reaching into the repellent object, in which the brain had already decomposed, he removed a set of false teeth. Just behind the right frontal bone of the skull, the police surgeon, who had been hurriedly summoned, found the bullet which had been fired into O'Connor's head. Shortly afterwards, the dentist who had made the false teeth identified them as belonging to his patient, the late Patrick O'Connor. It was now a murder case.

Hue and Cry

The word *sensation* was being frequently used in crime reporting to embody the spectacular character of the particular offence. The Manning case was the most sensational of its time.[10] It was unlike any others, in that the murderers were a London lower middle class married couple and the motive was greed. Few thought that the shambling alcoholic Frederick Manning had taken the lead. Maria was that hated figure, the woman who murdered. She was not a starving single mother or ill-treated wife, who could often rely on the sympathy of the jury. She was foreign; she had an aura of cold, arrogant sexiness about her, and it was probably she who had used a pistol to shoot her victim. Not only the murder but their flight on the railway, their capture using the telegraph and intelligent detective work, and the trial and execution of the murderers would 'go viral' in early Victorian London.

It was mid-August. The hunt was now on. Where were the Mannings? At first, a newspaper story was the origin of a red herring. An emigrant ship, the *Victoria,* had been lying in London docks, due to sail that same Friday, 17 August. A reporter questioned the baggage-master, who told him that there was luggage on board marked with the name Manning. Messages flashed to and fro on the telegraph and late that evening, Admiral Capel, in command of the naval base at Portsmouth, acted at the request of the police and the Home Office and ordered a fast frigate, the *Fire Queen*, to chase and stop the *Victoria*. At 1.45am on the Saturday, the *Victoria* was boarded, but the Mrs Manning who was on board was an American lady named Rebecca and not Maria.

Since Maria Manning had been seen leaving 3, Miniver Place the previous Monday afternoon in a cab. Detective Sergeant Shaw patiently tracked the driver down. When at last he found the man, whose name was William Kirk, he verified carefully that it was at 3, Miniver Place that he had picked her up. If defence counsel could suggest at a future trial that it was not from that address that Kirk had picked up a passenger in his cab, the case against Maria would collapse. Shaw then questioned Kirk in detail. It had probably never occurred to Maria Manning that detectives would interrogate the cabbie. Where had he taken her? Kirk said that he had taken 'a female of very respectable exterior' (this sounds like the police form of words rather than those which the cabbie would have used), to London Bridge, the nearby railway terminus. On the way, she had told him to stop at a stationer's where she had bought some labels. At the left-luggage office in London Bridge Station, she had asked for pen and ink and written on the labels 'Mrs Smith. Passenger for Paris. To be left until called for'. Detective Inspector Haynes went to the station and, though he had no power of compulsion, persuaded officials to allow him to open the trunks. In them were Maria's clothes. Was she laying a false trail? Or had she indeed taken the train and the ferry to France? Perhaps she did intend to go to Paris. It would probably have been a wise thing to do, and she could have continued to her native Switzerland. British consuls in the French Channel ports were asked to keep their eyes open for her. An inspector and a sergeant went to Paris, where the French police cooperated by searching the hotels and keeping a lookout at the railway stations.

It would have taken longer to trace Maria had she not unthinkingly re-engaged William Kirk's cab to drive her across the capital from London Bridge to Euston Square Station. Here she had stayed the night, perhaps taking a room at the Adelaide or the Victoria Hotel, both of which stood close by the station. Next morning, at 6.15, she left for Edinburgh.

At Euston, she had again unwittingly aided the detectives by labelling her remaining large number of trunks and boxes with the name 'Mrs Smith'. The porters who had loaded her baggage, for which Maria paid an excess charge, into the luggage van identified the owner as a woman and gave a description of her, which tallied with that given by the cab driver. Consequently, the detectives easily discovered that she had taken the train to Edinburgh. Inspector Haynes at once telegraphed her description to the Edinburgh police.

The expensive telegraph had not been used much by the police within London, though it had, famously, been employed to arrest the murderer Tawell four years earlier. Usually, the police sent a courier on horseback with 'route papers' around the various London divisional headquarters with information on recent crimes, lists and descriptions of items of stolen property and of wanted criminals. Each division added its own information and passed the details on.[11] But it would have taken twenty-four hours to send Maria's description by train to Edinburgh and she might have moved on by then. The 'wire', in contrast, reached Edinburgh within minutes.

Edinburgh police superintendent Richard Moxey was alert. When he received the telegraphic message or 'telegram' from London he saw at once that the description of Maria which it communicated corresponded to that of a woman who had been brought to his notice that very morning, Tuesday, 21 August, by the Edinburgh stockbrokers to whom Maria had tried to sell some of O'Connor's share certificates. Apparently also unaware of the efficiency of the mails, she did not know that on the morning she visited the stockbrokers, they had received a circular warning them not to deal in certain railway shares which had been stolen in London. The stockbroker noticed her French accent, although she said that her father's name was Robertson and that he lived in Glasgow. He notified the police at once. Maria had given the stockbrokers a note of the address where she had taken rooms, so the police had no difficulty in finding her. As she sat trying to compose herself with the aid of a glass or two of wine, the police searched her luggage and found seventy-three gold sovereigns, a banknote for fifty pounds, a five-pound note and six ten-pound notes: £188 in all, though it turned out that more than a third of this belonged to the Mannings themselves. Maria also had O'Connor's French railway shares and some certificates that he had been holding for her. She was at that point arrested for murder. Maria had made it easy for the police to discover that she had fled to Edinburgh. Her eagerness to cash in the share certificates had led the detectives straight to her.

As for Frederick, his addiction to the brandy bottle led him to boast and to draw attention to himself. He left No.3, Miniver Place on Tuesday, 14 August. The house was now empty, probably without even a bed, so Frederick slept at the Bainbridges', the dealer to whom he had sold the furniture. In any case, to sleep alone in the house where O'Connor's body was rapidly decaying under the kitchen floor would have been hard for even a stronger-minded man than Frederick Manning. On the Wednesday, he left the Bainbridge house. He travelled from the Waterloo railway terminus to the port of Southampton, stayed at a pub for a few hours and then sailed on the midnight ferry to the Channel Island of Jersey. Foolishly, he attracted attention in the hotel at St Helier, capital of the island, by his overbearing behaviour and his heavy drinking. He talked about going to France, a destination which the police were already investigating, but seems to have changed his mind. Did he know where Maria was? Had they made plans to flee to France and had Maria deceived him by going to Scotland but leaving clues which suggested she was indeed going to France? Had they made plans to meet when the hue and cry died down? Possibly, but, if they had, Maria had played him false, taken the money and abandoned him. No message between the two was ever discovered. She would not even speak to him as they stood side by side in the dock.

Frederick Manning continued to attract attention in the bar of the hotel, as he put away large quantities of brandy. It was almost as though he was consumed with guilt at the horrendous crime in which he had participated, and subconsciously wanted to be found. Yet, when he met a man who knew him from his home town, Taunton in Somerset, Manning decided that it would be safer to leave St Helier and take a room in a rural cottage. In any case, despite his loud boasting about how much money he had and what he intended to do with it, by then his funds must have been running low. He had left London with no more than the thirteen pounds that Mr Bainbridge had paid him for the furniture. Maria had taken their savings with her.

The police had begun their tracking of Frederick by questioning the cabbie who had driven him to Waterloo. He remembered Frederick's odd instruction to take the long way around when they could have gone straight along the Cut. Nevertheless, nobody at Waterloo or on the train remembered Manning, and the police were sent on a number of wild-goose chases up and down the line of the London and South Western Railway. However, they were fortunate enough to receive a report that he had been spotted on the ferry to Jersey by a woman who recognised him from when he had once stayed on Guernsey, another Channel Island. The police concentrated their attention on Jersey. Soon the local police, notified from London, discovered him quietly drinking himself into a stupor in a dwelling called Prospect Cottage. In the close society of the island, suspicions were aroused by Manning's excessive drinking and rude behaviour. The police went to the cottage. Late on Monday, 27 August, Detective Sergeant Langley and Constable Lockyer, from London, accompanied by Monsieur Chevalier, head of the Jersey police, arrested Manning as he lay in bed. Among his first words were 'Is the wretch taken?' This was what the newspapers reported, copying the police report, though he might well have said 'bitch'. When he learned that Maria was in custody he said 'Thank God. I am glad of it; that will save my life. She is the guilty party. I am as innocent as a lamb.'

Of course, he was not at all innocent, for even if Maria had fired the shot, it was never seriously alleged that anyone but Frederick had battered in their victim's skull with a crowbar. Frederick chattered to the detectives freely, accusing Maria. What he said would be read out at the trial as part of the police evidence. It would prejudice Maria's defence even though the judge advised the jury that they should ignore Frederick's words because in law, whatever he said was inadmissible evidence against his wife.

Early on 31 August Frederick, nonchalantly smoking a cigar, walked with the detectives through the streets of St. Helier to the harbour before boarding the ship to England. On the crossing, the police reported, he continued to chatter nervously. From Southampton he was taken by train to London. The police took him off the train at Vauxhall, shortly before Waterloo, probably to avoid the press of curious spectators. At Stone's End police station in Southwark, Frederick was charged with the murder of Patrick O 'Connor.

Thus, two and a half weeks after the murder, thanks to the post and the telegraph, as well as the alertness and hard work of the detective force, Maria and Frederick Manning had been arrested and brought back to London.

Dickens and the Detectives

It was probably the successful tracking down of the Mannings that impelled Charles Dickens to publish three long essays in his journal *Household Words* in high praise of the Metropolitan Police detectives.[12] The first article was by W.H. Wills, the sub-editor, who called it 'The Modern Science of Thief-taking'. Appearing on 13 July 1850, it compares the detective to an art critic, who knows who has painted the picture by the manner of its execution. In the same way, the detective can identify the criminal by the nature of the crime and the way it has been carried out. Dickens's own two articles, titled 'A Detective Police Party' (1) and (2), were written after Scotland Yard, as the detective branch was now habitually known, recognising the value of good publicity, had accepted the novelist's invitation to send a number of its detectives to the offices of *Household Words* in Wellington Street off the Strand. Here they sat smoking cigars and drinking brandy, though very abstemiously, as Dickens points out, and discussing their profession. Dickens gives the detectives barely concealed names, but present were the famous Inspector Field and a number of detective sergeants, including Thornton and Shaw, who had been involved in the Manning case.

Dickens, who idolised the detective force, noted that every man quietly took in the room and the editorial staff at a glance. Each one was an expert at pursuing a different class of crime, from housebreaking to selling stolen goods or 'fencing', and from safe-breaking to juvenile delinquency. Each deferred to his colleagues' superior knowledge and experience.

Detective Sergeant Thornton, who had boarded the *Victoria* when the Mannings were suspected of intending to flee to America, described going below to the lower deck of the ship, accompanied by the captain with a lamp in his hand, and speaking to the Mrs Manning who was on board, asking her to turn her head towards the light so that he could see that she was not the Maria Manning for whom he was searching. Sergeant 'Witchem' (really Jonathan 'Jack' Whicher), the original of Wilkie Collins's Sergeant Cuff, gave a long account of his detective work in running a well-known horse thief to ground.

The skill of the detectives often lay in their pretending to be what they were not and in playing dangerous roles, in one case for ten weeks. The detectives were keen, knowing and perceptive, professional, courageous and competent at their jobs, with the appearance of living lives of 'strong mental excitement', wrote Dickens.

Dickens's hero was Inspector Charles Frederick Field, since 1846 Head of the Detective Department of Scotland Yard. A man five foot ten in height, tall for the time, of massive build and ebullient personality, he had acted on the stage in his youth, which particularly endeared him to Dickens, who loved amateur theatricals, Field had been one of the first recruits to the new police, which he had joined in 1829 at the age of 25. On his first night on patrol in the dangerous St. Giles area, Field arrested a notorious robber. Within four years, and aided by the rapid turnover of the first recruits to the police, Field became an inspector, based in L Division in Lambeth.[13] Inspector Bucket in Dickens's novel *Bleak House* was modelled on Field. Introduced in Chapter Twelve on a sultry evening in Mr Tulkinghorn's house in Lincoln's Inn Fields, Bucket is described as attentive and composed. Dickens writes that 'He is a stoutly-built, steady looking, sharp-eyed man in black, of about the middle age'. Bucket and Mr Snagsby, the stationer, set out for Tom All-Alone's rookery, Bucket pretends not to know any policeman he passes in case an observant criminal realises that he is a plain-clothes detective. In the rookery, however, he is well-known and there is no need for concealment, so for added protection he calls on a constable at the beginning of the fetid street that leads into the slum. Provided with lanterns, they walk through the mud and foul puddles, keeping well away from the houses where people are known to be dying of infectious disease. Bucket speaks to men and women of all kinds with absolute self-confidence, in a jocular and even patronising tone, just as Dickens portrays Inspector Field doing in a piece he published in *Household Words* on 14 June 1851 in which the novelist describes a tour he made of the slums accompanied by the same famous inspector.[14] From the St. Giles rookery they went south over the Thames to Southwark, then crossed the river again to visit the Ratcliff Highway, with its sailors' taverns and brothels. According to Dickens's account, the brutal roughs of the district slunk off when warned to make way by the detective and the burly constables who walked with them. Self-possession and aplomb seem to have been the qualities that most struck Dickens in his descriptions of the London criminal detectives. Inspector Field, whose 'well-known hand has collared half the people here', is evidently feared. All the common thieves, local bullies and whores seek to propitiate him. Nobody would have lifted a finger to protect anybody from arrest by him.

Back in the fictional portrayal of Field in *Bleak House*, Mademoiselle Hortense, the French maid, is now introduced. Dickens based her on Maria Manning. He presents her as 'sufficiently good-looking', with an intense expression on her face and a harsh tone to her voice:

> My Lady's maid is a Frenchwoman of two-and-thirty, from somewhere in the southern country between Avignon and Marseilles – a large-eyed brown woman with black hair, who would be handsome but for a certain feline mouth

Hortense is proud, imperious and, like Maria Manning, has a tendency to violence. She shoots the lawyer Tulkinghorn because he refuses to pay her money which she claims is due to her. In Hortense's violent gestures and slightly imperfect English, Dickens, who may have attended the Manning trial, perhaps left posterity a record of Maria Manning's voice.[15]

'An extremely fine woman'

Popular rumour rendered Maria Manning both scarlet in her immorality and black in her cruelty. The press, unrestricted at the time by rules about what they could say before an accused person was actually found guilty, called her 'Lady Macbeth' and 'Jezebel'. By the power of the newspapers and the street balladeers, this woman became larger than life. Her French-accented voice, genuine in contrast with the fake Spanish accent of Lola Montes, who was being accused of bigamy at about the same time, her elegant neatness, her stillness as she stood in the dock, her aplomb, silence and apparently cold arrogance, combined to weave a legend about her.

Maria was born Marie de Roux in a village near Lausanne in Switzerland, where her father was the postmaster.[16] Her Swiss origin led people to think not so much of cuckoo clocks and picturesque chalets as of the notorious Swiss manservant François Courvoisier, who had cut his employer's throat and was hanged outside Newgate prison on 6 July 1840. Some of the press even put about the rumour that Maria was related to him.

Maria was described as being about thirty years old. She was five feet seven inches tall, which was a good height for a woman at the time. She was well-built, with a fresh complexion and long dark hair. The expression 'a fine figure of a woman', often used in press stories, was very fitting.

The sensationalist accounts published at the time of the Manning trial at the Central Criminal Court or Old Bailey make it difficult to sort out fact from fiction, especially when they discussed Maria's early life and tried to show that even then she had displayed the qualities expected of a savage yet seductive murderess. Robert Huish, whom the distinguished *Quarterly Review* described as an 'obscure and unscrupulous scribbler', was the author of the longest and best-known of these accounts: *The Progress of Crime, or: The Authentic Memoirs of Marie Manning*. The book was a collection of penny chapters written and hawked about the streets during the Manning trial. Huish narrated the possibly apocryphal tale that Marie, which was her real name, was engaged by an Irish couple who were touring Switzerland. The wife was impressed by Marie's ability to dress her hair, while the husband was attracted by the Swiss girl's beauty. Back in Ireland, the wife caught her husband and Marie in *flagrante delicto*. Marie was dismissed on the spot. The gentleman offered to set her up as his mistress in a house of her own, but Marie made off to London to collect a legacy. Here Huish linked his fictional account with the truth, for Marie had indeed been contacted by a London solicitor in connection with a bequest.

What is certain, however, is that, in about 1842 Marie, now in her early twenties, was taken on as a personal maid by Lady Palk, whose husband, Sir Lawrence, was a Member of Parliament. When Lady Palk died in 1846, Marie was engaged as personal maid to Lady Evelyn Blantyre, daughter of Harriet, Duchess of Sutherland. The Duchess was a stately and beautiful woman, who held the important royal office of Mistress of the Robes, so Marie may have been summoned to help out, perhaps even at Windsor Palace, with her not inconsiderable dressmaking skills.

Marie later called herself Maria, probably pronounced Ma-ry- a, because it sounded less foreign than Marie. She was competent and energetic, ambitious and self-confident. She was well-suited to her occupation, for ladies' maids were high up in the pecking order of servants, and enjoyed about the same status as the butler and the cook. As a personal maid, Marie would accompany Lady Blantyre everywhere she went. Most reports said that she met her victim, Patrick O'Connor, on a cross-Channel steamer in 1846 during one of Lady Blantyre's trips to some elegant Continental resort. O'Connor was tall and well-spoken, though over twenty years older than Marie. Journalists speculated wildly, though one may imagine that the older man relaxed in Marie's company and perhaps had a glass or two with her in the ship's saloon. A bachelor of sober habits and over fifty years of age, O'Connor did not often get the chance to talk to comely young women, especially one with an attractive French accent, which reminded him of Madame Celeste, at that time a French actress on the contemporary London stage. Marie made up her mind. She did not want to remain a lady's maid all her life. She was realistic enough to know that she was not going to marry much higher than herself on the social scale. Despite the difference in age, O'Connor was a good catch.

The Irishman seemed to be an ardent suitor, and followed Marie to London. She for her part assumed that they were engaged but he was slow in suggesting a date for the wedding. Marie complained about this in letters which O'Connor unchivalrously showed to his friends, which is how the newspapermen got to know about their contents. 'You never speak of marriage. Of what good is it to continue our correspondence?' wrote Marie plaintively.

Whether Marie and O'Connor were lovers in the sexual sense was never openly discussed, though the judge at her trial strongly hinted at it. However,

168

later on, after her unhappy marriage to Frederick Manning in May 1847, Marie ran away and lived briefly with O'Connor as 'Mr and Mrs Johnson'. It is not unlikely, then, that they had been intimate earlier.

As a lady's maid nothing, however private, would have been hidden from Marie. She would have been aware of the love affairs that took place in high society. When a lady's maid helped her mistress to undress before retiring to bed, the complications of wrongly united buttons and buttonholes and unmatched hooks and eyes would reveal if Milady had dressed herself without aid after a secret tryst with a lover during the day. In the early years of the new Queen's reign, the looseness of morals of the later Regency period had not yet been overwhelmed by Victorian austerity. Society drawing-rooms still echoed with the scandal of George Norton's legal action in the summer of 1836 against the Prime Minister, Lord Melbourne, whom he sued for *crim.con* or alienating the affections of his wife Caroline, a society beauty.

Now Marie Manning herself had become the talk of the town.

Chapter 11

Trial and Execution

Women who Murdered

When a woman committed a murder, the victim was not infrequently her newborn child. In 1849 Hannah Sandler, desperate with hunger, killed her child and had her death sentence commuted. She was one of many sometimes mentally deficient and starving single mothers who drowned their newborn infants and were usually treated with relative clemency by the courts.

Between 1847 and 1852, however, there was an epidemic of murders of adults by women. Thirteen were hanged for the crime and a further nine reprieved.[1] On 28 April 1849, *Punch* remarked that there had been six hangings of female poisoners in the previous six weeks alone. 1849, in effect, was an outstanding year for murderesses: Sarah Thomas, Mary Ball, Charlotte Harris, Rebecca Smith and Mary Ann Geering were all tried and sentenced. Sarah Thomas had murdered her employer. Charlotte Harris had killed her husband with arsenic. She wanted another man and married him, foolhardily, on the day of her first husband's funeral. Since she was pregnant the death sentence was commuted to transportation to Australia for life, Mary Ball caught her husband spying on her and her lover. Rebecca Smith poisoned eight of her children; there was no mercy for her. Women poisoners had proliferated in recent years. Wives poisoned their husbands and mothers their grown-up sons and daughters in order to claim the burial insurance, which would produce a small surplus after the interment. Women murderers were especially loathed because they appeared to betray the very nature of Victorian womanhood. A murderess was seen as an unsexed monster. She could not be a real woman because it was thought that no woman who had the sentiments and emotions proper to her sex could bring herself to commit murder, especially in the premeditated and often long drawn out way that was characteristic of poisoning.

The extraordinary number of murders by women suggested that fear of hanging did not seem to be a deterrent. Perhaps, it was thought, it would be better to make it harder to obtain poison. Arsenic, in particular, was

170

far too easy to buy. It was cheap, colourless, odourless and soluble. *Punch* published a cartoon on 8 September 1849 with the title 'Fatal Facility, or Poisons for the asking', in which a lisping child peeping over the counter asks the chemist:

> Please, mithter, will you be so good as to fill this bottle again
> with Lod'num, and let Mother have another pound and a half
> of arsenic for the rats?

How do you plead?

The accusation against Maria Manning was unique for the times. There were two prisoners in the dock, and they were middle class and married to each other. Maria had not used poison, the usual weapon of the premeditating murderess. O'Connor had been shot in the head and beaten to death with a blunt instrument. The motive of the murder was to seize O'Connor's money, which was also an original circumstance, for if a woman murdered her lover, it was usually out of jealousy.

On Thursday, 25 and Friday, 26 October 1849, the Mannings stood trial amid intense and feverish public interest. Throughout the weeks while they were in gaol, on trial, and awaiting execution, *The Times* carried 72 articles about them. So great were the notoriety of the circumstances and the fascination aroused by the press descriptions of Maria that seats were reserved at the Old Bailey for the ambassadors of several foreign countries. All eyes were on her as she was led into the dock. The reporters carefully listed the details of her clothes. She wore a close-fitting black dress, together with a multi-coloured shawl in which blue predominated, set off by primrose gloves and a white lace veil. It seemed that Maria wanted to have her dignified, modest and elegant appearance noted by all as she stood motionless in the dock during all that day and the following. Did she relish being the centre of attention? Undoubtedly, but perhaps also she judged that her demeanour was the best way she could arouse sympathy or even admiration among the all-male jury.

Frederick was charged with the murder of O'Connor; Maria only with having been present and aiding and abetting her husband. The Attorney-General, as prosecutor of both the accused, made a point of explaining to the jury that even if they thought that only one of the couple had actually committed the murder, if the other had been present and participated, or even had been absent but had prior knowledge of the intention to murder, the jury could convict them both of murder. Maria was a married woman, so the prosecutor quickly forestalled any assumption by the jurymen that the law considered her as under her husband's authority. In matters of murder, he underlined, a wife was responsible for her own actions.

The prosecutor went through the case in detail, suggesting that Maria had been on intimate terms with O'Connor. What fantasies went through the jurymen's minds as they gazed at the motionless, self-possessed and attractive woman in the dock? After listing all the facts in the evidence which pointed to the joint guilt of the Mannings, the prosecutor reminded the jury that, though Frederick had tried to throw the blame on Maria, he had not been able to tell the police who had battered in the victim's head. In the days before fingerprint identification, there was no proof that it was Frederick who had done this, but the jury was not likely to ascribe the deed to Maria. Could Maria have lifted the flagstone by herself and bundled O'Connor's corpse into it? Hardly. On the other hand, said the prosecutor, now attacking Maria, the jury would also find it difficult to accept that Frederick alone had shot O'Connor, finished him off with seventeen blows to the head with a crowbar, bound the body and pushed it into the grave, having lifted the stone. The evidence pointed to both Maria and Frederick being guilty.

The real conflict of evidence, never clarified, centred on the precise time that Maria had reached O'Connor's lodgings in Mile End. Defence for Maria claimed that she could not have been at 3, Miniver Place when the murder occurred. Possibly this was so, because O'Connor's landlady was vague about the time Maria was there. Nevertheless, the jury believed that she must have had prior knowledge of the intention to murder O'Connor, given the purchase and deliveries at the house of the crowbar and the quicklime. This was enough to convict her of murder.

Maria's defence counsel knew that there could be little doubt that it was Frederick who had beaten their victim to death with the crowbar. However, Maria's defence would have to deal with the embarrassing question of her relations with O'Connor, for it would be hard to endear an adulterous wife to the jury, especially since she was foreign into the bargain. These respectable male property-owners would also hear that when Frederick was arrested he had accused her. They could hardly ignore this, even though they were instructed by the judge not to take his words into account.

Frederick's defence counsel was unable to persuade the jury that the purpose of the quicklime, the spade or shovel and the crowbar was the innocuous one of installing a chimney piece in the front parlour. He had the difficult task of defending Frederick in the only way he could, which was by laying the blame on Maria. He suggested that Manning was weak, which nobody could deny, and that Maria had duped him. He tried to persuade the jury that she could have inflicted the injuries which finally killed the victim. She could also have buried him, he suggested to a probably incredulous jury. He was on stronger ground when he said that Manning was not a jealous man, given that he had already tolerated his wife's adultery. However, the jury might have thought that, with O'Connor dying on the floor, Frederick had given free rein to his anger. Frederick's defender also tried to suggest that Maria had acted quite independently of Frederick. Again, there was something in this, because Frederick had been surprised when Maria had disappeared, and she herself had told the Edinburgh police that she had left London without her husband's knowledge.

The jury was not, it seems, impressed by Maria's counsel, who also tried to imply that the quicklime and the crowbar had been purchased for work to be carried out on a chimney. As for the shares and the cash that Maria had taken from O'Connor's rooms, defence counsel claimed that she had asked him to buy shares for her and in her hurry might have accidentally picked up some that belonged to O'Connor. In the end, Maria's defender was reduced to attacking Frederick and his counsel for trying to lay all the blame on Maria. As for Maria's adultery, her defender used it cleverly as proof that she would not have wished her lover dead. However, reminding the jury that she was an adulteress would not necessarily help Maria. Consequently, her defence counsel alleged, without any evidence, that Frederick had mistreated his wife. Even more problematically, he tried to make the jury believe that Maria had no need to murder O'Connor for money, because she was young enough to get whatever she wanted out of a man who was twenty years older than her. The jurymen might well have judged that O'Connor was just as clever as his mistress and would not have been inclined to indulge her. However, the main point made by Maria's counsel was that she was not guilty unless she was actually present. He ignored the legal fact that Maria was indeed guilty if she had known of Frederick's intention to commit murder.

The Attorney-General claimed his legal right of reply, and confirmed what the jury must have been thinking. Maria on her own could not have shot, beaten to death, bound and buried O'Connor, nor replaced the flagstone. Frederick certainly participated, but he would not have had entry to O'Connor's rooms. It was she, not he, who took the cash and shares and fled to Scotland.

Summing up, the judge said that there was no suggestion that anybody but one or both the Mannings had committed the savage murder of Patrick O'Connor. Though Frederick's statement to the police that Maria had done the deed could not be admitted as evidence, it did establish that he had been present, so why had he not prevented Maria from murdering O'Connor, if in fact she was the only killer? Did the jury think this was likely? In other words, continued the judge, was it possible that the murder had been planned and carried out by one of the Mannings unknown to the other? This was clearly a rhetorical question. The answer was 'no'.

Within three-quarters of an hour, the jury returned with the verdict that both Maria and Frederick Manning were guilty. It was at this point that Maria spoke for the first time (defendants in murder cases did not give evidence). She spoke vehemently:

> There is no justice and no right for a foreign subject in this country. There is no law for me. I have had no protection, neither from the judges, nor from the prosecutors, nor from my husband. I am unjustly condemned by this court. If I were in my own country I could prove that I had money sent from abroad, which is now in the Bank of England. My solicitors and counsel could have called witnesses to identify shares that were bought by my own money.
>
> Mr O'Connor was more to me than my husband, and I ought to have been married to him. He was a friend and brother ever since I came to this country. I knew him for seven years. He wanted to marry me. I have letters which would prove his respect and regard for me; and I think, considering that I am a woman and alone, that I have to fight against my husband's statements, that I have to fight against the prosecutors, and that even the judge himself is against me, I think that I am not treated like a Christian, but like a wild beast of the forest, and the Judges and the jury will have it upon their consciences for giving a verdict against me.
>
> I am not guilty of the murder of Mr O'Connor. If I had wished to commit murder, I would not have attempted the life of the only friend I had in the world, a man who would have made me his wife in a week, if I had been a widow. I have lived in respectable families, and can produce testimonials of character for probity in every respect, if enquiry is made. I can account for more money than was equally to the trifling shares that were found on me. If my husband, through jealousy and a revengeful feeling against O'Connor, chose to murder him, I don't see why I should be punished for it. I wish I could have expressed myself better in the English language. That is all I have to say.

How accurate this is may be doubted, since the reporters present had not expected her to speak and would have had to take down what she said in hurried shorthand, assuming they possessed that skill. Nor does her protest look spontaneous. Had she written it previously, expecting a verdict of guilty? Whatever the case, one cannot avoid thinking that she made one or two good points, if it could be believed that she knew nothing about the planning of the murder and had not participated in it. Yet, if this was so, why had she gone to O'Connor's rooms and why was she in such a hurry that she had 'accidentally' taken his money and shares?

As for Frederick, only he could have struck the seventeen frenzied blows that had finished their victim off. The police also found a dealer who had sold a pair of small pistols to a man who 'looked like' Manning, and therefore was not a good witness and had not given court evidence. After the murder, Frederick pawned the pistols, giving a false name. He had no defence at all. As for Maria, she gave an impression of strength and determination which inclined the jury to believe that she, rather than the hopeless alcoholic Frederick was the dominant character in the marriage.

As the judge, with the square of black silk on his head, began to pronounce the death sentence, Maria shouted:

> No! No! I won't stand it. You are to be ashamed of yourselves.
> There is neither law nor justice here!

As she was led away she seized a handful of the rue which by tradition lay along the edge of the dock to disguise the body odour emanating from the prisoners, hurled it into the well of the court and cried out 'Base and shameful England! As she disappeared from sight she was heard to 'pour dreadful imprecations upon all around her' ending 'Damnation seize you all!'

They Swung for It

By the 1840s hanging, which in the early years of the century had been the sentence for a wide range of crimes, some of them mere petty theft, was restricted to those guilty of treason, piracy and murder. Even so, in 1845 49 men and women were sentenced to death, all for murder, in England and Wales, though only twelve were actually executed.

The Mannings were due to be hanged at 9am on Tuesday, 13 November. In those three weeks, the press and the rumour mills were full of reports about how Maria and Frederick were facing death. Many people applied for entrance to Horsemonger Lane Prison, on the site of today's Newington Gardens, hoping to catch a glimpse of the exotic and striking woman.

As the day approached, it was becoming apparent that the event would attract a large crowd. The hanging would take place in public view on the flat roof of the gatehouse. It would attract an unruly mob, anxious to see the spectacle of the suffering of the self-possessed and dominant Mrs Manning. There was little interest in Frederick.

Since 1783, hangings had no longer taken place at Tyburn, close to where Marble Arch stands now, but outside Newgate, the gaol where most prisoners sentenced at the Old Bailey were incarcerated. Hangings outside the prison avoided the disorder of the long ride through the main streets of central London.

Public executions were free spectacles which attracted all classes of people. Flashy young men, the type who liked bare-knuckle fighting and watching dogs tear each other to pieces, would make up parties. When James Rush was 'turned off' at Norwich in April 1849, one large group actually chartered a train, as if for a day at the races.

The Manning case was, however, quite exceptional because of Maria's strange fascination and her amazing aplomb. Did people want to see if she died proud and remote, or were they secretly looking forward with sadistic curiosity to the collapse, the shrieking and the begging for mercy of a woman who had at last lost her icy self-possession?

Rarely had there been a murder with so much drama and so much magnetic interest for Londoners, a murder by a seemingly ordinary lower middle-class couple who could be anybody's neighbours. The penny parts of Robert Huish's fictionalised biography of Maria Manning were being snatched eagerly, almost literally hot off the press. Newspaper supplements and hastily published copies of the trial proceedings repeatedly covered every single aspect of the murder, the house at 3, Miniver Place, the gruesome details of how the policemen had dug up O'Connor's corpse, and the depositions of the witnesses.

Interest grew now in how the Mannings were conducting themselves in prison. Journalists interrogated the wardresses who were with Maria in her cell. They recounted, or the journalists invented, juicy items such as that Maria had made a new pair of drawers to be hanged in, and that she was insisting on wearing a new pair of silk stockings for the event.

Windows and roofs in the streets facing or overlooking the gatehouse were being let expensively to spectators. Herman Melville paid 2/6d to stand on a neighbouring roof.[2] Enterprising businessmen rented front and rear gardens from landlords and kept carpenters busy erecting tiered platforms with seats at five shillings, irrespective of the wishes of the tenants of the houses, although the latter also let seats by their windows. Stands of often doubtful safety were quickly built and offered to anyone willing to pay. Legislation was inadequate; the authorities could do little to prevent unsafe scaffolding and seating. The best seats, costing £2 each, were on the terraces of two pubs which had an excellent view of the proceedings.

On the Monday night, 12 November, crowds began to assemble, ranging from the dregs of the capital's criminal population, eager to prey on the spectators, to well-off Mayfair men-about–town, with their champagne breakfasts laid on for the morning.

Probably a large proportion of the crowd had walked over the bridge to Southwark to see the Mannings hanged only half a mile or so from where they had committed the murder. Some would have come on the train to London Bridge Station, while the better-off and the hordes of journalists would have arrived in hansom cabs. As the night passed, a vast crowd steadily assembled outside the prison, barely controlled by hundreds of police whose task was to keep the mob away from the gaol itself. There was, in fact, no law to prevent such assemblies, and any attempt to do so would probably have provoked a riot. Such was the size of the crowd that *The Examiner* reported on 17 November that the area could have been filled even if it had been as large as Hyde Park.

Fast-food vendors set up stalls, lit by naptha flares. All sorts of peddlers made hay, as did the pickpockets and other petty criminals for whom a public hanging provided an unequalled opportunity.

In the meantime, Maria and Frederick were contemplating their approaching deaths. Frederick, having confessed to the murder, was reported to be reading the Book of Psalms almost continuously. The chaplain, however, could not find a way to persuade Maria to admit her part. However, he did administer the Sacrament to her because, when she met her husband at his request for the last time, in the prison chapel, not having spoken to him since the murder, she told him that she no longer bore him any resentment or animosity.

By early morning on Tuesday, 13 November, the multitude before the gaol was immense. Stalls were selling breakfasts of sausages and kidneys, to be washed down with beer. Ambulant vendors with their trays were offering biscuits and peppermints which they morbidly baptised as 'Mrs Manning's'. The crowd included 'the dregs and offscourings of the population', wrote *The Times,* as well as labouring men and clerks hoping that their employers would excuse their lateness for work. There were urchins and a mixed multitude of the curious and the prurient. Many had been there all that chilly night, drinking, smoking, dancing, fornicating with the cheap whores who had come to make a few shillings, singing obscene songs and, now and then, especially 'Oh! Mrs. Manning, Don't you cry for me', to the tune of Stephen's Foster's 'Oh, Susannah!'

A large variety of broadsides and ballads were hawked through the crowd, one including the following lines:

> At length they planned their friend to murder,
> And for his company did crave.
> The dreadful weapons they prepared,
> And in the kitchen dug his grave.
> And as they fondly did caress him
> They slew him – what a dreadful sight.
> First they mangled, after robbed him,
> Frederick Manning and his wife.
> Old and young, pray take a warning,
> Females, lead a virtuous life.
> Think upon that fateful morning
> Frederick Manning and his wife.[3]

Not surprisingly, the spectacle of a hanging attracted the interest of two of the great novelists of the period. In 1840, the hanging of François-Benjamin Courvoisier, the Swiss manservant who had cut his employer's throat, had been watched by both Dickens and Thackeray. The former was appalled by the behaviour of the people watching and wrote to the *Daily News*:

> I did not see one token ... of any emotion suitable to the occasion ... nothing but ribaldry, debauchery, levity, drunkenness and flaunting vice[4]

Thackeray's tone was different. He wrote that the crowd was well-mannered, joking, and the men were carefully protecting the women. He also noticed groups of 'debauched' men and women who had hired vantage points on neighbouring roofs. As the bell tolled eight, the men watching outside Newgate Prison removed their hats and 'a great murmur arose, more awful, bizarre and indescribable than any sound I had ever heard. Women and children began to shriek horribly.' He thought he was witnessing 'a hidden lust after blood' and that public hanging was beneficial because it was a deterrent, but it was so awful that it would have to stop because it was in itself murder. As he recorded in an article titled

'Going to see a Man Hanged', which he published in *Fraser's Magazine* of August 1840:

> I came away ... that morning with a disgust for murder, but it was for the murder I saw done[5]

This time, after the hanging of the Mannings, Charles Dickens wrote to *The Times* with all the power of his pen,

> I believe that a sight so inconceivably awful as the wickedness and levity of the immense crowd ... could be presented in no heathen land under the sun

The already famous novelist shuddered at the 'atrocious bearing, looks and language' of the spectators, the shrill cries and howls, screeching and laughter of boys and girls', together with 'every variety of foul and offensive' behaviour from the thieves, whores, vagabonds and ruffians who swarmed in front of the prison and in the streets around.

He continued in moving words which would often be quoted in the future, until public executions were ended:

> When the sun rose ... it gilded thousands upon thousands of upturned faces, so inexpressibly odious in their brutal mirth or callousness, that a man had cause to be ashamed of the shape he wore, and to shrink from himself, as fashioned in the image of the Devil. When the two miserable creatures who attracted all this ghastly sight were turned quivering into the air, there was no more emotion, no more pity, no more thought that two immortal souls had gone to judgment, no more restraint in any of the previous obscenities, than if the name of Christ had never been heard in this world, and there were no more beliefs among men but that they perished like the beasts[6]

Maria appeared at her hanging in a black satin dress with a large white collar. She died, wrote *The Times* with some degree of admiration, even for a woman who had behaved in a degree so inappropriate for her sex, 'exhibiting an amount of courage and nerve which contrasted with the terror-stricken aspect of her husband', though how this was visible to the journalist is questionable. The *Chronicle* referred to 'the remarkably fine contour of her figure as it swayed to and fro'.[7] The absence of horrified awe

179

at the hanging, that Dickens so condemned, is evident even in the novelist's own comment. He recalled Maria's body as:

> A fine shape, so elaborately corseted and artfully dressed, that it was quite unchanged in its trim appearance as it slowly swung from side to side.[8]

Both men and women spectators achieved perhaps a sort of sexual satisfaction. The former saw a dominant, aggressive woman being made to suffer, while the latter watched the punishment of a woman who had transgressed against the approved way for her sex to behave.[9] In this way, the spectators had the treat, as it were, of a double hanging, although it was Maria's death which they came to see and about whom they talked and sang ribald songs.

The issues were, however, more complicated. At a public meeting reported by the *Illustrated London News* of 24 November 1849, while all agreed that the crowd's behaviour at the Manning executions should never be repeated, numerous voices argued that the death penalty should be abolished.

Abolition, however, would not come for another century. Even public executions continued. That particular amusement for Londoners would not be stopped until the execution of the Fenian Michael Barrett, hanged at Newgate on 26 May 1868. The crowd, estimated at two thousand, booed, jeered and sang *Rule Britannia* and *Champagne Charlie* as his body dropped.

Maria and Frederick Manning were buried in the prison precincts. Nothing remains of them save their gravestones, now in Southwark's Cuming Museum. Perhaps the waxwork models of them that Madame Tussaud displayed until 1971 still exist in some remote place of storage. But the London where the Mannings lived, and most of the streets where they walked, are still there.

Chapter 12

Elation and Sorrow

The Great Exhibition

The first of May 1851 was the day of the formal opening of the Great Exhibition of Industry of All Nations in Hyde Park in central London. For weeks before, the streets were being resurfaced and shops repainted. The pageantry of the magnificent opening would make the Exhibition memorable for all time. Prince Albert, President of the Royal Society of Arts, Manufactures and Commerce, and Henry Cole, the civil servant who was largely responsible for the Penny Post, were the dynamic forces behind the idea of an immense international exhibition. 17,000 exhibitors would display more than 100,000 exhibits, half of which were foreign. For months Londoners had been climbing onto special viewing points to watch the Crystal Palace, thus named because it was made entirely of glass, rising above the green lawns and trees of Hyde Park. At the same time, and despite the requests of the conductors, passengers crowded unsafely on to the tops of omnibuses running along the Kensington Road to see what they could as they passed by. The Crystal Palace was erected in a few months by a labour force averaging two thousand.[1]

Between the well-off who had bought season tickets, others who bought day tickets for £1, the larger numbers who paid 5/- or 2/6, and the vast majority who visited the Exhibition on the days when entrance cost only a shilling, a total of over six million came to see it. What was there to see? There was the glass fountain in the centre of the building, with its 27 foot jet of water shining as the sun's rays came slanting down upon it through the glass roofs. Among the technical marvels were photography, mechanical agricultural machines, sewing machines, and the Colt revolver. In the machine-room were the power looms, the 'self-acting mules' or automatic machines at tireless work, drawing out long lines of thread; the huge Jacquard lace machines were busy weaving the finest hems; the pumps were throwing up huge cascades of water, while the steam printing-presses were pouring out printed sheets at great speed. One could marvel at the model locomotives snorting, whirring, and clattering. As one glanced down the avenues, objects of exquisite texture, form, or colour, met the eye everywhere. From the top of the galleries hung huge carpets, exquisitely coloured and designed tapestries, and rich silks. One could gaze at the fabulous Koh-i-Noor diamond and other precious stones, and admire the French exhibits of luxury garments, furniture, and porcelain. Looking down the nave, one could glimpse a colossal mirror, set in its massive gilt frame, and mounted on crimson cloth. At every corner were statues, with scarlet drapery arranged behind them, while immediately behind the throne set up for the Queen and Prince Albert to inaugurate the Exhibition were equestrian statues of the royal couple. Behind these was another fountain, and beside this rose palm trees embedded in moss, while at their feet was ranged a bed of flowers, whose petals seemed to have been dyed by the prismatic hues of the water drops of the neighbouring fountain. Then one's eye met the tall old elm trees of the park, which had not been felled but built into the glass structure itself.[2] Outside, on the Serpentine lake in the Park, sailed a model man o' war.

Over half a million people were reported to have congregated in Hyde Park on opening day. The usual omnibus routes had been suspended, and all the different companies' vehicles in their variegated colours were packed with passengers on their way to Hyde Park. There was not an unoccupied cab to be found. The main streets were empty of their usual throng of springtime strollers, shoppers and sightseers. Shops had closed to allow their owners and the assistants to go to see the Crystal Palace, at least from the outside. In the Park, there were tables and chairs to sit at and eat the picnics that people had brought with them or what wandering vendors were offering for sale.

The Queen mixed freely with the invited guests and ticket holders on Opening Day. In an often-quoted diary entry she wrote:

> This day is one of the greatest and most glorious of our lives ... it is a day which makes my heart swell.[3]

One story would be recounted down the years. To the delight, amusement or embarrassment of the invited dignitaries and the 25,000 season ticket holders who were allowed into the Crystal Palace for the formal Opening, a Chinese man in full ceremonial clothes made his appearance while the choir was singing the 'Hallelujah' chorus from Handel's Messiah. He had not been expected, though one suspects that he had been put up to it. He prostrated himself before an embarrassed Queen Victoria and a probably angry Prince Albert. Perhaps, he was a great nobleman. A whispered consultation took place, after which he was directed to take his place between the Archbishop of Canterbury and the Duke of Wellington. He turned out to be the captain, or perhaps a lesser member of the crew, of the Chinese junk moored at the time in the docks.

Ordinary Londoners would have to save up, even to pay the lowest entrance charge of a shilling. If they were among the three hundred who were fortunate enough to work for the brewers Truman, Hanbury and Buxton in Brick Lane, the firm gave them two days' leave and 2/6 each day.[4] The Admiralty also sent some of its dockworkers to London for six days, offering to send them in a ship from Portsmouth if the railway fares had not been significantly lowered.[5] A number of other employers also gave their employees leave and in some cases subsidised their visit to the Exhibition.

Inside the Crystal Palace, smoking and alcohol were prohibited, but filtered water was free and Schweppes had acquired the contract to sell soft drinks.[6] There were inevitably letters in the press complaining about the quality of the refreshments, among them the following: 'the worst and smallest sandwiches I ever tasted ... the coffee I have found always cold and good for nothing ... little, dry, sixpenny dollops of pork pie'.[7] A great many people, understandably, brought their own supplies and were seen to be eating them seated around the fountains. There were even complaints that mothers were suckling their babies in public.

One facility, much appreciated and probably also a novelty to most of the 827,280 people who used them, apart from the free-of-charge urinals for men, were the public water closets. They appear to have been bargains at a penny a time, which gave birth to the expression 'to spend a penny'. They were referred to euphemistically as 'halting stations', 'retiring rooms' or 'washrooms', while some called them 'monkey closets'. The water closets also provided a towel and comb, which suggests that a basin and mirror were fitted.[8]

Londoners, many of them for the first time, saw large numbers of people from other parts of the country, as well as from abroad. Geordie, Midlands, West of England, Yorkshire, Glasgow and Highland voices were to be heard all around.

All over Britain savings clubs and agents organised travel and suitable lodgings. Thomas Cook's sent 165,000 visitors to London on the Midland Railway, out of a total of between 750,000 and a million who came by rail.[9] On some days as many as twenty special trains drew into Euston from the North.[10] In her journal Queen Victoria noted that entire populations of some Kent and Surrey villages had saved up to come to London, while one Norfolk manufacturer had hired ships fully equipped with sleeping berths and cooking facilities to sail to London and tie up in the docks.[11]

Accommodation was scarce. London house owners or tenants were making a good income from letting rooms. £2.10s and upwards for bed and breakfast per person per week seems to have been about the norm, although rooms at 2/- per night were available.[12] The railway fare and incidental expenses would have to be added. The huge number of visitors indicates that many were able to accumulate the roughly £4 or £5 that the trip to London would cost, especially when helped by local gentry in the places the visitors came from.

Perhaps because visitors from abroad were not checked or even counted, one cannot be sure whether the frequent references to a large number of 'foreigners' – the word had a hostile connotation – were exaggerated. Was this what Henry Mayhew was suggesting when he wrote that for the fictional Sandboys family, 'one hundred thousand pairs of mustachioes will be tossed on our shores',[13] while rumour had it that Frenchmen would come wearing large beards, and perhaps British policemen would feel they had to grow whiskers. Again, as in 1848, there were fears expressed that foreigners would bring disorder and even revolution. Some worried that the Crystal Palace would repeat the biblical story of the Tower of Babel, whose builders suddenly began to speak in foreign languages. That summer, many Londoners and most provincials saw French, German and other nationalities for the first time. Perhaps they provided some enlightenment in a country where the French, leave alone the geographically more distant but often mentioned Spaniards, Italians and Turks, were assumed to be treacherous, violent and generally undesirable.

Summer 1851 may have been the first time also that public cigarette smoking was seen. Middle- and upper-class Englishmen smoked cigars; working men often had clay pipes in their mouths. It would take the cigarettes brought back from the Crimean war by officers, who had seen Turks and Russians smoking in that fashion, to make the habit normal in England.[14]

The Exhibition made an appearance in fiction also. In Wilkie Collins's *The Woman in White*, Monsieur and Madame Rubelle come to London from the French city of Lyons, taking a house near Leicester Square, which was the centre of 'Continental' London. They fit it out as a boarding house for foreign guests, who they expect will visit London in large numbers. However, fiction aside, there was a detective patrolling the Exhibition itself – his name was, rather awkwardly, Detective Serjeant – who could speak French and did so all day to the many French visitors, according to Dickens.[15]

Had Maria Manning not died at the hangman's hands, she might well have used her talents as an interpreter for the French, Swiss and Belgian visitors who came to London for the Great Exhibition. Maria – whose name was really Marie – was a highly presentable native speaker of French who spoke English well. Alternatively, the Great Exhibition would have offered her a commercial opportunity. Some of the Mannings' capital belonged to Maria personally, so even if she had decided to leave the alcoholic Frederick, it is feasible to imagine her starting up a prosperous little business of her own, an agency for rooms perhaps. She might even have taken a lease on a house that summer of 1851, and provided a continental breakfast and an evening meal to her guests' taste.

Apart from the fear of an influx of mustachioed, bearded, smoking, noisy and possibly revolutionary foreigners, *The Times* predicted on 26 June 1850 that Hyde Park would be turned into 'the bivouac of all the vagabonds of London'.[16] In reality, it seemed as though criminality had almost disappeared. On 5 May, a few days after the opening, the Queen was told that there had been no accidents, incidents or police reports on Opening Day, although it was calculated that between 500,000 and 700,000 people had been in Hyde Park.[17] Only twelve pickpockets were arrested in the Crystal Palace in the entire five months of the Exhibition.[18] There was, however, a large, permanent body of soldiers and police on duty.

Fears of mob disorder turned out to be unfounded. *The Economist* proclaimed at the end of the first week of cheap entry to the Exhibition:

> At the close of the first week of shilling days, we can say that
> no more orderly people ever existed than the multitude of
> London[19]

The overwhelming sensation was one of awe at everything that the Exhibition meant in terms of human, and particularly British material progress. The novelist Charlotte Brönte, recounted in her Autobiography that:

> It seems as if only magic could have gathered this mass of
> wealth from all the ends of the earth –as if none but supernatural
> hands could have arranged it thus

She adds how silent the people were:

> not one noise was to be heard ... the living tide rolls on quietly,
> with a deep hum like the sea heard from a distance.[20]

The Great Exhibition closed on 15 October 1851. 6,039,195 people had visited it, of whom 4,439,419 had paid the smallest entry fee. Its average daily attendance was fifty thousand, reaching over one hundred thousand in the final days. It recorded a profit of £180,000 when the Crystal Palace, now empty of its exhibits, was sold for £70,000 to the London and South Coast Railway, which re-erected it six miles south of London in a district which became known as Crystal Palace. There it remained till it was destroyed by fire on the evening of 30 November 1936.

Another satisfactory result of the Great Exhibition of 1851 was that it underlined the lack of suitable hotel accommodation, the narrowness of

London's streets, the poor quality of catering, the dire need for a major sewer system, for the embanking of the Thames and for a railway system within the city. These needs would be satisfied in the later years of Victoria's reign, much later, or perhaps never.

'A great man is fallen this day'. The Funeral of the Duke of Wellington

The Duke of Wellington celebrated his eightieth birthday on 1 May 1851, the day of the inauguration of the Great Exhibition. Still spry, he walked through the Park a number of times in the following weeks to visit the Crystal Palace. He was recognised once and, though in earlier years his reactionary stance on many matters had made him disliked, he was now seen as a great hero who had brought a long war to an end, defeated Bonaparte and created peace for Europe since 1815. The crowd cheered him. Others in the Crystal Palace heard the noise but, not seeing the cause of the excitement, panicked and rushed for the doors, and the police had to rescue the Duke.[21]

Wellington died at Walmer Castle, near Deal, on 14 September 1852.[22] His state funeral was fixed for 18 November. In the meantime his body lay in a closed coffin. On 10 November it was taken, embalmed, to Deal and thence by train to London. Here he lay, as was befitting, in the Chelsea Hospital, the national residence for old soldiers.

Between his death and his great state funeral, a diorama of his campaigns was shown in London twice daily. Portraits of him were on sale. One could buy a plaster bust of the Duke for five guineas or a bronze one for fifty. Less tasteful and more commercialised items could be bought, including 'Wellington Cake' and 'Wellington Wine', as well as plenty of catchpenny publications about his life and victories.

As Wellington lay in state, 260,000 people were estimated to have filed past the bier, many landing at Chelsea from river steamers, probably a quicker way to reach it from the City than the omnibus. On 17 November, the body was moved to Horse Guards, headquarters of the British Army.

In the meantime, official seats had been on sale along the route of the funeral cortège, while private rooms, windows and entire floors were let for high prices. Special trains came from all over the country, including one that Thomas Cook organised from Aberdeen in the north of Scotland. All streets were closed to traffic on the day of the funeral, and everybody was required to wear full mourning, while ladies were advised to wear dark clothes for some days afterwards.

At 7am on 18 November the Speaker of the House of Commons arrived at Horse Guards, accompanied by several carriages containing members of the royal family. At 8am the procession moved off, with the military band playing the *Dead March* from Handel's *Saul*. The funeral carriage was drawn by twelve horses. The body of the Duke lay covered by black velvet on a bronze catafalque 27 feet long and 10 feet wide, under a canopy 17 feet high. The soldiers reversed their arms; muffled drums beat out a slow tattoo, and the Duke's horse followed the cortège alone, with Wellington's boots hanging upside-down in the stirrups.

The route took a roundabout route to pass Buckingham Palace, thus allowing the Queen to view the procession. Protocol did not allow the monarch to attend the funeral of a subject who was not a close family member. From there the cortège climbed Constitution Hill, passed the Duke's own residence, Apsley House, where Prince Albert joined the procession, continued along Piccadilly, down St. James's Street into Pall Mall, where the gentlemen's clubs were draped in black, and on to Trafalgar Square.

Many spectators would have been present fifteen years previously, when the young Victoria had ridden along that same route in her coronation carriage. From Trafalgar Square she had descended Whitehall to Westminster Abbey, but the Duke's cortège was bound for St. Paul's. It processed along the Strand, having been joined by a group of 83 Chelsea Pensioners who would not have been able to march all the way from the Hospital. At the arch, called Temple Bar, now draped in black, marking the boundary between the Cities of Westminster and London, the procession was met by the Lord Mayor of the City of London, and then continued to St.Paul's Cathedral. All along the route, black-garbed and solemn people watched, amid the wind and the intermittent squalls of a late London autumn, silent and sadly aware that a long era was ending.

Inside the great Cathedral of St. Paul's, stands had been erected for selected guests. 17,000 mourners were estimated to have attended. The coffin was escorted by several retired generals who had served under Wellington, including the 84-year-old Marquess of Anglesey, who had lost a leg at the battle of Waterloo. Psalms and the *Nunc Dimittis* were sung together with verses from the Second Book of Samuel 'Rend your clothes and gird you with sackcloth, and mourn', as the coffin was slowly lowered into its grave, and trumpeters sounded a last, melancholy salute.

Victoria's coronation procession had been perhaps the first intimation that great occasions were for the entire public, especially the inhabitants of the capital. Wellington's funeral marked the definite change from a world of heraldic pageantry for the interest of a few to one of public participation and the reflection of national events in mass media.

These two events, the Great Exhibition and the death and funeral of the Duke of Wellington, national in interest but taking place in London, mark the end of the first quarter of Victoria's reign. The next quarter would begin with the tramp of soldiers' boots marching through London's streets to the railway stations to entrain for the Crimean War of 1854-1856, the first time in the almost forty years since the battle of Waterloo that British troops would go to war on European soil.

Plus ça change...

Writing in 1832, after a wave of cholera infections in London, the diarist Charles Greville observed that the London mob was as ignorant as that of St Petersburg and other European capitals, where the poor thought that the doctors themselves were creating the illness. In St Petersburg, the mob killed one German doctor and severely beat six others. Doctors were seen as part of the hated governing class, rather like the police. In London, people refused to observe the precautions advised against cholera, believing that the whole thing was an attempt at deceit. A patient who had been taken to the cholera ward in a special hospital in St. Marylebone was carried back home. The chair on which he sat was destroyed and the bearers and the surgeon barely escaped with their lives. Scenes of uproar, violence and brutal ignorance had occurred. Boards of Health were ignored, parishes refused to provide money to carry into effect the recommendations and even orders of the Privy Council. In this town, Greville wrote 'the mob has taken the part of the anti-cholerites'.[23]

Inevitably, one thinks of the opposition to vaccination against mumps, measles and whooping cough as well as the refusal of so many people to be vaccinated against the various strains generally known as 'Covid-19'.

Refusal to adopt measures for the general good continues. And, despite nearly two centuries of reforming governments and London administrations, many of the problems of the early Victorian epoch are still unsolved. Water companies are still accused of pouring sewage into the Thames, housing is too expensive for most Londoners, and public transport costs more than in probably any capital city in the world. The appalling behaviour at public hangings, and at the Manning execution in particular, could be said to continue at some football matches, street demonstrations and protest meetings, while in contrast, the conduct of the public at major royal or national events remains strangely exemplary. Many things are completely different, but much is the same. Such is history.

Bibliography

(the editions cited are those used in writing this book)

Manuscript Sources

Records of the Manning trial: National Archives (Kew) CRIM 12/9, DPP 4/2
Manning Case: Police Record: National Archives MEPO 3/54
Rev. D. Greatorex, Manuscript Diary (London Borough of Tower Hamlets P/GTX)

Printed Sources (all books, unless otherwise stated, were published in London)

Ackroyd, P., *Dickens* (Sinclair-Stevenson, 1990)

Ackroyd, P., *London: the Biography* (Vintage Press, 2001)

Adburgham, A., *Shops and Shopping 1800-1914* (Allen & Unwin, 1964)

Altick, R., *The English Common Reader: a Social History of the Mass Reading Public 1800-1900* (Chicago: University of Chicago Press, 1957)

Altick, R., *The Shows of London* (Cambridge, Mass: Harvard University Press, 1976)

Altick, R., *The Presence of the Present: Topics of the Day in the Victorian Novel* (Columbus: Ohio State University Press, 1991)

Auerbach, J.A., *The Great Exhibition of 1851: a National Display* (New Haven and London: Yale University Press, 1999)

Barker, T.C. and Robbins, M. A., *A History of London Transport*, 2 volumes (Allen & Unwin, 1963)

Bermondsey Murder. The. A Full Report of the Trial of Frederick George Manning and Maria Manning for the Murder of Patrick O'Connor...etc. (W.M. Clark, 1849)

Borowitz, A., *The Bermondsey Horror* (Robson Books, 1989)

Briggs, A., *Victorian Cities* (Harmondsworth: Penguin Books, 1968)

Briggs, A., *Victorian Things* (Harmondsworth: Penguin, 1988)

Burnett, J., *A History of the Cost of Living* (Harmondsworth: Penguin, 1969)

189

Burnett, J., *Plenty and Want: a Social History of Diet in England from 1815 to the Present Day* (Scolar Press, 1979)

Burnett, J., *A Social History of Housing 1815-1870* (Methuen, 1980)

Calder, J., *The Victorian Home* (Batsford, 1977)

Chesney, K., *The Victorian Underworld* (Temple Smith, 1970)

Colman, H., *European Life and Manners in Familiar Letters to Friends*, 2 volumes (Boston.Mass.: Little & Brown, 1850)

Corton, C., *London Fog, the Biography* (The Belknap Press of Harvard University Press, Harvard, Mass., 2015)

Cruickshank, D. and Burton, N., *Life in the Georgian City* (Viking, 1990)

Day, J., *The Story of the London Bus* (London Transport, 1973)

Diamond, M., *Victorian Sensation* (Anthem Press, 2003)

Dickens, Charles, *Sketches by Boz, Nicholas Nickleby The Chimes, Dombey and Son, David Copperfield, Bleak House, Little Dorrit*

Dickens, Charles, *Dickens's Journalism*, ed. Slater, M., 4 volumes (Dent, 1996), volume 2, 'The Amusements of the People and other Papers, 1834-1851')

Dodd, G., *The Food of London* (Longman, Brown, 1856)

Dodds, J.W., *The Age of Paradox: A Biography of England 1814-1851* (Gollancz, 1953)

Dyos, H., and WOLFF, M., *The Victorian City: Images and Realities*, 2 volumes (Routledge, 1973)

Finestein, I., *Anglo-Jewry in Changing Times* (Vallentine, Mitchell, 1999)

Flanders, J., *The Victorian City: Everyday Life in Dickens' London* (Atlantic Books, 2013)

Gibbs-Smith, C.H., *The Great Exhibition of 1851: a Commemorative Album* (Victoria and Albert Museum, 1951)

Grant, J,. 'Penny Theatres' in *Sketches in London* (1838)

Greer, Germaine, *Sex and Destiny* (Secker & Warburg, 1984)

Hardyment, C., *From Mangle to Microwave: the Mechanisation of Household Work* (Cambridge: Polity Press, 1988)

Harrison, J.F., *Early Victorian Britain 1832-1851* (Fontana, 1979)

Hayter, Alethea, *A Sultry Month: Scenes of London Literary Life in 1846* (Robin Clark, 1992).

Hayward, D., *The Days of Dickens* (Routledge, 1976)

Head, Sir Francis Bond, *Stokers and Pokers* (John Murray,1849)

Holme, T., *The Carlyles at Home* (Oxford University Press,1965)

Hoppen, K.T., *The Mid-Victorian Generation 1846-1886* (Oxford: Oxford University Press, 1998)

House, H., *The Dickens World* (Oxford: Oxford University Press, 1941)

Huish, Robert, *The Progress of Crime; or Authentic Memoirs of Maria Manning (a Romance)* (author, 1849)

Jackson, J., 'The Irish in London' (London University MA thesis, 1958)

Jackson, L., *Dirty Old London: the Victorian Fight against Filth* (New Haven and London: Yale University Press)

James, A., *The Post* (Batsford, 1970)

Jerrold, D., *Mrs Caudle's Curtain Lectures* (Richard Edward King, no date, 1898?)

Johnson, E., *Charles Dickens, His Tragedy and Triumph*, (Harmondsworth: Penguin, 1986)

Kent, W., *Mine Host London: a Chronicle of Distinguished Visitors* (Nicholson Watson, 1948)

Knelman, J., *Twisting in the Wind: the Murderess and the English Press* (Toronto: University of Toronto Press, 1998).

Laver, J., *Manners and Morals in the Age of Optimism 1848-1914* (Weidenfeld & Nicolson, 1966)

Laver, J., *A Concise History of Costume* (Thames & Hudson, 1969)

Leigh, P., *Manners and Customs of the Englyshe, Drawn from ye Quick by Rychard Doyle. To which be added some extracts from Mr Pips hys Diary* (Gutenberg digitised version of edition published Edinburgh: Foulis, 1911)

Levitt, S., *Victorians Unbuttoned* (Allen & Unwin, 1986).

Lewis, J., *London, the Autobiography* (Robinson, 2009)

Longmate, N., *King Cholera, the Biography of a Disease* (Hamish Hamilton,1966)

Mayhew, Henry, *Life and Labour of the London Poor*, 3 vols. (first published 1851) (Charles Griffin & Co., 1861-1862).

Mayhew, Henry, *The World's Show 1851, or the Adventures of Mr. And Mrs. Sandboys and Family* (George Newbold, 1851)

Melville, H., *Journal of a visit to London and the Continent 1849-1850* (Cohen and West, 1949)

Mottram, R.H., 'Town Life' in Young, G.M. (ed.), *Early Victorian England 1830-1865,* 2 vols. (Oxford: Oxford University Press, 1934)

Muir, R., *Wellington: Waterloo and the Fortunes of Peace 1814-1852* (New Haven and London: Yale University Press, 2015)

Murray's Handbook to London (John Murray, 1851)

Nowrojee, J. and Merwangee, H., *Journal of a Residence of Two Years and a Half in Great Britain* (W.H. Allen, 1841)

Pearsall, R., *The Worm in the Bud: the World of Victorian Sexuality* (Harmondsworth: Penguin, 1971)

The Penguin Book of Comic and Curious Verse (Harmondsworth: Penguin, 1952)

Perkin, J., *Women and Marriage in Nineteenth Century England* (Routledge, 1989)

Picard, L., *Victorian London, the Life of a City 1840-1870* (Weidenfeld & Nicolson, 2005)

Pool, D. *What Jane Austen ate and Charles Dickens knew (from fox-hunting to whist. The facts of daily life in 19th century England)* (New York: Simon & Schuster, 1993)

Porter, B., *The Refugee Question in Mid-Victorian Politics* (Cambridge: Cambridge University Press, 1979)

Porter, R., *London, a Social History* (Harmondsworth: Penguin, 1996)

Porter, R., *A History of Medicine* (Cambridge: Cambridge University Press, 1996)

Rappaport, H., *Beautiful for Ever: Madame Rachel of Bond Street* (Ebrington, Gloucestershire: Long Barn Books, 2010)

Reade, C., *It's Never too Late to Mend* (Richard Bentley,1856)

Reynolds, G.W.M., *The Mysteries of London* (ed. Thomas, T.), (Keele: Keele University Press, 1996)

St-Aubyn, G., *Queen Victoria: a Portrait* (Sinclair Stevenson, 1991)

Sala, G.A., *Gaslight and Daylight* (Chapman & Hall, 1859)

Sala, G.A., *Twice round the Clock*, first published 1859 (Intro. Collins, P, Leicester: Leicester University Press, 1971

Seaman, L.B., *Life in Victorian London* (Batsford, 1973)

Seymour, R., *Lola Montez* (New Haven: Yale University Press, 1996)

Sheppard, F., *London 1808-1870: the Infernal Wen* (Berkeley: University of California Press, 1971)

Slater, M., *An Intelligent Person's Guide to Dickens* (Duckworth, 1999),

Sponza, L., *Italian Immigrants in Nineteenth Century Britain: Realities and Images* (Leicester: Leicester University Press, 1988)

Stanley, M.L., *Marriage and the Law in Victorian England 1850-1895* (I.B. Tauris, 1989)

Sutherland, J. *Is Heathcliff a murderer? Puzzles in 19th-Century Fiction* (Oxford: Oxford University Press, 1996),

Swift, R., and Gilley, S., *The Irish in Britain 1815-1939* (Pinter, 1989)

Taine, H., *Notes on England* (translated Fraser, W.) (Strahan,1872)

Thackeray, W.M., *Pendennis*

Tristan, Flora, *Promenades dans Londres* (Paris: Delloye, 1840)

Trudgill, E., *Madonnas and Magdalens* (Heinemann, 1976)

Vega, de la, V.*Cartas familiares inéditas* (Madrid, 1873)

Walker, G., *Gatherings from Graveyards, particularly those of London* (Longman, 1839)

Weightman, G., *Bright lights: Big City* (Collins & Brown, 1992)

Weinreb B. And Hibbert.C., *The London Encyclopaedia*: Macmillan, 1983)

Wilson, A.N (Ed.), *The Faber Book of London* (Faber& Faber, 1993)

Wilson, A.N., *The Victorians* (Hutchinson, 2002)

Notes

Chapter 1: The Largest, Richest, Most Populous and Refined City in the World

1. Dodd, G., *The Food of London* (London: Longman, Brown, 1856), pp.127-128
2. Taine, H., *Notes on England* (New York: Holt and Williams, 1872), p.76
3. Porter, G.R., *The Progress of the Nation* (London: John Murray, 1847), p.575
4. Tristan, Flora, *Promenades dans Londres*, (Paris: Delloye, 1840), Preface, p.xvii
5. Melville, *Journal of a Visit to London and the Continent 1849-1850*, ed. Eleanor Melville Metcalf (London: Cohen and West, 1949), p.21
6. *Murray's Handbook to London* (London: John Murray, 1851), p.49
7. Anon., *The Bermondsey Murder: Full Report of the Trial of Frederick George Manning and Maria Manning for the Murder of Patrick O'Connor* (London, Printed and Published by W. M. Clark, 1849), p.36
8. Mayhew, H. and Binney, J., *The Criminal Prisons of London and Scenes of Prison Life*, first published 1862 (London, Frank Cass, 1968)
9. Sheppard, F., *London 1808-1870, the Infernal Wen* (Berkeley, University of California Press, 1970), p.26
10. Seaman, L.B., *Life in Victorian London* (London, Batsford, 1973), pp.17-19
11. Holme, Thea, *The Carlyles at Home* (London: Oxford University Press, 1965), p.154
12. Ibid., p.4
13. Tristan, pp. 3 and 9
14. For multiple references to fiction, see Altick, Richard, *The Presence of the Present: Topics of the Day in the Victorian Novel* (Columbus: Ohio State University Press, 1991), specifically to Jo and crossing sweepers, pp.391 and 615

15. Colman, H., *European Life and Manners in Familiar Letters to Friends*, 2 volumes (Boston: Little and Brown, 1850 and London, John Petherham, 1850), Vol.1, p165

16. Ibid., Vol.II, p.117

17. Sala, G.A., *Twice Round the Clock* (Leicester: Leicester University Press, 1971), pp.351-152. It had appeared first as magazine articles in the 1840s and was published in book form in 1859 (London: J. and R. Maxwell)

18. Quoted in Sutherland, J., *Is Heathcliff a murderer? Puzzles in 19th-Century Fiction* (Oxford: Oxford University Press, 1996), p.95

19. Mottram, R.H., 'Town Life' in Young G.M. (ed.), *Early Victorian England 1830-1865*, 2 volumes (Oxford: Oxford University Press, 1934), Vol.1, pp. 155-223

Chapter 2: A Woman's Place?

1. St, Aubin, G., *Queen Victoria: a Portrait* (London: Sinclair-Stevenson, 1991), p.118

2. See the US *Saturday Evening Post* of 28 July 1838.

3. For illegitimate births see the Annual Report of the Registrar-General of Births, Marriages and Deaths

4. On London prostitution, see among others, Flanders, Chapter 15

5. Altick, *The Presence of the Present* ,pp.533-534

6. Ibid, p.534

7. Pearsall, R., *The Worm in the Bud; the World of Victorian Sexuality*, (Harmondsworth: Penguin, 1971 ed.), p.313

8. *Notes on England*, quoted in Laver, J., *Manners and Morals in the Age of Optimism, 1848-1914* (London: Weidenfeld and Nicolson, 1966) p.36

9. Flanders, p.403

10. Tristan cit., pp. 114-118

11. Weinreb, B., and Hibbert, C., *The London Encyclopaedia* (London: Macmillan, 1983) under 'Crime'

12. https://victorian   web.org>authors>dickens>rogers   (accessed 7 December 2021)

13. Ibid

14. Quoted in Trudgill, E., *Madonnas and Magdalens* (London: Heinemann, 1976), p.107

15. Seymour, B., *Lola Montez* (sic), (New Haven: Yale University Press), 1996

16. Dodds, pp.371-372
17. Altick, p.542 note
18. On Madame Rachel, see Rappaport, H., *Beautiful for Ever: Madame Rachel of Bond Street, Cosmetician, Con-Artist and Blackmailer,* (Ebrington, Glos. 2010)
19. Trudgill, p.132, Chesney, K., *The Victorian Underworld* (London: Temple Smith, 1970), pp.239-245
20. Trudgill, p.176
21. Quoted by Hoppen, K.T., *The Mid-Victorian Generation 1846-1886* (Oxford: Oxford University Press, 1998), p.319
22. Stanley, M.L., *Marriage and the Law in Victorian England 1850-1895* (London: I.B. Tauris, 1989), p.37
23. Trudgill, p.4
24. Quoted in ibid. p.56
25. Altick, p.308
26. Slater, Michael, *An Intelligent Person's Guide to Dickens* (London: Duckworth, 1999), p.138, quoting Dickens in his magazine *Household Words*, 8 November 1851
27. Perkin, J., *Women and Marriage in Nineteenth Century England* (London: Routledge, 1989), p.128; *History Workshop Magazine* No.4 (1977), pp.57-60, 71; Greer, Germaine, *Sex and Destiny* (London: Secker& Warburg, 1984), p.133
28. Trudgill, pp. 28, 76

Chapter 3: What They Ate, Where They Shopped and What They Wore

1. Burnett, J., *Plenty and Want: a Social History of Diet in England from 1815 to the Present Day* (London: Scholar Press, 1979), pp.78-79
2. Reynolds, G.W.M, *The Mysteries of London,* ed. Thomas, T.(Keele University Press, 1996), p.234
3. Tristan, p.297. Dickens, speaking of France in his *A Tale of Two Cities* of 1859 (Chapter V) mentions 'husky chips of potato, fried with some reluctant drops of oil'.
4. Sala, G.A., *Twice Round the Clock,* was first published in 1859 but had appeared as magazine articles earlier (Leicester: Leicester University Press, 1971), p.298
5. Quoted in Ackroyd, P., *London, the Biography* (London: Vintage Press, 2001), p.317

6. Hoppen, p.346
7. Burnett, J., *A History of the Cost of Living* (Harmondsworth: Penguin, 1969), p.209, Clapham, J.H., 'Work and Wages', in Young, Vol.1, pp.1-77
8. Burnett, *Cost of Living*, pp.212-213
9. Dodds, J.W., *The Age of Paradox: a Biography of England 1841-1851*, (London, Gollancz, 1953), p.430
10. Burnett, J., *Plenty and Want*, p.89
11. Holme, T., *The Carlyles at Home*, (London: Oxford University Press, 1965), p.34 and 166
12. Dodds, *Age of Paradox*, p.299.
13. Briggs, A, *Victorian Things* (Harmondsworth: Penguin1990), p.216
14. Greatorex, Rev.D. Mss diary, kept at Tower Hamlets Local History Centre (Ref. P/GTX), 8 October 1856
15. Sheppard, pp.189-190
16. Burnett, *Cost of Living*, p.216
17. Dodds, *Age of Paradox*, pp.121-123. Dickens, *David Copperfield*, Chapter 11. Dickens published this novel in serialised form in 1849-1850. His reference may have been contemporary, though the novel itself is set ten years earlier
18. Pool, Daniel, *What Jane Austen ate and Charles Dickens knew* (New York: Simon and Schuster, 1993), p.209
19. Ibid, pp.205-206. See also Burnett, *Plenty and Want*, pp.103-115
20. House, H., *The Dickens World*, (London: Oxford University Press, 1941), pp.184-185
21. Burnett, *Plenty and Want*, p.119
22. Holme, p.85
23. Colman, Vol.1., p.141
24. Burnett, *Plenty and Want*, quoting from the anonymous *Memoirs of a Stomach*
25. Melville, pp.31-32
26. Kent, William, *Mine Host London, a Chronicle of Distinguished Visitors* (London: Nicholson and Watson, 1948), p.159
27. Sala, *Twice Round the Clock*, pp.322-324.
28. Dickens, C., *Sketches by Boz* (London: Chapman and Hall, 1913 edition), Chapter 11, 'Greenwich Fair'.
29. Altick, *The Presence of the Present*, pp.220-22
30. Adburgham, A., *Shops and Shopping 1800-1914* (London: Allen and Unwin, 1964), pp.141-142
31. Ibid, p23

32. Ibid, p.12
33. Ibid, p.14
34. Colman, Vol.1, pp. 127-128
35. Quoted in Adburgham, pp.141-142
36. Quoted in Laver, p.86
37. National Archives (Kew) MEPO 3/54
38. Hardyment, C., *from Mangle to Microwave, the Mechanisation of Household Work* (Cambridge: Polity Press, 1988), p.43
39. Briggs, p.281
40. Borowitz, p.15
41. Ibid, p.282
42. Quoted by Seaman, *Life in Victorian London*, p.128
43. Colman, Vol.1, pp.21-22
44. Ibid, p.166
45. Laver, J., *Taste and Fashion from the French Revolution until Today* (London: Harrap, 1937) p.57
46. Briggs, p.267
47. Jerrold, D., *Mrs Caudle's Curtain Lectures*, Lecture XX
48. Melville, p.61
49. Holme, p.103-106
50. Jerrold, pp.84-85
51. Dickens, *Dombey and Son*, (first published 1846-1848), Chapters 10 and 31
52. Altick, *The Presence of the Present*, p.237
53. From a New Year message by E. Moses and Son, quoted in Dodds, *Age of Paradox*, p.279
54. Quoted Lewis, J., p.292
55. Sala, G.A., *Gaslight and Daylight* (London, Chapman and Hall, 1859, p.260
56. Sheppard, p.168
57. Levitt, S., *Victorians Unbuttoned* (London: Allen and Unwin, 1986), p.12
58. Hoppen, p.350
59. Dodds, p.279

Chapter 4: In Sickness and In Health

1. Holme, pp.42-43
2. Dodds, p.283

3. Altick, *Presence of the Present*, p.552 note
4. Ibid, p.551
5. Dodds, pp.282-283
6. Picard, p.187
7. St, Aubyn, pp.257-258
8. Picard, p.188
9. Picard, pp.182-183
10. Hoppen, p.326
11. Ibid
12. Burnett, J., *A Social History of Housing 1815-1870* (London: Methuen, 1980), p.101
13. Ackroyd, *Dickens*, p.384
14. Holme, p.155
15. For details, see Jackson, Lee, *Dirty Old London: the Victorian Fight against Filth* (New Haven and London: Yale University Press), p.50
16. Sheppard, p.256
17. Ackroyd, *Dickens,* p.382
18. Ibid
19. Wilson, E.N., *The Victorians* (London: Hutchinson, 2005), p.155
20. Sheppard, p.270
21. *Illustrated London News*, 8 September 1849, p.163
22. Sheppard, p.189
23. *The Times*, 31 January 1851
24. Reynolds, p.163
25. Walker, G. A., *Gatherings from Graveyards, particularly those of London* (London: Longman, 1839), p.168
26. *Dickens's Journalism*, (ed. Slater) Vol.2, pp.147-156, specifically p.150
27. *The London Encyclopaedia*, pp.930-931
28. Ibid
29. Quoted by Longmate, N., *King Cholera, the Biography of a disease*, (London: Hamish Hamilton, 1966), p.180

Chapter 5: Money, Housing and Class

1. Dodds, p.360
2. Burnett, *History of the Cost of Living*, pp.200-201
3. Sheppard, p.71.
4. Altick, *The Presence of the Present*, p.641
5. Holme, p.28

6. Altick, *The Presence of the Present*, pp.662-663
7. Greatorex, Rev. D., *Diaries* (Tower Hamlets Local History Centre, Mss P/GTX) 1 October 1855
8. Hoppen, p.339
9. Sheppard, p.95
10. Johnson, E., *Charles Dickens, His Tragedy and Triumph*, (Harmondsworth: Penguin, 1986),p.28
11. Ibid
12. Hardyment, pp.17-18
13. All details of the Carlyle's house are from Holme, pp. 9-11 and 76 and ff
14. Holme, p.48
15. Burnett, *Social History of Housing*, p.145.
16. *The London Encyclopaedia*, p.624
17. National Archives (Kew), MEPO 3/54
18. Burnett, *A Social History of Housing,*p.211
19. Holme, p.10
20. Burnett, *A Social History of Housing*, p.171
21. Cruickshank, D. And Burton, N., *Life in the Georgian City*, (London: Viking 1990), p.78
22. Altick, *The Presence of the Present*, pp.343-344
23. Ibid, p.126
24. Cruickshank and Burton, p.74
25. Burnett, *A History of the Cost of Living*, p.242
26. Holme, pp.141-147
27. *Dickens' Journalism,* Vol.2, pp.234-241
28. Pearsall, p.79

Chapter 6: Learning, Literature and Liturgy

1. 'Ignorance and Crime', in *The Examiner* 22 April 1848, quoted in *Dickens's Journalism*, Vol. 2, 91-95
2. Ibid, p.94
3. Cruickshank and Burton, p.88
4. For a discussion of literacy and reading, see Altick, R., *The English Common Reader: a Social History of the Mass Reading Public 1800-1900* (Chicago: University of Chicago Press, 1957), p.170
5. Maria's books are listed by Borowitz, p.301
6. Hoppen, p.388
7. Altick, *The English Common Reader*, p.321, citing Forster's *Life of Dickens*

8. Sweet, M., *Inventing the Victorians*, (London: Faber, 2001), p.67
9. Quoted in Ackroyd, P., *Dickens*, pp.195-197
10. Reynolds (ed. Thomas), p.169
11. Ibid. Introduction, p.15
12. Michael Slater, in *Dickens' Journalism*, Vol.2, Introduction, p.xv
13. Zeldin, T., *France 1848-1945*, (New York: Oxford University Press, 1980) 4 vols. Vol.1, p.7
14. Weindling, D. and Colloms, M., *Kilburn and West Hampstead Past* (London: Historical Publications, 1999), pp.23-24 (W.H. Smith lived in Kilburn)
15. Dodds, p.374
16. Trudgill, pp.220-221
17. Altick, *English Common Reader*, p.301
18. Ibid, p.103
19. Ventura de la Vega, *Cartas Familiares Inéditas*, (Madrid , 1873), p.9
20. Cruickshank and Burton, p.192
21. Ibid
22. Sala, p.294
23. Hoppen, p.465
24. Ibid. p.431
25. Ibid., p.453
26. Ibid, p.453. On the likening of religion to opium by both Marx and Kingsley see/www.theguardian.com/notesandqueries/query/0,5753,-1987,00.html (accessed 29 December 2021)
27. *Sybil*, Vol.2, p.289 (quoted by Trudgill, p.176)
28. Russell, G.W.E. *Collections and Recollections* (1898), quoted by Cruickshank and Burton, p.173
29. Altick, *Presence of the Present*, pp.423-425
30. Hoppen, p.463; Altick, *Presence of the Present*, p.102

Chapter 7: Outsiders

1. Altick, *English Common Reader*, p.116
2. Hoppen, p.445
3. Lytton Strachey's essay on Cardinal Manning, in his *Eminent Victorians* of 1918 is vivid on this
4. Quoted in Hoppen, p.145
5. Dickens's Journalism, Vol.2, pp.297-305
6. Picard, p.73

7. Quoted in Lewis, J., *London, the Autobiography* (London: Robinson, 2009), p.254

8. Engels, F., *The Condition of the Working Class in England* (eds. Henderson, W. and Challoner, W.),(Oxford: Oxford University Press, 1958, p.123). See also Swift, R. And Gilley, S., *The Irish in Britain 1815-1939* (London: Pinter, 1989)

9. Mayhew, H., *Life and Labour of the London Poor*, 3 Vols, first published 1851 (London: Charles Griffin & Co. 1861-1862), Vol.1, pp. 108 and ff

10. Thompson, D., *In Camden Town* (1983) quoted in Wilson, A.N., *The Faber Book of London* (London: Faber & Faber, 1993), pp.290-293

11. See Jackson, J., 'The Irish in London' (London University MA thesis, 1958); Alpert, M., 'The Church of the Sacred Heart: Irish Catholics in 19th century Kilburn' (*Camden History Review*. September 2001)

12. Carlyle, T., *Collected Works* (London: Chapman & Hall, 1857), Vol.1, p.67

13. Sponza, L., *Italian Immigrants in Nineteenth Century Britain: Realities and Images* (Leicester: Leicester University Press, 1988), pp.21-22. I thank Dr Sponza for guiding me around Little Italy

14. Ibid, p.62

15. Altick, *The Presence of the Present*, pp.527-528

16. Sala, *Twice Round the Clock*, pp.106-107, and Sponza, Chapters 5 and 6

17. *Nicholas Nickleby*, Ch.2

18. Nowrogee, J. and Merwangee, H., *Journal of a Residence of Two Years and a Half in Great Britain* (London: W.H. Allen, 1841), p110

19. Sponza, p.133

20. Flanders, J., *The Victorian City*, (London Atlantic Books, 2012), p.345 note.; see also http://breweryhistory.com/wiki/index.php?title=The_Story_of_General_Haynau (accessed 3 January 2022)

21. Porter, R., *London, a Social History* (Harmondsworth: Penguin, 1996), p.16

22. Porter, B., *The Refugee Question in Mid-Victorian: Politics* (Cambridge: Cambridge University Press, 1979), p.42

23. Ibid, p.76

24. Ibid, p.25

25. Picard, p.222

26. Holme, p.83

27. Porter, *The Refugee Question*, p.92, quoting a private diary

28. Wilson, *The Victorians*, pp.117-118

29. Picard, pp.213-214

30. Seaman, p.44

31. Sheppard, p.332
32. Salbstein, M., *The Emancipation of the Jews in Britain* (London: Associated University Presses, 1982), pp.37-38
33. Finestein, I, *Anglo-Jewry in Changing Times* (London: Vallentine, Mitchell, 1999), p.31
34. Mayhew, Vol2, p.112
35. Ibid, p.44
36. Ibid, p.45
37. Ibid, p.135
38. Jerrold, Lecture XVI

Chapter 8: Communications

1. *Comic Almanack, 1842,* in Altick, R., *The Shows of London* (Cambridge, Mass.: Harvard University Press, 1976), p.181
2. Altick, *The Presence of the Present*, p.135
3. For the early history of the London omnibus see Day, John R., *The Story of the London Bus* (London: London Transport, 1973)
4. *The Penguin Book of Comic and Curious Verse* (Harmondsworth: Penguin,1952), p.239
5. Holme, p.47
6. Melville, p.26
7. Day, p.9
8. Altick, *The Presence of the Present*, p.373
9. Hayward, A.L., *The Days of Dickens* (London: Routledge, 1926), pp.7-8;) Melville, p.37
10. Holme, pp.68 and 170
11. Dickens, *The Uncommercial Traveller* (1851), quoted in Hoppen, p.290
12. Altick, *The Presence of the Present,* p.608
13. Lewis, J E., *London, The Autobiography* (London: Robinson, 2009), p.256
14. Barker, T.C. and Robbins, M., *A History of London Transport*, 2 vols. (London: Allen and Unwin, 1963), Vol.1, p.46
15. Burnett, *History of the Cost of Living*, p.216
16. Thackeray, *Pendennis*, Chapter 8
17. 'Terminus' meaning the end of a railway line, dates from 1836 (Oxford English Dictionary)
18. Cruickshank and Burton, p.97
19. Melville, p.20
20. Ventura de la Vega, pp.20-21

21. *Quarterly Review*, vol.74, p.250, cited by House, H., *The Dickens World* (Oxford: Oxford University Press, 1941), p.151

22. Cruickshank and Burton, p.95

23. Quoted in House, p.140

24. Sheppard, p.135

25. *Manners and Customs of Ye Englyshe in 1849,* (Edinburgh: Foulis, 1911,digitised Gutenberg 2011), p.41

26. Sir Francis Bond Head, quoted by Freeman, M., *Railways and the Victorian Imagination* (New Haven and London: Yale University Press, 1999), p.42

27. *Punch*, 1 September 1849

28. Altick, *The Presence of the Present*, p.212

29. Hayward, A. L. *The Days of Dickens* (London: Routledge, 1926), p.209. I have changed 'ran-tan' to 'rat-tat' (MA)

30. *Illustrated London News*, 15 September 1849

31. Ventura de la Vega, pp.17 and 42

32. *Illustrated London News*. See illustration in Altick, *The Presence of the Present*, p.208

Chapter 9: 'A burst of applause which made the building ring': London amusements

1. Barret-Ducrocq, F., *Love in the Time of Victoria* (London: Verso, 1991), p.13

2. Burnett, *History of the Cost of Living*, p.263

3. Hoppen, p.353

4. 'A Gin-Shop' in *Sketches by Boz* quoted in Wilson, *The Faber Book of London* (1993), pp.369-371

5. *Dickens' Journalism*, Vol.2, p.137

6. Altick, R., *The Shows of London*, (Cambridge, Mass.: Harvard University Press, 1976), p.171

7. Melville, p.30

8. Nowrojee, J. and Merwangee, H., *Journal of a Residence of two years and a half in Great Britain*, (London: W.H. Allen, 1841), pp.138-139

9. *Dickens' Journalism*, p.180

10. Altick, *The Shows of London*, p.514 and ff

11. There are many interesting references to Tom Thumb in Alethea Hayter's *A Sultry Month: Scenes of London Literary Life in 1846* (London Robin Clark, 1992)

12. Altick, *The Shows of London*, pp.514 and ff
13. Sala, G.A., *Gaslight and Daylight* (London: Chapman and Hall, 1859), p.177
14. *Sketches by Boz* (London: Chapman and Hall, 1913), p.98
15. Hayter, p.46
16. Altick, *The Presence of the Presence*, p.435
17. Ibid
18. Vega, pp.25-26
19. Weightman, G., *Bright Lights, Big City* (London: Collins and Brown, 1992), pp. 19-20
20. Kent, p.143. See also Dickens's *Sketches by Boz* 'Greenwich Fair' in *Dickens' Journalism*, Vol.1, p.115
21. According to Weightman, p.65, the 'Minstrels' were all 'blacked-up' white men
22. Sala, p.293
23. Altick, *The Shows of London*, pp.323-331
24. Nowrogee and Merwangee, pp.102-103
25. *Dickens' Journalism*, Vol.2, p.171
26. Ibid, p.159
27. *Dickens' Journalism*, Vol.2, pp.182
28. Ibid, pp.193-197
29. Quoted in https://www.victorianlondon.org/publications/sketchesin london-5.htm (accessed 1 February 2022)
30. https://en.wikipedia.org/wiki/Canterbury_Music_Hall (retrieved 1 February 2022)
31. Kent, pp.164-165. For the Coal Hole see Flanders, pp.362-363
32. Altick, *The Shows of London*, p.454.

Chapter 10: Crime, Police, Detectives and the Manning murder

1. Holmes, pp.89-90
2. *Dickens' Journalism*, Vol.2, p 266.
3. For details of the creation of the Metropolitan Police see Sheppard pp.37-39
4. Pool, p.136
5. Kent, p.160
6. Vega, p.21
7. The *Polytechnic Magazine*, 28 January 1903. Hogg commented that the word 'ecilop' was still used for the police.

8. *Chamber's Journal*, No. XIII, p.54
9. Clark, pp. 9 and 15
10. Sweet, pp.4-5, who places the beginning of the use of *sensation* in that sense to the 1860s, although it could certainly have been applied to the Manning case.
11. Lock, p.36
12. Most of the following is drawn from Michael Slater's introduction and notes to Dickens's two articles about detectives. See his edition of *Dickens' Journalism*, Vol.2, pp.265-282
13. Lock, p.34
14. *Dickens' Journalism*, Vol,2, pp. 356-369
15. This is suggested by Borowitz, although Maria did not speak except for her outburst when found guilty. See Borowitz, p.306
16. For personal details I have relied on Borowitz, E., *The Bermondsey Horror* (London: Robson Books, 1989)

Chapter 11: Trial and Execution

1. On the subject of women who were hanged see Knelman, J., *Twisting in the Wind: the Murderess and the English Press* (Toronto: University of Toronto Press, 1998)
2. Melville, p.26
3. Quoted in Diamond, M., *Victorian Sensation* (London: Anthem Press, 2003), p.163
4. Quoted in Flanders, p.389
5. Ibid, and Ackroyd, p.300
6. Quoted in Borowitz, p.261
7. Knelman, p,262
8. Ibid
9. Ibid, pp.261-262

Chapter 12: Elation and Sorrow

1. Victoria and Albert Museum (Gibbs-Smith, C.H., Compiler), *The Great Exhibition of 1851* (London: HMSO, 1950), p.13
2. Detailed descriptions of the Exhibition can be found in *The Great Exhibition: A Documentary History* (ed. Cantor, G.), 4 vols. (London: Pickering and Chatto, 2013), and Auerbach, J., *The Great Exhibition of*

1851: A Nation on Display (New Haven and London: Yale University Press, 1999)

3. The full entry can be found in *The Great Exhibition* (Ed. Cantor), vol. 2, pp.291-293
4. Auerbach, p.150
5. Gibbs-Smith, p.29, quoting the *Portsmouth Guardian*
6. Ibid, p.7
7. Ibid, p.27
8. https://en.wikipedia.org/wiki/George_Jennings,accessed 23 February 2022. There was probably an attendant who wiped the seat and provided the hand towel in exchange for a tip and, if required, the square of newspaper which was the usual medium. Paper for the specific purpose of personal toilet was not invented until 1857 by Joseph Gayetty in the US. (My thanks to Professor Barry Kudrowitz of the University of Minnesota for his information on this subject)
9. Auerbach, pp.137-139
10. Sheppard, p.135
11. Picard, p.224
12. Auerbach, pp.141-142. I thank Professor Auerbach for kindly providing more details about the cost of accommodation in London during the Great Exhibition
13. Mayhew, *The Adventures of Mr. and Mrs. Sandboys and family, who came up to London to enjoy themselves and to see the Great Exhibition* (London: George Newbold, 1851) Gutenberg digitised version, 2021
14. Altick, *The Presence of the Present*, pp.269-270
15. *Dickens' Journalism*, Vol. 2., p.359
16. Gibbs-Smith, p.8
17. Ibid, p.18
18. Picard, p.222
19. Quoted in Auerbach, p.148
20. Quoted in Picard, p.219
21. Auerbach, p.148
22. For details of the funeral of Wellington, I have relied on Flanders, pp.335-346, and Muir, R., *Wellington, Waterloo and the Fortunes of Peace 1814-1852* (New Haven and London: Yale University Press, 2015), pp. 568-572
23. https://spartacus-educational.com/Discholera.htm (accessed 24 February 2022)

Index

Abortion, 23
Acton, Dr. William,
    gynaecologist, 21
Acton, Eliza, cookery writer, 29, 30
Adelaide Gallery, 37, 134, 139, 140
Aldgate, 43, 119
Aliens' Act 1848, 110
Amusements, 134-153
Anaesthesia, 50, 62, 139
'Angel in the House, The', 19, 23
Anti-Catholicism, 97-9
    and Dickens, 99-100
    and Maria Manning, 98
Apsley House, 12, 187
Area, 71
Arsenic (used in murder), 47, 48, 170
Astley's circus, 135, 143, 144

Bacon, 26
Balham, 134
Bank of England, 118
Bankruptcy, 67, 68
Banvard's Panorama, 136
Bathrooms, showers, 72
    baths, public, 72
Bazalgette, Joseph, sewer
    builder, 63
    (See also SEWERS)
Beards, 45, 105, 107, 184 (See also
    FOREIGNERS)
Beer, 135
Belgravia, 68
Berkeley Square, 46

Bermondsey, 4, 5, 69, 157
    sewers, 54
    slums, 70
Bethlehem Hospital, 58, 141
Birth rate, 52
Blackwall, 37
Blanc, Louis, French socialist, 104
Bond Street, 43
Books, 84
    (See also NOVELS, HISTORY,
        RELIGIOUS PUBLISHING)
Boot blacking, 45
Bread, 26
Brighton, 124, 125
British Museum, 5, 84-5, 152, 153
Brixton, 134
Broad Street pump, 62
Brontë, Charlotte, novelist, 20
Brougham, Henry, Lord Chancellor, 83
Buckingham Palace, 12
Budgets, family, 26-8
Building, 69, 70
Burlington Arcade, 14, 136
Bus conductors and drivers, 119, 120
    (See also OMNIBUSES)
Butter, 27, 28

Cabs, 116
    Dickens and, 117
    fares, 117
Cafés, 107
California, 65-6
Camden Town riot, 102

Carlyle, Thomas, historian, 7, 28, 30, 42, 69
Carlyle, Jane, 7, 28, 30, 33
Catholics, 98-100
Catholic Revival, 99
Catnach, J, publisher, 84
Cemeteries, 56
Chamber of Horrors, 142
Charing Cross, 13, 121
Chartism, 108-9
Chartist demonstration, 110-1
Chelsea, 7, 70, 122, 123
Chinese junk, 140
Cholera, 57-8, 60, 188
    and *Punch*, 32
Christmas cards, 132
Church, 90, 91, 93, 94, 96
Church attendance, 94
    (*See also* SUNDAY OBSERVANCE)
C.I.D (*See* Detectives)
City of London, 1, 7
City Road, 118
Clapham, 134
Class, 75-6
Clement's Inn, 119
Clerkenwell, 103
Clothes, 39-44
    Carlyles, 42
    Maria Manning's, 39-41
    men's, 41-46
Coaches, short-stage, 117, 120
Coaching inns, 125
Coal, 8, 73
Coal Hole, The, 65, 142
Cole, Henry, civil servant, 181
Collins, Wilkie, novelist, 40, 64, 95, 119, 165, 184
Colman, Henry, US Unitarian minister, 8, 9, 34, 38, 41, 91
Colosseum (*See* Royal Colosseum)
Concerts, 148

Consolidated Fund, 66
Contraception, 73
Cook, Thomas, travel agent, 186
Cookery books, 29, 30
Cooking, 73
Count d'Orsay, 67
Covent Garden, 13, 65
Covent Theatre, 149
Coventry Street, 35
Cremorne Gardens, 65, 145-146
Crime, 154
    Jane Carlyle and, 154
    Dickens and, 154, 156
Crimean War, 188
Croydon, 123
Crystal Palace, 181
    facilities, 27, 28
    and Carlyles, 73
    and Mannings, 73
Cubitt, Thomas, builder, 68
Currency, ix, x
Customs and Excise, 3
Cyder Cellars, The, 65, 142

Daguerre's Diorama, 137
Daguerrotype (*See* Photography)
Daily Telegraph, 87
Death Rate, 51-2
Department stores, 37
Detectives, 156-7
    Dickens and, 164-5
    investigate murder of O'Connor, 161-3
    use telegraph
Dickens, Charles, novelist and journalist, 8, 16, 22, 30, 32, 34, 42, 46, 50, 55, 59, 64, 67, 68, 77, 79, 80, 81, 82, 83, 86, 89, 92, 93, 99, 100, 104, 113, 123, 129, 135, 136, 139, 143, 144, 147, 149, 150, 164, 165, 166, 167, 178, 179, 180

Diseases, 47, 49, 51, 52
Divorce, 21
Dressmaking, 14
Drury Lane, 148
    Theatre Royal, 149
Dry cleaning, 45-46
Dulwich Art Gallery, 138
Dupin (Baron), French mathematician
    and politician, 2

Eating out (*See* Food, Restaurants)
Edgware Road, 14, 118
Edinburgh, 124
Education, 76, 81-3
    Dickens on, 82, 83
    (*See also* UNIVERSITY
        COLLEGE, MECHANICS'
        INSTITUTES)
Egyptian Hall, 136, 141, 142
Erotica, 89
Euston Square (later Euston) Station,
    13, 127-8, 129
Evangelicals, 83, 94-5
Examiner, The, 87
Exeter Hall, 94, 98, 148

Field, Inspector, 164
    Dickens and, 164
Finance and financial swindles, 66-7,
    and railways, 123-4
'Finishes', 15
Firman, Hannah, 75
Food, 24-36
    Dickens and, 25, 27, 35-36
    shopping for, 31
    supply to London, 30-31
Foreigners, 106-7 (*See also*
    ITALIANS, POLES, SPANIARDS,
    BEARDS)
    British attitude towards, 105
    fear of, 184

Fortnum and Mason, 36
France, 21, 22
    Mr and Mrs Caudle visit, 134
Fried fish, 113
    and chips, 24
Frith, William, artist, 138
Fruit, 28, 30
Furniture, 73

Gas lighting, 7, 74
Gin palaces, 135,
    Dickens and, 135
Gold reserve, 66
Golden Square, 104
    Dickens and, 104
Gordon Square, 68
Gravesend, 2, 3, 34, 122, 124
Gray's Inn Road, 68
Great Exhibition of 1851, 2, 181-3, 185-6
    water closets at, 183
Great Marlborough Street, 37
Greenwich, 35, 122, 124,
    Fair, 147
Greenwich Mean Time, 126
Green Park, 13
Gunter's, 36

Hair, women's, 19
Hairstyles, Maria Manning's, 41
Hampstead, 119
    Heath, 147
Hampton Court, 125
Hanging, 175-7, 178, 180
    Dickens, Thackeray and, 178-9
Harrod's, 37
Hatton Garden, 103
Haymarket, The, 13, 14, 35, 37, 148
Haynau, Austrian general, 105
Her Majesty's Theatre, 148
Herzen, Alexander, Russian
    intellectual, 104

Highbury Park, 68
Highgate, 120
History, 84, 88, 188
Holborn, 103
Holywell Street, 20
Hornsey, 134,
Hospitals, 51-55
Hotels, 8
'Hottentot Venus', The, 148
House of Commons, 138
Housing, 68-71
   Carlyles' house, 70-1
   Dickens family house, 71
   Mannings' house, 69-70
   Marx's house, 70
Housing for poor people, 11
Hudson, George, railway financier,
   124-5
Huish, Robert, author, 167
Hyde Park Corner, 12
Hygiene, lack of, 52-5 (*See also*
   WATER, SEWERS)

Illegitimate births, 13
Illness, 47-63
Illustrated London News, 87
Incomes, 64
   Dickens's, 64, 77
   Mannings's, 76-7
   servants', 75
Income tax, 77-78
Investment, 66
Irish in London, 9, 100-1 (*See also*
   CAMDEN TOWN RIOTS,
   O'CONNOR)
Irish priests, 102
Islington, 118
Italians in London, 103

Jerrold, Douglas, author and playwright,
   134, 149 (*See Mrs Caudle's Curtain
   Lectures*)

Jews, 112-115
   atttitude towards, 114
   civil rights of, 114
   Dickens and, 115 (*See also*
     PETTICOAT LANE, FRIED
     FISH)
Jullien, Monsieur, choirmaster, 138

Kensington, 70
Kilburn, 128
King's College, 103
Kitchens, 71
Kossuth, Lajos, Hungarian
   revolutionary, 105

Lambeth, 150
Laudanum, 47
Laundry, 74-75
Lavatory (*See* Privy, Water Closet)
Leicester Square, 103, 143
Letterboxes, 133
Libraries, 88 (*See also*
   MUDIE'S)
Lind, Jenny, singer, 148
Literacy, 81
   Dickens and, 81-2
'Little Italy', 103
London, (congestion, docks, fog,
   gloom, government, industry,
   labour force, manners, mud,
   population, recent building, size,
   smoke, social conditions, writers
   on), 1-8
London Bridge, 119, 122, 124
   London Bridge Station, 13
London districts, 9 (*See also* under
   local place-names)
Louis Napoleon, President and
   Emperor of France, 104
Louis-Philippe, King of France, 104
   and Thackeray, 106
Lowther Arcade, 37, 139

Macassar Oil, 45

Madame Tussauds's, 142-3

Mannings, Frederick and Maria, 3, 21, 23,
  murder of O'Connor and trial, 157-175
  and religion, 98
  waxworks and grave marker, 180

Manning, Frederick, 158
  flight and arrest, 163-4

Maria Manning, 161, 167-9
  clothes, 171
  Dickens and, 166-7
  flight and arrest, 162
  marriage, 20
  under sentence of death, 176-7

Margate, 3, 122, 134

Marylebone Theatre, 149

Marx, Karl, founder of Communism, 84, 104
  and Hampstead Heath, 147

Massey, William, 70, 142, 148

Mayhew, Henry, investigative journalist and comic novelist, 4, 25, 45, 86, 114 (*See* '*Mr and Mrs Sandboys, visit the Great Exhibition*')

Mayne, Richard, Commissioner of Police, 3

Mazzini, Giuseppe, Italian revolutionary, 103

Meal times, 24

Meat, 27, 28

Mechanics' Institutes, 83

Medical skills, 49-51

Medicines, 47, 48 (*See also* Patent Medicines)

Melbourne, Lord, Prime Minister, 12

Metropolitan Police (*See* Police)

Metropolitan Railway, 6

Melville, Herman, US novelist, 3, 7, 8, 35, 120, 122, 126, 138, 148, 150, 176

Middlesex Street, 43 (*See* Petticoat Lane)

Mile End, 119

Milk, 26, 30

Minories, The, 43

Minstrels, 147

Moneylending, 67 (*See also* O'CONNOR)
  Dickens and Reade on, 67

Montes, Lola, adventuress, 17-18, 21

Moses, Elias and Sons, 43, 106

Moxey, Richard, Superintendent of Police, 129, 162

'Mr and Mrs Sandboys, visit the Great Exhibition', 45 (*See also* MAYHEW)

Mrs Caudle's Curtain Lectures, 42, 114, 134 (*See also* JERROLD)

Mudie's Library, 87-8

Murder by women, 171-2

Music, 148

Music halls, 151

Muswell Hill, 134

Mysteries of the Court of London, 24, 86-7 (*See also* Reynolds)

National Gallery, 6, 92, 95, 138

New Bond Street, 19

New Cross, 123, 125

New Cut, 151

New Oxford Street, 43, 45

New Road, 118

News of the World, 85, 87

Newspapers, 85

Nichol, H. J., Men's outfitter, 45

Nitrous Oxide, 139 (*See also* ANAESTHESIA)

Novels, 87, 89
  serialisation of, 85

Novelists, (*See* Collins, Dickens, Reade, Thackeray)

O'Connor, Patrick, 3, 4, 23, 100, 134, 158
  murder and discovery of corpse of, 159-60
'Oh, Susannah', 136
'Old Vic' (*See* Royal Victoria Theatre)
Omnibuses, 6, 117-22
  Dickens and, 121
  Maria Manning and, 119
  Melville and, 120
  Thackeray and, 121
Oratorios, 148
Oxford Circus, 38
Oxford Movement (*See* Tractarianism)
Oxford Street, 37

Paddington Green, 118
Pall Mall, 13, 148
Palmerston, Lord, Foreign Secretary, 20
Panoramas, 136
'Paradise at Tooting, The', 58-60
  Dickens and, 59
Pantheon, The, 37
Patent medicines, 48-9
Peel, Sir Robert, Home Secretary, 154-5
Penny Dreadfuls, 86
Penny Gaffs, 151, 153
Penny Post, 131-3
Pentonville Road, 118
'Pepper's Ghost', 139
Petticoat Lane, 44, 114
Photography, 139, 181
Physicians, 47-8
Piccadilly, 13, 23, 36, 125
Piccadilly Circus and surrounding streets, 13, 14
Pimlico, 68
Pineapples, 30
Poles, 103, 106

Police, 20, 32, 80, 92, 102, 109, 110, 111, 129, 130, 154-5, 155-6;
  arrest Mannings, 185 (*See also* DETECTIVES)
Pornography, 20 (*See also* EROTICA)
Poses Plastiques, 143
Post (*See also* PENNY POST), 132
  Dickens and, 131, 132
  speed of, 132
Postal districts of London, 132
'Pretty little Polly Perkins', 118
Press, 84-5 (*See also* NEWSPAPERS, REYNOLD'S NEWS, DAILY TELEGRAPH, THE TIMES)
Primrose Hill, 128
Privy, 55, (*See also* GREAT EXHIBITION and WATER CLOSETS)
  in Manning house, 72
Prostitution, 13-17
  Dickens and, 16
  Taine, Flora Tristan, and, 15
Public houses, 135
Public transport (*See also* CABS, SHORT-STAGE COACHES, OMNIBUSES, RAILWAYS)
Punch, 29, 32, 44, 45

Rachel, Madame, cosmetician, 19-20
Railways, 30, 123-30 (*See also* HUDSON)
  Dickens and, 123, 129
  Maria Manning's railway journey to Scotland
  Melville and, 126
  'Mr. Pips' and, 126
  John Turner and, 123
  finance and speculation, 123-4
  Punch and, 124
  Thackeray and, 123, 124

Ramsgate, 134

Reade, Charles, novelist, 67

Red Indians (Native Americans), 140-1

Reform and protest associations, 111-2

Reform Bill of 1832, 12

Reform Club, 13

Refugees in London, 103-8 (*See also* FOREIGNERS, ITALIANS POLES, SPANIARDS)
   British tolerance of, 107
   spying on, 108

Regent Street, 13, 14, 16, 37, 38, 139

Regent Circus, 38

Regent's Park, 137 (*See also* ZOO)

Religion, 84, 90-1 (*See also* CATHOLICS, CHURCH)

Religious publishing, 89, 90, 92, 98

Rent and rates, 70-1

Restaurants, 33-37
   Dickens, Jane Carlyle and Henry Colman on, 34

Reuter, Julius, founder of press agency, 72

Revolutions of 1848, 106
   and fears in Britain, 109

Reynolds, G. A., journalist, and Chartist leader, 24, 86, 109

Reynold's Weekly, 86

Richmond, 2

Ritualism, 97

Rookeries, 6, 9, 11, 14

Round House, 102, 128

Royal Colosseum, 137

Royal Polytechnic Institution, 138-9, 153

Royal Victoria Theatre, 150

Sadler's Wells Theatre, 149

Saffron Hill, 103

St. George's Hospital, 12

St. Giles, 103

Sala, G. A., journalist, 10-11, 24

Saville House, 143

Schools, 81

Scotland Yard (*See* Detectives)

Sewers, 7, 53, 54, 55, 60-2

Sewing machines, 40

Sex and 'seriousness', 21

Shellfish, 35

Shillibeer, George, omnibus proprietor, (*See also* OMNIBUSES)

Shopkeepers, attitude of, 39-40

Shopping, 37-9

Short stage coaches (*See* Coaches)

Simon, Dr John, pathologist, 54-55

Singing, 148

Smith, W.H., stationer and bookseller, 98

Smithfield, 8, 55-6
   Dickens and, 55

Smoking, 105, 184, 185

Smuggling, 3, 4, 9, 80

Snow, Dr John, anaesthetist and epidemiologist, 62

Snow Hill, 125

Social class (*See* CLASS)

Soho, 103

Soho Bazaar, 37

Southampton, 124

Southwark, 122

Soyer, Alexis, chef, 13, 29, 74

Spaniards in London, 103

Steamboats, 122, 134, 186
   Carlyle and, 123
   Melville and, 123

Strand, The, 14, 65, 119, 122, 139, 143

Street entertainments, 146

Stulz, George, gentleman's tailor, 43

Sugar, 26, 28

Sunday observance, 91
   and Dickens, 91-2
   and Disraeli, 91

Surgeons and surgery, 49-50
Surrey Gardens, 148
Swan & Edgar, 41
Sweating trades, 45

Taine, Hippolyte, French historian, 2,
    6, 15, 39, 41, 51
Tax (*See* Income Tax)
Tea, 26-27
Telegraph, 130-1
    and arrest of criminals, 130
Thackeray, William, novelist, 44, 68,
    89, 145, 178
Thames, River, 1, 2
The Times, 16, 55, 56, 62, 87, 98, 110,
    141, 171, 179, 185
Theatres, 149-50 (*See* Covent Garden,
    Drury Lane, Her Majesty's,
    Marylebone, Theatre Royal,
    Sadler's Wells)
Theatre Royal (*See* Drury Lane)
Toilet (*See* Privy)
Tobacco, 3, 54, 9, 80
Tottenham Court Road, 43, 135
Tractarianism, 96, 99
Trafalgar Square, 6, 109, 137, 187
Tristan, Flora, French socialist, 3, 7, 8,
    15, 24

Uncle Tom's Cabin, 89, 141
University College London, 83, 103
Utilitarianism, 83

Vauxhall, 122, 123
Vauxhall Gardens, 14, 45, 144-5
Vegetables, 28

Victoria, Queen, coronation procession
    and celebrations, 12-13, 141-2
    visits Great Exhibition, 182
Victoria Park, 153
Victoria Station, 13

Water closets, 53, 60
    at Great Exhibition, 183
Water supply, 55, 61-3, 71-2
    and cholera, 60-1
Waterloo, 124, 128
Waterloo Bridge, 15
Waterloo Road, 15
Waterloo Station, 13
Waxworks (*See* MADAME
    TUSSAUD'S)
    Anatomical, 143
Wellington, Duke of, 12
    death and funeral, 186-7
Westbourne Terrace, 68
Westminster, 122
Westminster Abbey, 12
Westminster Bridge Road, 143
Whicher, Sergeant, 165
Whitechapel, 43, 119
Wiseman, Cardinal, 99, 103
Woburn Place, 68
Women, 12-23
    legal status of, 20
Workhouse, Dickens's description,
    79-80
Working class, clothes, smell and
    speech, 79-80
Working conditions, 77

Zoological Gardens, 153